CHASING THE GAME

ALSO BY FILIP BONDY

*Tip Off: How the 1984 NBA Draft
Changed Basketball Forever (2008)*

*Bleeding Pinstripes: A Season with the Bleacher
Creatures of Yankee Stadium (2005)*

CHASING
THE GAME

America and the Quest
for the
World Cup

FILIP BONDY

DA CAPO PRESS
A Member of the Perseus Books Group

Cataloging-in-Publication data for this book is available from the Library of Congress.

First Da Capo Press edition 2010
ISBN: 978-0-306-81606-2

Published by Da Capo Press
A Member of the Perseus Books Group
www.Dacapopress.com
Da Capo Press books are available at special discounts for bulk purchases in the U.S. by corporations, institutions, and other organizations. For more information, please contact the Special Markets Department at the Perseus Books Group, 2300 Chestnut Street, Suite 200, Philadelphia, PA, 19103, or call (800) 810-4145, ext. 5000, or e-mail special.markets@perseusbooks.com.

10 9 8 7 6 5 4 3 2

For my dad and my son,
who keep the
spotted ball rolling

CONTENTS

FOREWORD

You only had to sit inside the stadium or mill about the crammed platforms of the tiny Kaiserslautern train station in Germany that one night on June 17, 2006, to feel the overwrought passion of United States soccer fans. Americans stumbling over Americans, with knowing, appreciative glances. The Stars and Stripes draped around otherwise naked bodies, or stitched more formally into collared shirt patterns. These avid supporters had come that day to watch their flawed national team, the United States of right-footed kickers, earn a 1–1 draw in the first round against Italy, the eventual World Cup champions. The result had been a pleasant surprise, a bit of a fluke achieved despite a ten-on-nine manpower advantage for Italy during the second half of the match. But the size and bent of this crowd at Kaiserslautern station was no accident. Decades of soccer evolution at all levels of American society had finally produced physical evidence of progress—off the field, at the very least. For the first time at a World Cup tournament outside the U.S., American fans were represented in numbers substantial enough to alter the tenor of a match.

The national team's supporters, tens of thousands of them, booed lustily inside the stadium when a fire-engine red card was shown to U.S. defender Eddie Pope. At times, these jeers drowned out the more familiar, indignant European-style whistles. Americans had joined with impressive force the mobile, global sports community, traveling to soccer matches in migratory herds, arranging itineraries on the fly while speaking loudly into cell phones. This wasn't true as recently as 1998 in France, where only true-blue Sam's Army and a few hundred other

American supporters were spotted in the sometimes quarter-empty stadiums. It certainly wasn't the case in Korea, an inconvenient outpost for a breakthrough run to the quarterfinals in 2002. In Germany, though, trains were packed with flag-waving, chant-challenged Americans who had yet to coin a decent nickname for their beloved side. These supporters were not the most colorful contingent at the tournament, but they definitely had joined the party—stomping and cheering in the stands, commuting with élan and camaraderie, drinking and bouncing around the platforms and streets just like their English and Dutch counterparts. They *got* it, finally. And when a U.S. player scored a goal in Germany—there was only one such moment, actually—the hero, Clint Dempsey, suddenly had a choice: should he head to the east or west stands toward American supporters for his choreographed celebration?

The 2006 World Cup did not end well for the U.S. national team. Requiring only one victory—against upstart Ghana—in their final Group E match, the Americans lost in Nuremberg, 2–1, and left the tournament convinced a referee had robbed them. Markus Merk of Germany whistled a wrongheaded penalty kick against U.S. defender Oguchi Onyewu just before halftime. There was no great conspiracy involved, however; just a slice of misfortune and a larger failure of skill and tactics from the Americans. They were built to counterattack against a stretched offense, never to chase the game from behind. When the U.S. desperately needed two goals against Ghana to advance with a victory, the Americans were unable to mount a comeback. After three matches, the team finished last in its group with one point on two goals (one of them an own goal by Italy). The U.S. was saddled with two player ejections and managed a total of just four shots on goal. This was not quite the lights-out disaster of 1998, but hardly the adrenaline rush of 2002.

The eight-year tenure of U.S. head coach Bruce Arena ended quickly. Like most two-term politicians, he had worn thin his welcome. Arena's contract would expire in December 2006, and he seemed to indicate that day in Nuremberg that enough was enough. A fresh start was in order, on all fronts. "If you ask me now, probably not," he said then, about enduring the World Cup cycle again. By the standards of international soccer coaches, Arena's length of stay with the U.S. team had been substantial and relatively successful. He'd led the Americans all the way to a quarterfinal in Korea, an unlikely accomplishment aided somewhat by the luck of the draw. He understood the complicated variables of the qualifying process and the limitations of his uneven talent pool. At the same time, Arena failed to develop a cohesive midfield or discover reliable finishers. Injuries were a factor, too, but so was Arena's impatience. His lineup changes wore on goalkeeper Kasey Keller and on his fleetest attacker, DaMarcus Beasley. He had his favorites and they didn't always return the favor. Arena lived and died with Claudio Reyna, a frail, possession midfielder whose slower pace was tremendously useful in theory. In actual matches, however, his leisurely tack rarely jived with the breakneck attacks of Landon Donovan and DaMarcus Beasley.

Despite such disappointment in Germany, the sport continued to chug along steadily in the States. The final of the 2006 World Cup, between France and Italy, garnered a 7.0 television rating on ABC. Altogether, nearly 29 million viewers in the U.S. watched either on that network or on the Spanish-language network Univision. Those numbers were considerably higher, in fact, than the ratings for the NBA Finals. The World Series, contested that same year by the Detroit Tigers and St. Louis Cardinals, drew a 10.0 network rating, but lacked the big bump from Univision. Americans cared about soccer. They were watching, and would keep watching – in both languages.

A slow, grinding, contextual revolution had begun when the immortal Pelé himself came out of retirement back in 1975 to sign a $7 million, three-year deal with the New York Cosmos of the North American Soccer League (NASL), vowing "to make soccer truly popular in the United States." In the broadest of evolutionary terms, the NASL of the seventies and eighties begat a burgeoning youth movement, which begat a competitive World Cup squad and brought the 1994 World Cup to America, which begat Major League Soccer (MLS). Youth soccer is no longer just about playtime for America's kids. It is a giant, multi-tentacled scouting and feeder system. The sport has seeped methodically into the consciousness and vocabulary of U.S. citizens, from the roots up.

Soccer moms . . . travel teams . . . Bend It like Beckham . . . Freddy Adu . . . Zinedine Zidane's head butt. Soccer-specific stadiums and Major League Soccer franchises—expanding toward twenty clubs—are sprouting across the nation. Magazines and websites, from *Soccer America* to Soc-cerbyIves.net, serve a knowledgeable audience. There is a growing awareness and hunger for media coverage among new generations of fans and among older immigrants who grew up playing and loving the sport. On cable and online, via sites like You Tube, Americans regularly watch touch passes from Kaká of Brazil or the mesmerizing footwork of Cristiano Ronaldo from Portugal, teammates on Real Madrid. They follow Lionel Messi, the Argentine considered by many the greatest player in the world, during his club matches with Barcelona. ESPN, under the soccer-supportive leadership of programming exec John Skipper, has aggressively and presciently contracted for Confederations Cup matches, for World Cup qualifying and finals matches, for English Premier League rights, and for any soccer that might fill a growing viewership appetite. "There's been a huge difference from [Skipper's predecessor at ESPN] Mark Shapiro to Skipper," said Alan Rothenberg, former president of the United States Soccer Federation. "Shapiro inherited soccer and hated it. Skipper was with his teenage son traveling all over Germany at the World Cup long after the U.S. was eliminated, going to twenty-one games. That tells you a lot. He can feel something about the sport."

And then there is the growing belief that the Americans just may be able to play this game, after all. We glimpsed such possibilities again at the 2009 Confederations Cup in South Africa, where the U.S. upset Spain, the top-ranked team in the world and European champions, then very nearly beat Brazil for the title before another impressive television audience back home. Granted, this was not the World Cup. Still, it was a lesson learned: Sometimes, it doesn't matter *how* you win, but when you win. The United States finished that Confederations Cup with a modest 2–3 mark, yet enhanced its international reputation and very nearly stole a major FIFA (Fédération Internationale de Football Association) trophy. The ball is round, the saying goes. Anything can happen.

"All of my dreams end the same way, with us winning the World Cup," said Sunil Gulati, president of the U.S. Soccer Federation, (usually shortened to U.S. Soccer), about the men's team. "But if we talk about when that will happen, it starts getting a little fuzzy." It almost certainly won't happen soon. But if the U.S. men's national team ever wins the World Cup, the triumph will likely produce a cathartic sporting moment in this country on a scale never before experienced. Most Americans go about their daily lives acutely unaware or only vaguely interested in such a possible script. To them, the World Cup is a bit like a distant meteor spinning and hurtling through space, periodically spotted, unlikely to affect them in the slightest. Its potential impact, however, is enormous. "The moment the U.S. wins the World Cup will be the moment that soccer will take on the other pro leagues in America," said Don Garber, commissioner of Major League Soccer. "It would be a story on a global scale."

Gulati believes a World Cup title for the U.S. men's national team would become the greatest sports achievement in his country's history. Americans may not have an innate affinity for their national sports teams, but they make an ardent exception if both drama and precedence are afoot. They adore the big event, the very bracketology of it all. The World Cup finals, a thirty-two-nation elimination tournament watched internationally by billions, meet all criteria. There was already a considerable stir when the top-ranked American women captured a World Cup title on home soil in 1999. Back in 1980, an ice hockey gold medal at Lake Placid once taught Americans to love a national team the way Europeans, Africans, and South Americans more naturally embrace their own. While the 1980 run was a stirring upset, that U.S. hockey team was ranked fourth or fifth in the world at the time. The U.S. soccer team, by comparison, has been ranked lately only among the top fifteen teams in the world. If the Americans were able to beat Brazil, Germany, or Italy on such a stage, they would be Princeton finally making that last-minute shot to defeat Georgetown in the NCAA basketball tournament—with the whole world watching. "Are we going to win the World Cup in 2010? Of course not," Gulati said. "At the same time you have to say, 'Why not?' The goal is still the same." Since their renaissance in 1990, the Americans owned a sober-ing mark in five World Cups of 3–12–3 (this book uses the American method of listing a team's record, wins–losses–ties; not the global stan-dard, wins–ties–losses). When they scored first in those matches, how-ever, their record had been 3–0–1. And whenever they tied or won their first group match, they advanced to the second round. So the formula was clear: Score first. Win first. If only it were that simply executed.

Soccer is the most democratic of all sports. It is played in all the nooks and crannies on Earth, by men and women of every age, race, and shape. It demands only a ball and four old shoes for goal markers. Even at the very highest levels, players don't need to be particularly tall or muscular, just agile and adept. There are forward positions readily avail-able for fleet sprinters and midfield spots custom-made for slower, more instinctive playmakers. It is true: Spectators require considerable patience to love the sport. In a society nurtured on instant replays and gaudy video graphics, this viewing experience demands a different mindset. Americans have for years been spoon-fed National Football League games with a series of convenient, four-down packages punctuated by a touchdown, field goal, or punt. Timeouts are frequent. Baseball is sim-ilar, with nine, neatly packaged innings and climactic, structured mo-ments when the bases are loaded and two men are out. The 24-second clock propels offenses in the National Basketball Association, creating a countdown on every possession. And the power play is hockey's way of rousing spectators, warning them a goal is more likely over the next two or five minutes.

Soccer is different. Goals often arrive without such countdowns, constructed from a slim advantage. They may be the product of a lengthy siege, or appear suddenly against the run of play. Each half is forty-five minutes of running time, of unpredictable attacks and counter-attacks. There is no guaranteed payoff. The dreaded nil–nil score always looms as a real possibility. Yet patience is rewarded with a flow and rhythm unmatched in any other sport.

Gulati likes to say that America is just starting the second half of its soccer odyssey. By this fifty-year timeline, which arguably gives short shrift to the NASL days, the chase began in earnest when the stadiums were filled by enthusiastic, paying customers at the soccer matches during the 1984 Olympics in Los Angeles. That sight convinced FIFA officials to stage the 1994 World Cup in America, and from there a professional league was born. One thing is certain: No other athletic event delivers such an ultimate payoff. The World Cup is the grandest of all televised sporting events, a tournament of both enormity and relative simplicity. An American might watch his side go up in flames yet again in South Africa over the course of just two hours. But he can also dream of a match-changing goal, right through to the end of injury time.

There is considerable joy to be found in the cyclical four-year quest—in the challenges faced while choosing a coach, surviving qualifiers under extremely hostile conditions, and preparing a team for the rigors of the World Cup. This book takes that journey. It joins the Americans in their run-up to South Africa 2010, with one hopeful eye to the future and an appreciative review of the past.

CHAPTER 1

The American Coach

THE NEW COACH WASN'T REALLY NEW AT ALL. BUT ON MAY 16, 2007, Bob Bradley appeared inside a ballroom at the New York Marriott Marquis for his official introduction as head coach of the United States national soccer team. Here, just off Broadway, the unwanted appendage "interim" would be ceremoniously stripped from his title. A blue curtain, along with the usual series of corporate logos, provided the backdrop to the dais. A dozen enlarged, glowering photos of Bob Bradley lined the walls. Bradley was not known as a sideline celebrator. He was wholly analytical, glum, flirting with dour. If you looked closely enough, there seemed to be a half-smile on his face in one of the photos. That was about as much as he would give the world. Bradley was a thorough professional and a dedicated family man. Many people loved to work for him, or with him, but he was often a tough interview subject for the media. He tightly guarded his opinions about players. His post-match debriefings, although informative, were performed only in the broadest of strokes. Everybody knew what they were getting with Bradley, for better or worse. There would be no surprises.

An insular attitude came naturally to Bradley, who was at heart devoted utterly to a soccer life. It had been a long road here, sometimes detoured or thwarted by limited opportunity. The international soccer community might be largely indifferent to the American player, but its lowest opinion was always reserved for that of the American coach. John Harkes, the former U.S. midfield star and ESPN analyst, harbored great ambitions one day of landing an international coaching job. Yet after several false starts, Harkes decided that his storied playing career had been considerably easier to launch than a coaching career. "You're more in control of changing opinions when you're playing," Harkes said. "You don't need to rely as much on somebody else's ignorant view." It was the general consensus among those in the international soccer community that coaching required a strong cultural base, and that the U.S. had neither the soccer history nor infrastructure to provide such underpinnings. There also was no great reservoir of former superstars in the U.S. In other nations these golden athletes, from Frank Rijkaard in Holland to Juergen Klinsmann in Germany, were often permitted to leap-frog several learning stations and advance directly into big-time technical positions. Could there have been a crazier idea than promoting erratic Diego Maradona to head coach of Argentina's national side?

Long ago, coaching soccer in America came to be viewed as an import trade, not a domestic or export business. Coaches at all levels of the sport—from local teenaged travel teams to national sides—were recruited from Britain and from non-English-speaking nations to teach both young and prime-time players. Meanwhile, there were few opportunities abroad for even the most seasoned of U.S. coaches. No discriminating Premier League team in England would ever consider such a hire, for fear of intense mockery. Steve Sampson, a very nice man and questionable tactician who headed the U.S. team's 1998 World Cup fiasco in France, was signed to coach a notable foreign national team, Costa Rica, in 2002. But he was afforded only a short leash. After going undefeated in 2003 and guiding the Costa Ricans to the number seventeen ranking in the world, Sampson was dismissed the next year following a short rough patch during World Cup qualifying matches.

Other than Sampson's underwhelming position in Central America, there had been very little employment available. The exceptions were few, and not necessarily lucrative. Iranian-born Afshin Ghotbi, who came to the U.S. at age thirteen, was hired in 2009 as national coach of Iran, a position with laughably little job security. American coaches instead took great pleasure in any polite confirmation of their talents. Bradley savored moments when opposing coaches or players from top international sides at various age levels complimented his team's play. But, yes, he still wished very much to coach abroad at some later stage of his career.

"As the game continues to grow in this country, as players get opportunities to show what they're about, hopefully that will happen with coaches," Bradley said. "Professionally you think as a coach and as a person, 'I'm ready for more challenges.' You put whatever you have into the group you're with. No job is a stepping stone. But at the end of the day, a lot of American coaches would hope the day will come when there are opportunities at the international level."

Even in America, homegrown coaches competed with foreigners for sideline spots at colleges, on national teams, and on Major League Soccer clubs. When the head coach position opened for the U.S. national team leading to the 2010 World Cup, it was only natural that Sunil Gulati, president of U.S. Soccer, took a long look outside his nation's own borders to fill the job vacancy. It was also predictable when a roar of protest arose from the protective, domestic inner circle of American coaches.

There had been considerable debate among the sport's aficionados throughout time about the influence and impact of any soccer coach—American, European, or multinational. At the youth level, where teaching was a critical skill, the importance of a strong technical director was self-evident. At the professional club level, the impact of a coach varied greatly, according to his power in choosing personnel. A club coach could impose a general philosophy of attack or caution, changing formations and substitution patterns. He set the psychological tone for a long season. He might act as a recruiting magnet for certain players. But the world of soccer was littered with famous, well-regarded coaches who failed miserably with one club after succeeding magnificently with another. Ultimately, soccer was not at all like American football and a coach who wished to control the flow of play, once a match began, was inevitably a frustrated man.

On the national team level, a coach assumed responsibilities well beyond the playing field. He kept track of a sprawling player pool, and negotiated delicately with club teams at home and abroad for the release of his best players during key World Cup qualifiers. He was required to maintain the respect of his full roster during a lengthy and grueling schedule, often in hostile stadiums. He set the schedule of exhibitions. Ideally, he would also be schooled in the fine art of public relations. The coach of a national team represented his country abroad and spoke for the sport of soccer at home.

Bruce Arena, arguably the most qualified American coach in the history of our country, did not necessarily wish to leave his national post after the World Cup in Germany. He sounded tired after the loss to Ghana in Nuremberg. He had hinted in the past about potential employment in Europe. Then reality intervened. Arena had only one viable prospect: The Major League Soccer franchise New York Red Bulls offered him a head coaching position. Arena preferred to remain as national team head coach, a far more prestigious position, but he needed a quick commitment from Gulati. Otherwise, he would accept the Red Bulls' contract. Gulati was considering several candidates, most notably Klinsmann, the enormously popular head coach and former star for Germany. There was no wiggle room.

"We had to make a tough decision coming out of the World Cup," Gulati said. "I've never said this, but I'm not sure I would have come to the same conclusion about Bruce if Bruce hadn't pushed us on the timetable because of the Red Bulls' offer. Bruce had been extraordinarily successful." Arena also was not the easiest of employees to manage. Gulati and Arena forged a fragile association, at best. Gulati traveled everywhere with the team, and was constantly in the mix. His influence on the team and its players was apparent everywhere. Coaches did not always appreciate his sagging body language in the locker room after a tough defeat, or his commitment to answering every negative email from fans. Arena felt Gulati was too much the micro-manager. "He was trying to get rid of me long before he did," Arena said, when he was coaching the Red Bulls. "You get some people to vote you president and then you do what you want." Arena's tenure coincided with the growing financial solvency of the U.S. Soccer Federation, and he believed that Gulati was afforded too much of the credit. "When I came over there, when (former U.S. Soccer president Alan Rothenberg) and Sunil were there, the Federation was within one year of going bankrupt," Arena said. "Now they're fine."

For his part, Gulati stipulated that the sometimes prickly Arena had done a sound job, despite the dreary World Cup showing in 2006. There was, after all, that idyllic advancement to the quarterfinals in 2002. But Arena was not an aggressive spokesman for soccer in America. He was no friend at the time of Don Garber, commissioner of MLS [Major League Soccer], who felt Arena too often griped about the level of play in his league. Arena was very much the realist, not an inspirational dreamer. Gulati was reminded of that again after his decision.

"I go to the first day of [U.S. national team] training camp in January [2007] at Home Depot and it's rough," Gulati said. "I go to Fort Lauderdale for the MLS combine and Bruce is there coaching the Red Bulls. He asks how it was. I say, 'Rough, not a lot of talent.' And he says, 'Sunil, we're not going to win the World Cup.' And I said, 'Bruce, after you lose to the Czechs 3–0 [in 2006], and you're walking out to face Italy for the second match of the World Cup, is the last thing you say to them in the huddle, 'Guys we got no chance to win this game?'"

The two men parted ways and worked hard in future years, with success, to repair their strained relationship. Arena accepted the job with the forever-doomed Red Bulls, then became coach of the Los Angeles Galaxy and revitalized that franchise, taking it to the MLS championship in 2009 where it lost to Real Salt Lake in a shootout. Gulati would look elsewhere, and his hunt for Arena's successor was at first centered on Klinsmann, who positively glowed with internal and eternal optimism. "Juergen in many ways was the dream candidate," Gulati said. "Not only of the general public, but of the media. He was coming out of a very successful [semifinal] run as World Cup coach. He didn't have a lot of coaching experience, but he was well-spoken, successful, charismatic, good looking, all of those things. It was natural to look at that. He'd been a successful player as well."

Before negotiating, Klinsmann requested a couple of months off after the World Cup. Gulati put out feelers to several other international coaches. He spoke with Roberto Donadoni, the former Italian star of AC Milan, just three days after the World Cup, but Donadoni would soon accept the coaching position for Italy's national team (a brief, unhappy tenure). Gulati eventually contacted many candidates from abroad: Sven-Göran Eriksson of Sweden, the dismissed coach of England who would take jobs with Manchester City and the Mexican national team (also ill-fated); Gerard Houllier of France, head coach of Olympique Lyonnais; Luiz Scolari of Portugal, who would become for a short time the wealthy coach of Chelsea; Carlos Queiroz of Portugal, an assistant coach at Manchester United with long-held ties to U.S. Soccer; Ruud Gullit of the Netherlands, a former star who would serve a particularly unsuccessful stint with the Los Angeles Galaxy; Jose Pekerman, the former head coach of Argentina; and Carlos Alberto Perreira of Brazil, who accepted a lucrative position with the South African national team. Most of these candidates would have been far better off coaching the U.S. national team—a relatively secure, low-pressure situation—if only they'd have sacrificed some money and willingly lived abroad.

Gulati also talked with five domestic candidates, including Peter Nowak and Bradley, who was the final interviewee. Gulati was focused all along on Klinsmann, though. "I knew if I signed him I'd be a hero," Gulati said. "If I didn't I'd be an idiot, which is how it turned out." The two sides were extremely close to an agreement after meeting for weeks. So close, in fact, that Klinsmann laid out preliminary U.S. player rosters and pools. In anticipation of his signing, the Federation readied a press release with quotes from the German.

The sticking point wasn't money—the Americans were prepared to throw millions at Klinsmann. Gulati and Klinsmann's agent, Andy Gross, couldn't come to an agreement on contractual terms that would give Klinsmann the sort of final say he demanded on virtually all matters. Gulati never planned to overrule Klinsmann on such issues as the selection of assistant coaches or the scheduling of a minimum fourteen matches per year for the national team. But he couldn't in good conscience sign away the rights of U.S. Soccer on these items. Gulati wasn't George Steinbrenner, representing his own professional franchise. He was a bureaucrat, fronting a national sports federation. There was also considerable skepticism from those around him about the whole deal. Klinsmann was a handful in many ways. The cult of personality surrounding him in Germany had been a divisive force. Top officials there were resentful about Klinsmann's popularity and his power, so they were not totally unhappy when the coach decided to quit his job with the national team, even after reaching the semifinals at the 2006 World Cup. Klinsmann was a players' coach, whose nature and experience encouraged freedom of expression rather than specifically drawn tactics. He was a "Go get 'em, boys!" kind of leader, consciously lacking in Xs and Os. "He'd make a lousy coach here," one former U.S. Soccer official grumbled. As it turned out, nobody would ever find out.

Talks fell apart during the first week of December, after Gulati informed Klinsmann that the Federation couldn't make those final, contractual concessions. Gulati was now in an uncomfortable bind. The national team faced upcoming international exhibitions and regional tournaments. There was the Gold Cup, which was the championship of CONCACAF (Confederation of North, Central American, and Caribbean Association Football) and Copa America, the South American regional championship, which had extended a special invitation to the Americans. On December 8, 2006, Bradley accepted from Gulati the position as "interim head coach" of the national team, hoping against most thoughtful odds that he might prove himself worthy of a permanent position. The deal was much easier to strike than the Klinsmann pact. Gulati and Bradley hammered it out quickly one night in Gulati's office at Columbia University on the Upper West Side of Manhattan.

Bradley was nothing like Klinsmann, a stark contrast in personality and philosophy. Bradley was a videotape junkie who broke down replays at his home until the wee early morning hours. He was less intuitive than Klinsmann; more schematic. Bradley admired talent, but respected hustle. He had one particularly favorite way of gauging readiness and talked about it often: *What did a player do after he lost the ball?* Everybody laid off a bad pass occasionally during a match, or was stripped (soccer vocabulary nerds call it "dispossessed") off the dribble. Bradley cared more about how the player reacted to these turnovers. If the player tracked back and remained active on the ball, Bradley took note. If the player moped or walked away, the coach was not pleased. "When you lose the ball you are, in a pure soccer sense, the guy who can help your team the most," Bradley said. "You can save guys from a lot of running. You can do a lot of things that can help your guys, put them in the right position to get the ball back. It's one of the things you see in the best teams. When Wayne Rooney (the brilliant English striker) loses the ball, you see a competitiveness and fire that makes you say, 'I would want him on my team.' Other guys, it's somebody else's job or, 'I was fouled.' That's not a mentality that has a chance to win something. You try to hold up that standard."

Gulati had first met Bradley at a Princeton soccer camp and was immediately impressed. "I knew he could, would, should eventually be coach of the national team," Gulati said. "He's an intellectual about the game." Bradley's connections to all strata of the domestic sport were inter-generational. He'd played college soccer in the seventies. His son, Michael, was now a top prospect in the national team pool. His appointment was therefore embraced with great enthusiasm in most quarters, as the U.S. team went undefeated under his supervision for ten games in five months. Pressure increased on Gulati to appoint Bradley the national coach on a fulltime basis. Whenever the Americans played a match telecast by ESPN, analysts such as Arena and former U.S. forward Eric Wynalda would ratchet up the pressure on the U.S. Soccer president. They argued the Americans could not afford this period of uncertainty when the buildup for the Olympics and the next round of World Cup qualifying already loomed. The U.S. senior national team had gone seven full months without an international match, following its ouster from the World Cup. But now it had resumed a full schedule of exhibitions beginning with a 5–0 victory over Norway in Carson, CA, heading toward the Gold Cup competition in June 2007.

Gulati refused to budge on Bradley's interim label, even under withering on-air interrogation from the ESPN analysts. He'd given up on Klinsmann, but there were other possible European coaches whose seasons would end in May. Gulati had this vision of a perfect international coach, whose assets included an ability to speak Spanish—or, at least, the willingness to learn the language—in order to mine the mother lode of Hispanic talent so famously ignored by national team selectors. Nobody really knew if these players with gorgeous technical skills and American passports existed in substantial numbers, or were merely a myth. The success stories were few and far between, but Gulati was more a believer than a skeptic on this subject. He had witnessed firsthand the development of former U.S. star Tab Ramos, who came to the States from Uruguay at the age of eleven. Gulati was also monitoring the evolution of José Francisco Torres, a gifted Mexican-American midfielder and candidate for the senior national team. Gulati wanted his coach to speak conversational Spanish. This was not a guarantee of success, however. Bora Milutinovic of Serbia had been multi-lingual, yet sometimes befuddled American players and reporters with sentence fragments in several tongues during his run as national team coach in the 1990s.

In May 2007, Gulati finally made the call to Bradley after his options and his own timetable ran down. Since Klinsmann's withdrawal, other foreign candidates did not appear particularly eager, either. There were reasons why Gulati felt better about Bradley at this time than if he had made the decision six months earlier. During his tenure as acting coach, Bradley very much played the part correctly. He treated the team's string of scheduled exhibitions exactly as that. They were just friendlies. Bradley hadn't fielded his top lineup for every match, but rather studied a broad sample of his player pool. He rotated captains while his lineups varied wildly, yet purposefully: Bradley did not waste elite players Tim Howard, Carlos Bocanegra, and Clint Dempsey on the first exhibition against Denmark, but brought them into the starting lineup in the next game, two weeks later against rival Mexico. Bradley tried not to rely heavily or capriciously on European-based players, who were needed by their pro clubs. His restraint was appreciated by those foreign teams, and it was rewarded by Gulati. "Right from the beginning, Bob treated this job as if it was his," Gulati said. "We saw results. We saw he was playing the young guys and not calling up others unnecessarily to save his job." Gulati first mentioned in March to Bradley that the interim title might be removed. The coach had carefully avoided bringing up the subject on his own.

All along, win or lose, Bradley's intensity was an impregnable shield against those who might distract him from his appointed duties. Reporters were not exactly the enemy, but they were never confidantes. It had always been like this with him. On one occasion when Bradley was coaching the MetroStars, the club's public relations director, Nick DiBenedetto, said to him, "You know, you're actually a nice guy." Bradley responded, "Don't let anybody know. I don't want them to bother me." The coach occasionally prodded DiBenedetto to perform some informal spying on beat reporters during late-night drinking sessions. Bradley wanted to know what questions and issues might be out there, so he would be prepared. He was a protective den father with his team. Journalists were uncomfortably outside his zone of influence.

Still, at his inaugural press conference in 2007, Bradley tried his best. He talked easily with soccer writers, a small, familial breed, and told stories sometimes at his own expense. The Spanish-speaking prerequisite, so hopefully spelled out by Gulati as part of the job description, already was a running joke. Bradley had coached a great number of Spanish-speaking players at Chivas, but he found his fitful language skills unnecessary most of the time. Nearly all the players spoke better English than he spoke Spanish. His efforts were often greeted with grimaces. "I told them once I wanted them to play with *mucho gusto*," Bradley said. "They thought I was an idiot."

Bradley was proud, excited, honored. "Being on the national team is not something you're entitled to," he said. "That's what makes the national team different." He cited Youri Djorkaeff from France, one of his players on the MetroStars, who seemed always to know the difference between competing for a club team and for the world champion French national team. "He liked doing his own thing," Bradley said. "When he was playing for a professional club, he would stay at the center city penthouse. But he always said it was different when he went to the national team."

These circles of friendship and responsibility were important to Bradley. He used the term, "on the inside," all the time. You were either there on the inside with him, as a player with the national side, or you were observing from the outside. "We can't have everybody in there," he warned. "I have not always been open with the media." He surely would never become as welcoming or beaming a figure as Klinsmann. Bradley was unlikely to be as quote-worthy or frank in his analysis as Arena. But he did not offend with the practiced condescension of Arena, who might preface his reply to a reporter's question with, "Obviously, you have never played this sport," or, "How many World Cups have you watched?" Promoting the game, Bradley promised, was a priority. "If you asked me a few years ago, I would have said, 'Not much,'" Bradley said. "But I've learned there is more to it. I'm not as good as maybe I could be. I get criticized for not smiling. When we score, I'm already thinking, 'Can we hold that lead?' My wife Lindsay has the toughest job. She asks me, 'Can't we just enjoy it for a few minutes?'"

Bradley had a theory about the recent failures of U.S. teams, and how those disappointments extended beyond the soccer fields, into the ice hockey rinks, and onto the basketball courts. He felt the emphasis on the individual, and on professional careers, had drained the national teams of a more communal personality.

"In 1980, the U.S. hockey team was together for months, and they played for a coach who purposely established an environment where he was hard on them, and didn't want them to like him. We must become a real team like that. We have to value our time together, play collectively with belief. We must develop that kind of attitude. The Italian team (World Cup champions in 2006), they were blood brothers. We must build on that first. On the inside, I don't choose to play mind games. Do they like me? Some do, some don't."

Bradley required as many allies as he could muster. His national team already had endured a long, fragmented history. There was no "American style" of play per se. The national team was not yet technically proficient enough for a possession, or short passing, game. Against the best sides, its strength lay more often in the counter and in tactics based on an opponent's strengths or weaknesses. Traditionally, the U.S. merely tried to wear down foes, employing willpower and fitness as its chief weaponry. When it came to first and finishing touches, it remained somewhat lacking. Among international opponents, it was always felt that the U.S. team as a whole was greater than its parts. The perception abroad about American soccer could be summed up in four words: Great will, little skill. After all these years, America was still forging its identity on the soccer pitch.

CHAPTER 2

1863 . . .

SOCCER IS NO MORE NATIVE TO AMERICA THAN CLOTTED CREAM.
It was conceived in England, mother to all that is footy. The birthday is
recorded very carefully—more accurately, in all likelihood, than the
birthdays of many international youth players—and it occurred on the
morning of October 26, 1863, during the first meeting of a dozen football clubs at the Freemason's Tavern on Great Queen Street in London.
Until this session, the rules of the sport had varied by region and by
whim. But during this gathering and then five more meetings that took
place over nearly three months' time, laws were formalized and the
Football Association (FA) was created. The process was painful and divisive. One club from Blackheath quit the association on the very last
day, when it became apparent the other clubs would not permit carrying the ball downfield by hand or allow tackling with arms. Blackheath
had something a bit more brutish in mind, and joined other clubs
around the region as part of the breakaway Rugby Football Union. But
there were still eleven clubs left in the FA, directed by a man with the
Dickensian name of Ebenezer Cobb Morley, playing football almost
exclusively with their feet.

The original Thirteen Laws of the Game required some tinkering
over the next few years, as a crossbar was added and other rules were
refined. In 1872, the first international match ever officially recorded
was played between England and Scotland at Hamilton Park in Glasgow. Detractors of the sport or of these two particular federations can

delight in knowing the final score was 0–0, although a rematch the following year produced a decisive 4–2 victory for England. As these international matches increased and spread across the European continent, FIFA (Fédération Internationale de Football Association) was formed on May 21, 1904, in Paris. None of the British sides was an original member. Instead, the charter nations were Belgium, Denmark, France, Netherlands, Spain, Sweden, and Switzerland (Germany joined soon after, before FIFA actually began operations that September). To join, each federation paid the equivalent of about ten dollars in French francs. The founding rules were quite sensible. Players could only perform for one national association at a time, and all the members would recognize the suspension of a player in any association. In 1905, England bowed to lobbying efforts by FIFA member Baron Edouard de Laveleye and joined the association. The addition of this football giant allowed FIFA to begin sponsoring international tournaments, including events at the 1908 and 1912 Olympic Games, won by Britain.

By this time, the sport had spread all over the world, including America. It is difficult to pinpoint a true evolutionary ground zero, but easier to trace a myriad of roots and hot pockets around the country—from north Jersey to southern Massachusetts to St. Louis. The Oneida Football Club of Boston began playing some form of the sport in 1862, and an obelisk was erected at Boston Common to honor the team as "the first organized football club in the United States." It was along the banks of the Passaic River in New Jersey, however, where a wave of immigrant textile workers may have begun to compete by the sacred Laws of the Game, as established by the Football Association. The Paterson Football Club was formed in 1880, with three teams that played in the American Football Association: Paterson Rangers, Paterson True Blues, and Paterson Thistle. The True Blues became something of a dynasty, winning the American FA Cup three times. There was photographic evidence of the Paterson F.C., an 1884 picture of 23 players, several in horizontal-striped uniforms, sitting around captain Peter Wright. The caption read, "The first club playing the Association Game in the United States."

But it wasn't just in Paterson that this import was taking root in Jersey. Balls were being booted all along the banks of the Passaic River, wherever mills and textile plants had drawn fresh immigrants from Europe during the Industrial Revolution. The town of Kearny, named after Civil War General Phillip Kearny, seceded in 1867 from the larger municipality of Harrison. Although Kearny had a population of only 11,000 in 1900, it played a disproportionately large role in the growth of soccer at the time, and then again much later. Clubs, leagues, and associations were formed there, as ambitious Scots came to start new lives working at the Clark Thread Company, a corporation with headquarters back in Paisley, Scotland. Another group of players was recruited from the local linoleum plant, Michael Nairn & Company. According to research by David Wangerin, author of *Soccer in a Football World*, Clark's new soccer team in 1883 was named ONT, after Our New Thread, a product the company advertised at the time as "a filament which was the first suitable for use in sewing machines."

The American Football Association was created in the Hose House of Clark's thread factory. ONT of Kearny captured the American FA Cup in 1885, and also that year staged a match on Clark Field with a visiting team from Canada. That was the first time an American club had played host to an international opponent. The next year, Canada visited again on Thanksgiving. The teams split the two matches. A description of conditions at that second game, a 3–2 soggy victory for ONT, was reported in the *Newark Evening News* and cited by soccer historian Roger Allaway:

> Fast falling rain was making a big marsh of the foot ball grounds in Kearny yesterday afternoon when the members of the Canadian foot ball team, dressed in their showy uniforms, made their appearance. The citizens of the Dominion arrived in the city shortly after noon. By the time they had shaken hands with all their friends and eaten dinner at the Continental Hotel it was nearly 3 o'clock. Most people supposed that the game would be postponed on account of the miserable weather, but the Canadian players found the American team practicing and ready to receive them, while 2,000 enthusiasts

stood shivering in the rain anxious to witness the contest. The ground was soft and slippery, and the spot where the spectators stood was a little lake.

While expansion by overseas manufacturers drove the sport in the East, soccer spread through a Midwest hotbed, St. Louis, by a different agent: the Catholic Church. The church pushed soccer as a healthy recreational program as far back as 1886. This led to leagues, tournaments, and provincial dabbling with the rules. Halves were shortened from the standard forty-five minutes to thirty and there was free substitution for injured players. A relatively primitive style of play emerged from the area, one more dependent on speed and on aggressively stripping the ball from opponents with feet-first "tackles" than on the finer art of passing. The St. Louis Soccer League was founded in 1903, and then leagues sprouted exponentially in the area. Wangerin uncovered some old soccer poetry from St. Louis, entitled *Arabella's Favorite Game,* written at the time of World War I and attributed to sportswriter W.H. James:

Miss Arabella Simpkins Brown would leave her book and rocker
And travel half across the town to see a game of soccer.
For there's a sport that's full of thrills, excitement, 'pep' and action,
Of snap and ginger, bumps and spills, to lend its rare attraction,
A baseball game is lame and tame, or so it seems in winter
Compared with this quick-moving game where every man's a
   sprinter . . .

Soccer continued to evolve in the U.S., as it did everywhere else in the world. But unlike other sports in America, it did not gain much impetus from college campuses. There had been some early interest at Princeton, but in 1876 that school turned toward the more hard-boiled version of American football, joining other institutions that had already followed that path. It would be left to the immigrants, to the church, and to the working man to make a go of soccer in America, while the game found less resistance across the pond.

FIFA first declared an intention to create a world championship back at its birth in 1904. After two decades of infighting and considerable procrastination, FIFA decided at the 1924 Paris Olympics to sketch out details for the first World Cup. If the Olympics back then had permitted professionals to compete, there would never have been a need for such a tournament. But Olympic officials were steadfast in their adherence to the slippery concept of amateurism. The Europeans were para-professionals, earning scant pay for play, and were therefore ineligible. By the 1928 Olympics in Amsterdam, FIFA was prepared to award the World Cup to a worthy host for 1930. Two FIFA officials in particular were the guiding forces: president Jules Rimet and secretary Henri Delauney. Five nations bid for the event: Holland, Italy, Spain, Sweden, and Uruguay. The South American country was the only one that agreed to pay the travel and hotel bills for all visiting teams and to build a new stadium expressly for the World Cup. Uruguay was anxious to celebrate the one-hundredth anniversary of its independence with great flourish, despite somewhat limited resources. There were very hard feelings after Uruguay was awarded the tournament. The four losing bidders boycotted the inaugural World Cup, along with soccer powers England, Hungary, Germany, Switzerland, and Czechoslovakia. From a historical perspective, it would be a great loss to all these stubborn, shortsighted federations. Only four European teams—Belgium, France, Romania, and Yugoslavia—agreed to take the long, two-week journey by sea.

The United States was among the thirteen countries that participated in the first World Cup. The Americans, coached by Jack Coll, were hardly Americans, however. The team's starting eleven included an English professional, George Moorehouse, plus five Scotsmen: Andrew Auld, Jimmy Gallagher, Bart McGhee, James Brown, and Sandy Wood. Wood was the only naturalized American. The other four were still Scottish citizens, though with very limited or no professional experience in Britain. Brown's son, George, would play for the U.S. in the late 1950s and was inducted into the Soccer Hall of Fame, along with his father. At the Hall in Oneonta, New York, in 2002, George Brown spoke about his dad's hope even back then for a more diverse American team. "He always believed that for the United States to be successful on the world level, it must attract minority players, have an established professional league and possess a strong youth program," George Brown said. The U.S. team that went to Uruguay received very limited compensation. Players were offered about $30 for each World Cup victory and $25 for each draw. After spending three months in South America altogether, they left with $130 apiece for their trouble. A few players managed to hook on with British professional teams after the tournament. Brown played for both Manchester United and Tottenham Hotspur.

That 1930 team was effective but hardly an elegant side. A French journalist dismayed by the physical brand of football labeled the U.S. side "the shotputters." Despite such derogatory criticism, the Americans were strong enough to dominate weak opponents Paraguay and Belgium in Group 4 play with a pair of 3–0 victories. The U.S. also made history. The team's first match against Belgium at the *Estadio Gran Parque Central* was one of two simultaneous games that kicked off that first World Cup. The hero of the two U.S. wins was a native-born American, Bert Patenaude, twenty-eight, from Fall River, Massachusetts, who scored four goals in those two matches—including the first World Cup hat trick in the team's second win over Paraguay. Patenaude, who died at age sixty-five in 1974, managed to forge a semi-professional soccer career by playing for teams in virtually every American hotbed of the sport. On July 17, 1930, he scored his three goals against Paraguay in the tenth, fifteenth and fiftieth minutes. His second goal was originally credited to a teammate, Tom Florie. But decades later, on November 10, 2006, based on evidence from soccer historians and the U.S. Soccer Federation, FIFA declared that it was in fact Patenaude who scored the first hat trick at the World Cup. As it turned out, this would be the one and only time the U.S. won its group at any World Cup tournament. The Americans would lose their semifinal, 6–1, to Argentina, a team that was fleeter and technically superior. There was virtually no coverage of these events in U.S. newspapers, but the World Cup had been a great success, a boost for the sport everywhere, by osmosis and word of mouth.

Soccer in America was at this juncture something of a regional success story, and Patenaude was very much part of it. On April 5, 1931, playing for what was described in the *New York Times* as "the soccer Yankees," he scored five goals during a 6–2 victory over the Chicago Bricklayers before 12,000 fans at the Polo Grounds, during the first match in a best-of-three national championship series staged by what was then called the U.S. Football Association. A match report appeared in the *New York Times:*

> Chiefly, . . . [the Bricklayers'] eventual defeat was due to the great work of the Yankees' centre forward, Bert Patenaude, a native American and product of Fall River's amateur ranks. Patenaude, after shooting the three goals in the first half, added two more, thereby clinching the victory for his side at a time when Chicago stock was booming. . . . Chicago kicked off at 3:47 o'clock to start the game. Play had been under way only three minutes when Patenaude intercepted White's cross and headed the ball over Neate's shoulders into the net for the first goal."

But any sense of momentum for the sport was quickly lost, frittered away at the 1934 World Cup. The top European teams had joined the tournament, now that it was staged more conveniently in Italy. Dictator Benito Mussolini turned the event into a roaring propaganda machine, much as Adolf Hitler would do with the 1936 Berlin Olympic Games. Several countries felt uncomfortable about such fascist pomp, and the defending champion, Uruguay, declined to participate—in part as a protest against Italy's absence four years earlier. The Italian players offered a fascist salute to Mussolini before every match, and would eventually win the title in overtime, 2–1, over Czechoslovakia. The Americans were required to qualify for this tournament, becoming the very last team to earn a berth by defeating Mexico three days before the World Cup began. The U.S. then suffered the misfortune of facing the hosts in a first-round knockout match. The result was a 7–1 thrashing by Italy that did nothing to lift the sport from America's shadows.

The debacle was reported by the Associated Press:

"Although play was constantly in American territory, the invaders held Italy scoreless for the first eighteen minutes of the game but thereafter it was a procession of Italian goals. Italy led by 3–0 at half time and although Aldo (Buff) Donelli of Curry, Pa., netted the first goal in the second half to make the score 3–1, the Americans really had no chance against the fine team play of their rivals . . . A crowd of 30,000, including Premier Mussolini, saw the match."

Donelli, who died in 1994, epitomized the American player navigating these times. He loved soccer above all else, yet found it impossible to make a living in the sport and instead later coached two different American football teams during the same season. In 1941, Donelli led his alma mater Duquesne University to an undefeated season and also coached the Pittsburgh Steelers of the National Football League to five straight losses. Later in his coaching career, he guided Columbia University to its only Ivy League football title. Donelli's goal at the World Cup was a source of great pride for the man, but that one-sided defeat, plus tense global politics, sent American soccer officials scampering for cover. From 1934 to 1947, the U.S. Soccer Federation skipped all international competition and paid a heavy price for its bunker mentality. Soccer stagnated, while college football claimed a large chunk of the nation's autumn sporting scene. It wasn't until 1950 that yet another Scotsman, Penn State coach Bill Jeffrey, put together a team to compete at the World Cup in Brazil. The result would be one of the greatest upset victories in the history of football of any variety.

CHAPTER 3

The Odyssey Begins

THE QUALIFYING PROCESS FOR THE 2010 WORLD CUP IN SOUTH Africa was a tortuous path, though certainly more grueling for some nations than for others. A middling soccer team such as the U.S. was far better off assigned to CONCACAF or to the Asian region than to Europe, where the talent pool was overwhelming and even the minnows bite with considerable ferocity. Regardless of grouping, however, this was no cake walk. For most federations, the journey required nearly a year and a half of passionately physical matches at far-flung venues before hostile fans in extreme climatic, altitudinal, and stadium conditions.

There were only thirty-two of these precious berths available—actually thirty-one, because one was allotted to the host, South Africa—and they were carefully parceled out by zone. As qualifying began for 2010, the U.S. was one of only seven countries to have earned a place in all the World Cup tournaments since 1990. The others were powerhouses Germany, Italy, Spain, Argentina, and Brazil, plus another regional stalwart, South Korea. Even such giants as England and France had faltered along the way, while Mexico was disqualified in 1990 for fielding over-aged players in youth competitions.

By the official entry deadline of March 15, 2007, FIFA had received 204 applications to participate in the 2010 World Cup qualifying tournaments. Five nations—Bhutan, Central African Republic, Eritrea, Guam, and Sao Tome and Principe—subsequently withdrew. That left the number just shy of 200. Fewer than one in six of these teams would survive all the way to South Africa.

FIFA made some effort every four years to adjust the number of qualifiers from each region, according to various power ratings. But if sheer ability were the only measure, then Europe would probably get about eighteen berths, South America would receive six, Africa four, Asia two, and CONCACAF two. That mix wouldn't be international enough for organizers or sponsors, who were desperately trying to act with global correctness and to sell this extravaganza as a democratic affair. So Europe received just thirteen berths for 2010, while CONCACAF was granted three and a half. The fourth-place finisher in CONCACAF would play off against the fifth-place finisher in South America for a final spot.

This meant that at least one and possibly two marginal CONCACAF teams—other than traditional powers U.S. and Mexico—could win a trip to the World Cup finals. Not many years earlier, there was reason for considerable optimism about soccer in this region. Jamaica had been steadily improving while Trinidad and Tobago was exporting some of its top players abroad for proper honing. But for one reason or another, progress halted spectacularly in the early 2000s. Everybody noticed, even if it were impolitic to admit such a thing. Bruce Arena would never speak to that point until he was out of office. Then, and only then, he admitted the obvious.

"Everything is falling apart in CONCACAF," Arena said. "Jamaica was going to be the next good team, and they've taken a step backward. Costa Rica stopped making progress. The money and organization just aren't there."

The players noticed this, too. After a shutout victory over Trinidad and Tobago during the run-up to Germany 2006, the famously left-footed Eddie Lewis declared that "everybody else except us and Mexico is stalling. Our depth, our federation, is getting better and better. The gap is getting bigger and bigger." The Americans weren't complaining about such lopsided circumstances. If you asked the players whether they felt the least bit guilty about their overwhelming advantage in CONCACAF play, they understandably responded that their only concern was a letdown on the field as such heavy favorites. The men were very different in this way than the women. When Mia Hamm was asked a similar question about beating up on smaller, underfinanced countries, she responded thoughtfully that she hoped the U.S. team could become an example to other federations in the region. Hamm wanted to believe these other countries would come to realize how allotting adequate funds for a women's team might lead to great things. The U.S. men didn't think like that. On an international scale, they were still the playground pushovers, grabbing whatever victories where they could.

The CONCACAF qualifying process began in downright silly fashion, as top teams were forced to play two aggregate-score knockout matches, home and away, against under-financed and over-matched opponents from tiny Caribbean islands. In general, Central American opponents were far more formidable in terms of passion, governmental commitment, and home field advantage than Caribbean teams. Fans from the Caribbean islands were usually more interested in cricket or baseball. They were polite and welcoming to soccer visitors and also hampered by another factor, geography. These isles were by nature low-lying, and therefore it was impossible to stage high-altitude matches that might be of a considerable disadvantage to visitors. The condition of the home field was the only true variable. Jamaica, for example, was virtually unbeatable for years in the national stadium nicknamed, "The Office," in large part because of the rock-hard ground and the baked blades that were more hay than grass. Goats commonly grazed outside the stadium, a further indication to visitors that this rickety building was more a public right of way than it was Wembley Stadium in London.

Starting in spring of 2008, the Americans faced the daunting prospect again of eighteen qualifying matches in sixteen months required to reach the tournament in South Africa. The first round opponent was Barbados, an island nation with a population of 281,000 and a mucky home pitch. There was a history between these two teams. Back in November 2000, the U.S. had found itself in alarming straits during the semifinal round of qualifying, needing a victory in Waterford, Barbados, in order to advance toward the 2002 World Cup in Japan and Korea. The match was set for a Wednesday. On that Tuesday, the Americans pulled into National Stadium aboard a chartered shuttle bus for a scheduled practice. The Barbados soccer players arrived too, by more modest means. One rode a bicycle while three car-poolers, each wearing a different uniform, were stuffed into a mini-compact. Within an hour, everyone was ordered to leave the place. Emerson Mathurin, Canadian match commissioner for the World Cup qualifying game, decided the field was in such terrible shape that it could not support training sessions by either side.

"This is as bad as it gets," said Arena, then the U.S. coach, after stepping over the potholes and slogging through some muddy bare spots. The Barbados federation had endured four player strikes in the previous year, a funding crisis that was only solved after FIFA donated $150,000 toward minimal player stipends amounting to $200 per month, plus bonuses of $300–425 per match. At the time, the goalkeeper, Horace Stoute, was expected to retire soon to become a full-time barber. Soccer was not the first love of Barbados, where highway roundabouts were named for adored, local cricket stars.

The Americans came within thirty minutes of a disastrous 0-0 draw that Wednesday in Waterford before they salvaged the 2000 qualifier with an explosion of four late goals. This time around there would be far less drama, because the first match against Barbados took place on June 15, 2008, in Carson, CA, where there was plenty of grass and no realistic threat of elimination. The Americans were ranked number twenty-one in the world at this time by FIFA, exactly 100 positions ahead of Barbados. Leading into the game, the U.S. warmed up with exhibitions against the mighty triumvirate of England, Spain, and Argentina. Meanwhile, Barbados played Bermuda and lost, 3–0. "You are playing to go to the World Cup," Landon Donovan insisted. "You can't underestimate anyone on the planet."

Not many people really bought into that notion and only 11,476 Southern California fans showed up at the Home Depot Center for the match, which immediately became a rout. The 8-0 final score represented the largest victory margin in the ninety-year history of international play for the U.S. team. Maybe Mia Hamm's teams would have pulled back a bit, but the men just kept pouring it on. Clint Dempsey broke another record, the team's fastest goal ever, scoring in just fifty-three seconds. Brian Ching and Michael Bradley added two more in the match's first twenty minutes. Dempsey and Ching netted two goals apiece. Donovan, Bradley, and Eddie Johnson scored one each. Daryl Ferguson of Barbados managed a humiliating own goal. After failing to score even once during those three tune-ups against the giants of soccer, the U.S. found it almost impossible to miss against Barbados. Donovan's goal in the fifty-ninth minute was the one that bugged Barbados the most. The midfielder scored on a free kick while his opponents were still setting up their wall, before any whistle from the referee. It hardly mattered. "You can't say, 'OK, we're ready to win the World Cup after beating Barbados,'" Dempsey said. "We're not going to get a false sense of hope. It's a totally different team today than we played before. It's not like we're doing so well. It's difficult to score against the best teams in the world. We'd like to score more goals against the better teams." The result effectively eliminated any meaning from the return match at Barbados, on the cricket grounds in Bridgetown. "We have to go to Barbados and make sure we don't lose 9–0," Dempsey joked. Instead the Americans won by a modest score, 1–0.

More meaningful than the one-sided, nine-goal aggregate victory was Bradley's lineup for that first match against Barbados, which foretold a somewhat cautious reign. At the start of this qualifying run, there appeared to be seven core players who were givens, likely to start most matches: Donovan, the twenty-six-year-old attacking midfielder and mainstay for the Los Angeles Galaxy of MLS, who already had scored thirty-four goals for the national side through 2007; Dempsey, twenty-five, another natural wide midfielder playing for Fulham of the English Premier League; DaMarcus Beasley, twenty-six, the swift midfielder for Glasgow Rangers who had seventy-two caps, or appearances, for the U.S. national team in seven years; Carlos Bocanegra, twenty-nine, the veteran defender who was transferring at the time from Fulham to Rennes in France; Michael Bradley, twenty-one, the coach's son and midfielder who had scored twenty-one goals for Heerenveen in the Netherlands and was headed for Borussia Mönchengladbach of the Bundesliga in Germany; Oguchi Onyewu, twenty-six, the giant, six-foot, four-inch middle defender starring at Standard de Leige in Belgium; and Tim Howard, twenty-nine, the starting goalkeeper at Everton in the Premier League.

That left four spots for Bob Bradley to fill, more or less at his whim. And while there had been some imaginative, aggressive selections available for this Barbados match—including defender Jay DeMerit, young attacking midfielders Freddy Adu and Sacha Kljestan, plus swift forward Eddie Johnson—the opening lineup was far more practiced and conventional: Brad Guzan in goal, replacing Howard, who was suffering from a sore back; Steve Cherundolo and Heath Pearce at outside backs; Onyewu and Bocanegra at center backs; Michael Bradley and Pablo Mastroeni, the holding midfielders; Donovan and Beasley, the attacking midfielders; Brian Ching and Dempsey at forward. Of all these selections, the choice of Ching was arguably the most telling. He was a perfectly competent, conventional striker in the MLS, and would score fourteen goals during the 2008 season for the Houston Dynamo. But his upside was not particularly notable on the international level. Ching was mostly tough and big. He played the target striker role filled more effectively in previous years by Brian McBride. Bradley might have moved either Donovan or Dempsey up top, with Adu or Kljestan trailing, to create a potentially dynamic setup. But he was not the first soccer coach to choose consistency and work ethic over creativity. Such decisions had been made for decades, by American and international coaches alike. Arena, for one, had lost patience back in 2002 with lurker Clint Mathis, despite some spectacular goals. Several coaches in England abandoned David Beckham, who was seen as something of a one-trick pony. That trick—Beckham's ability to cross the ball onto a teammate's head from fifty yards, or to bend a free kick into the upper corner—was worthy of a place on any roster. But coaches were coaches. They simply didn't want to look out onto a field and spot a player trotting about listlessly, biding his time, risking a counter-attack by opponents, until a golden opportunity arose.

Any lineup debate for the Barbados match was quickly forgotten, after a half-dozen goals were netted in the first half. There were still vacancies to be filled—most notably at left back, a stubborn, traditional landmine for the U.S. side. The Americans moved on nonetheless to the semifinal qualifying round, a relatively safe round-robin tournament in which they were required only to finish among the top two in a four-team group comprised of themselves, Cuba, Guatemala, and Trinidad and Tobago. Advancement was all but clinched again in the very first match, when the U.S. posted a difficult, physical 1–0 victory in Guatemala City on August 28, 2008—which included a red card for both sides.

This was the first time the U.S. had ever won a World Cup qualifier in Guatemala, a breakthrough of sorts. But there were extenuating factors. The Guatemalans made a serious tactical error by staging the match at *Estadio Mateo Flores*, a 25,000-seat stadium, named after a Guatemalan runner who won the 1952 Boston Marathon. The place had recognizable infrastructures such as a rooted grass field and a conventional visitors' locker room. It was, in other words, a real stadium. Once the site of a horrible soccer stampede in 1996 that cost more than eighty lives before a qualifier against Costa Rica, the building's capacity had been reduced and tighter security was put into place. This venue was far more comfortable for visitors now than the alternatives. During a previous qualifier against Guatemala in 2000, the Americans were forced to trek across jungle by bus to reach the disconcerting, disorienting, mosquito-riddled soccer grounds in Mazatenango. The decision to go with *Estadio Flores* came down to a matter of height: Guatemala City had an elevation of 4,921 feet, nearly a mile high, while Mazatenango lay on a coastal plain at just 1,217 feet. The Guatemala National Football Federation felt high altitude was a requisite edge against the U.S. side, which struggled on a regular basis with elevation problems in Mexico City. The Americans braced themselves for trouble. "I have friends in England who say, 'Oh, it's just Guatemala, that's an easy three points,'" Howard said. "They don't understand that there's nothing easy about it."

The air proved inadequately thin, however, and the Americans were just lucky and plucky enough to win. Guatemala, ranked one-hundredth in the world by the FIFA computer, outshot the U.S., 16–9, and forced Howard to make seven saves, a couple of them quite difficult. The Guatemalans were known around CONCACAF to be a dirty side, and this match was marred by forty foul calls—including one that nullified a Guatemala goal. Carlos Ruiz kicked Howard during a play that eventually resulted in a goal by Guillermo Rodriguez, which would be disallowed. Afterward, Howard fumed at Ruiz while Guatemala coach Ramon Maradiaga aimed his wrath at the official, Enrico Wijngaarde of Suriname. "They annulled a goal that was ours, and that happens because they name referees that lack the preparation to call a game at this level," Maradiaga said. "But that is what FIFA does. Their decisions are unappealable."

The match was in doubt from the start, and became extremely dicey after Cherundolo was ejected in the sixtieth minute with a second yellow card for tripping Freddy Garcia. Tim Howard's play was remarkable, as was that of defender Carlos Bocanegra, who never lost sight in the box of Guatemala's chief scoring threats, Carlos Manuel Contreras and Carlos Ruiz. Eventually the Americans demonstrated their pedigree on a goal in the sixty-ninth minute, when Bocanegra used Ching as a pick to clear himself in front of the net, then headed a DaMarcus Beasley corner kick for a goal. Beasley had entered the match as a substitute just three minutes earlier, after Eddie Lewis was carried off the field with a five-stitch wound to his head from a forearm by Jose Manuel Contreras. It was Bocanegra's tenth goal for the national team in fifty-nine appearances. The reliable defender, approaching age thirty at the time, had not skipped a single step in his determined rise to the U.S. national team's captaincy. The son of a Mexican-American father in Alta Loma, California, Bocanegra played college soccer at UCLA, then was drafted in 2000 and was voted Rookie of the Year for the Chicago Fire of MLS. He signed with Fulham in 2004 and played more than a hundred matches for that side until he was viewed to be in decline and was released to play for Rennes. The center back was far from the most colorful of American players, yet Bocanegra was respected by both teammates and coaches as a defensive anchor and a cautious spokesman.

His goal against Guatemala, however, left the home team incensed. One local journalist asked Bradley outright, "How does it feel to win a match with the help of the referee?"

"The referee did a very solid job trying to deal with a very hard-fought game," Bradley responded. "For us, it was a hard-fought three points. It was pure determination of the team which is necessary to win games like this one." Bradley's core group had come through, and his somewhat suspect outside defensive backs had held. Much credit belonged to Howard. He was the chief organizer in the back, the most passionate of participants. He had patiently awaited his turn for many years, and was now savoring every save, seizing every moment.

CHAPTER 4

A Yank at Goodison Park

TIM HOWARD STOOD ALONE IN THE MIDDLE OF A SOCCER FIELD, totally ignored for one of the last times in his life. This was back in June 2001, when Howard had just earned his spot as starting goalkeeper on the New York MetroStars of Major League Soccer. He had generously volunteered to appear in support of a breast cancer fundraising event in Montclair, New Jersey, sponsored by Goals for Life. All around him, men, women and children were kicking around balls, earnestly scrimmaging, failing to acknowledge the emerging star among them. Virtually nobody recognized him or even knew his name. A few short years down the road, Howard would need to be protected from a very different public: from aggressive English fans at Manchester United and Everton. But for now, he stood alone, peering at the ground. Finally a local sportswriter walked up to Howard, who seemed glad for the company. He spoke about his schedule, his hopes for the season, and in this light, at this time, Howard was clearly comfortable with his own virtual anonymity. Howard owned aspirations to become a top-level athlete, to star on the professional and international levels. But he could wait. He didn't covet the fame that accompanied such achievement.

Howard had his reasons for this reluctance, beyond an inherent shyness. He'd been tremendously successful on the playing fields throughout his young life, working his way up through the New Jersey scholastic, developmental, and pro ranks until he earned a spot as resident starter on the MetroStars. But he was fighting a second battle simultaneously.

He needed to focus doubly hard, to conquer a case of Tourette's syndrome that occasionally caused a tic of the eye, a twitch of the arms, a flick of the neck.

"My case is worse than some, better than others," said Howard, who decided to make his condition known and to become involved in foundation work to help children afflicted with the same problem. "It's neurological, provoked by anxiety, and naturally a soccer match is a nervous time. Maybe off the ball it may happen. But once my eye and mind click over to the ball, I am focused and nothing happens. Never on a kick or a save."

He was the son of an African-American truck driver, Matthew, and a white Hungarian immigrant, Esther, a sales manager. Growing up in North Brunswick, New Jersey, Howard remembered getting teased by classmates as early as fifth grade, when he first became conscious of his problem. He would come home exhausted each day, after fighting to restrain any tics or vocal outbursts in school. While busy soul-searching, he became a big fan of Louisiana State basketball star Chris Jackson, who later changed his name to Mahmoud Abdul-Rauf. Abdul-Rauf suffered from a more severe case of Tourette's, which led him to blurt out incoherent phrases at random times during practices and games. "I saw this star, and I thought, 'He's making it,'" Howard said. "My dream is, I still want to meet him, get his autographed jersey." Howard's case was more subtle, nothing like the "poop"-blurting character, Melanie West, played with comic flourishes back in 2001 by Anne Heche on *Ally McBeal*. "If I curse," Howard said, "it's just because I'm ticked off." Not every teammate on the MetroStars even knew he suffered from Tourette's. "He considered it a gift, part of him," said Mike Petke, his roommate on the road with the MetroStars. "Look where it got him. Look where he is, and what he's accomplished." For some time, Howard did not wish to talk about it. Then he decided to go public. If his own story inspired a fifth-grader somewhere with Tourette's, Howard could feel that much better about his own condition.

"At first, I backed away from talking about it," Howard said. "It was a comfort zone I was in. But now, it's a coming out. Why not put it in the media guide?" And so, he did. His MetroStar teammates were less concerned with his Tourette's than with his play. They were depending on a twenty-two-year-old goalkeeper that season to take over from former team leader Mike Ammann. Howard was listed in a lot of league previews as the team's primary question mark, which upset him. "Here's an obvious answer to that question mark," Howard said. "A pro organization with lots of money on the line supports me. I have their respect. The only questions come from the outside."

It was still early in his career, but Howard was doing all the right things, consorting with the right people. When choosing his place of residence, Howard made an important symbolic gesture. After talking with former U.S. star Tony Meola, he moved to Kearny, New Jersey, birthplace of American soccer. Howard's physical strengths were obvious, even then. At 6-feet, 3-inches and 210 pounds, rock solid, he was always a formidable presence inside his own box. He was aggressive off the line, with extraordinary reflexes. "A great shot-stopper, vocal in the back, easy to get along with," said Clint Mathis, a teammate on both the MetroStars and the national team. The nicest thing you could say about Howard, really, was that nobody didn't like him. Howard was a professional, and treated others the same way. When an opponent scored a goal against him, he didn't necessarily take it out on his defenders.

"I've played with a number of goalkeepers in college and growing up who like to bark orders, point fingers when a goal is scored," Petke said. "I never understood that. Their number one job is to stop the shot. We limit the shots to two or three on goal, and then goalies yell, 'How'd they get that shot off?' That flat-out pissed me off. We don't turn around and point fingers when the ball goes in. Timmy was proactive. But when he did have something to say, he was so professional, you didn't take offense. He has a very commanding voice. You listen. You know he's not bitching. He's never been that type of guy. You'll see a ball go in, and he'll get angry at himself."

Petke remembered his MetroStar days with Howard fondly, though the two bachelors were hardly the wildest pair on the road. They'd drink some beers, trash talk each other and order a lot of room service. Petke knew from the start that Howard was a great talent, and that his temperament would serve him well. "Even when he was sitting behind Tony Meola and Mike Ammann, he was fine with that, always trying in practice. Once he got a shot, he took it by the reins."

Howard was only the latest in a long line of potentially world-class American goalkeepers. While the U.S. struggled to develop international standouts at all field positions, there was never a shortage of talent over the decades when it came to guarding the net. The keepers just seemed to be getting better and better. Meola was a fine reader of the game, a passionate leader, even if he wasn't on an athletic par with the very best European keepers. Then came Brad Friedel and Kasey Keller, two rivals who survived all anti-American prejudices to become durable successes in the Premier League.

There was considerable debate about how this was possible; how America had produced such a lopsided talent pool in goal. The most obvious theory was that the country was a hands-first, feet-second nation, and that in this way the U.S. would always have an advantage over others. A strong goalkeeper also could emerge from weaker youth teams. He required less talent around him in order to shine. He wasn't as reliant as a midfielder on passing or teamwork. It was more important to face the challenge and searing shots of high-level opponents than to play on the same side with such stars. Finally, there was considerable depth in the coaching ranks at this position. Good goalkeepers created good goalkeepers in America from generation to generation, by sheer example and by coaching the younger prospects.

Soon, even the skeptical scouts abroad had come to respect and covet U.S. goalkeepers. It was quite a leap of faith for all when Howard transferred in 2003 from the MetroStars to mighty Manchester United. The soccer world was small enough, however, that no jewel went un-plucked for long. Manchester United owned a pervasive scouting system and MLS was on the radar. Howard had won the MLS Goalkeeper of the Year award in 2001 after recording 4 shutouts and 146 saves. His talent was undeniable. He was also brilliantly athletic. Des McAleenan, the Irish goalkeeper coach with the MetroStars, knew from the start he had someone special in his net. "He wasn't as tidy or complete a package as you see now, a little sloppy in training, but he had the ability to dominate and take over games," said McAleenan, who had tapes of every save Howard made with the MetroStars. "Come game time, boy, could he play. It was amazing the ability he had to switch on. I look back at some of the stuff he'd done, it's pretty impressive, a lot to be proud of. Every year he got better and better. He was exceptional—lightning quick reflexes, very good hands, explosive power, a real competitor. This was a great athlete. He was a gentleman, very level-headed. Good family. Well-grounded. It was an easy sell. All you had to do was get somebody's attention to his talents."

McAleenan did his part, making his own pitch. By sheer chance, he was a confidante of Dan Gaspar, the goalkeeper coach with Portugal. Gaspar, in turn, was a longtime friend of Carlos Queiroz, the Portuguese assistant coach at Manchester United. Queiroz asked Gaspar to help him find a replacement for Fabien Barthez, the French keeper who was driving the club crazy with his flightiness. "Gasper asked me to put together a list of top ten goalkeepers in the world," McAleenan said. "Then he asked me if there were any others. I said, 'We've got a fellow here who's among the top three young goalkeepers in the world.'" Gaspar made the recommendation to Queiroz. Whether or not this was a major factor is debatable. But United scouted Howard during a high-pressure match against Mexico at Reliant Stadium in Houston on May 8, 2003, before nearly 70,000 fans. Soon enough, he was signed.

"Manchester United didn't turn Tim into a fantastic goalkeeper," McAleenan said. "Within one month, he was playing for them at Charity Shield. They got a player who could already play."

By the early summer of 2003, Howard was starting on the U.S. national team at the Confederations Cup in France, and heading for Manchester. He would stop only long enough back in New York's Central Park to marry Laura Cianciola, an all-city basketball player from Memphis, Tennessee, who had been introduced to him by her cousin, Ross Paule, another MLS player. Then it was off to England, to play for head coach Sir Alex Ferguson.

No native American player had ever managed to crack the lineup of one of the Big Four Premier League teams: Manchester United, Arsenal, Liverpool or Chelsea. But fabled Man United thought enough of

Howard, just twenty-four years old, to pay a $3.4 million transfer fee to Major League Soccer and a $1.4 million salary directly to Howard—the same fellow who two years earlier was being totally ignored on a rutted field in Montclair, New Jersey. Traditionally, goalkeepers didn't peak until they were close to thirty years old, if only because experience and knowledge of the angles trumped physicality at this position. But Ferguson almost immediately anointed Howard a starter at Old Trafford, ahead of the French World Cup star Barthez, and Howard roared off to a fast start over his first ten matches.

Not all was sweetness and light. There remained a startling absence of sensitivity in this region of the world. "I had no idea what I was getting myself into," Howard said. Americans learned long ago to curb their tongues, to think before taunting, or else face communal disapproval. In much of Europe, there was far more tolerance for intolerance. The God-given right to utter offensive phrases at will was considered a great freedom to some. Howard was a perfect target in this unfiltered world of tabloid headlines and vulgar supporter chants. He was large, he was of mixed race descent and he suffered from Tourette's syndrome—though Howard would argue there was no suffering involved. The tabloids had fun at Howard's expense, and then the creative fans at Old Trafford invented some chants that were in theory supportive but were largely insulting. One went, "Timmy Tourette's is in our nets; Fuck off, Fuck off, Fuck off." Another, sung to an old "Mary Poppins" tune, went, "Tim-Timer-ee, Tim-Timer-ee, Tim-Tim-Ter-oo; We've got Tim Howard and he says, 'Fuck you.'" You get the idea. "People aren't afraid of Tourette's," Howard said, about the experience. "They just need to be educated. Only four percent of people with Tourette's curse."

As long as Howard performed well in the nets, this sort of teasing would remain good-natured enough. And because Manchester United threw around mad money to purchase the very best players in the world, his success was more or less assured. If Howard made a mistake here or there, world-class strikers and defenders playing in front of him likely would compensate. Howard started seventy-seven matches at Manchester, assuring himself a lucrative career and numerous high-pressure situations.

"I expected to have to be patient at United," Howard told the *Miami Herald* at the time. "You are coming into a legendary club, and you have to pay your dues. Maybe I didn't have to pay as many as some people. People say I'm doing so great, something bad is bound to happen. But I am not touching wood. If it turns, I believe I can handle it. I like to think I have pretty thick skin, thicker than other people."

Nothing lasts forever, especially in the world that spins so rapidly atop the Premier League. Clubs like Man United were forever searching for the next bright star in the galaxy, another way to sell their brand. Howard famously misplayed a critical ball from a free kick by Benny McCarthy of Porto, costing United a 2004 Champions League match. Then before the start of the 2005–2006 season, United acquired Edwin van der Sar, a nimble goalkeeper for the Dutch national side. It became immediately obvious that Howard's reign as a starter had ended, following two impressive seasons and an FA Cup title. Suddenly, Howard found himself in the uncomfortable position of benchwarmer that too often sabotages the development of American players in England or other top leagues abroad. His U.S. national teammates Freddy Adu, DaMarcus Beasley, Carlos Bocanegra, Eddie Johnson, Landon Donovan, and Jozy Altidore all would suffer, at one time or another, longer periods of diminished participation, despite good health. If Howard did nothing about this, his skills were certain to deteriorate and he would likely lose his projected spot on the U.S. national team. He went to Ferguson directly and suggested he be loaned out to another team—that peculiar, yet humane process in Europe by which a player remained under contract with one side, while playing with another. The only caveat in this sort of arrangement was that the athlete in question sat out matches against his original, contracted team. Man United had absolutely no intention of loaning Howard to one of its three chief rivals. As it turned out, however, Everton was the perfect middle-of-the-table alternative. The Toffees had finished eleventh in the twenty-team league the previous season. They were a solid side from Liverpool, but they weren't Liverpool. Everton played next door to that more fabled club, while forever hoping to relocate from its own aging stadium.

So Howard was sent to Goodison Park, where he was a great hit. There was pressure with Everton, aspirations of greatness, but not the outrageous presumptions present at Manchester. "At Man United, you knew each season that you would lose only four games," Howard told the *Boston Globe*. "There's a weird joy in not knowing." In 2006–2007, Everton exceeded expectations by finishing sixth, qualifying for European competition and whipping its archrival Liverpool, 3–0, in one match. That victory was greeted with such joy that the club issued a Christmas DVD of the game.

In 2009, by now fully under contract with Everton, Howard would beat Manchester United with two brilliant penalty kick saves in an FA Cup semifinal. If he were seeking revenge—which he was not—it might have been very sweet. Instead, he was busy assimilating, quietly living with his wife and two children in Liverpool. After six seasons overseas, Howard was starting to develop a trace of an English accent. "Uh-oh, I hope I don't have an accent. Maybe so," he said. "But I'm a Jersey boy, born and bred. I'll always be from Jersey."

Another thing hadn't changed. Howard would not take any medication to control his Tourette's symptoms.

"I've been dealing with TS for twenty years, more than twenty years," he said. "For me, it's something that is as normal as breathing. You get up everyday, it's just there. It's not something at this stage that I think about. It's not something that I worry about what people will think or how they react. It's a part of me. And I've gotten to the point where I've realized Tim Howard could not be Tim Howard without TS. I would be a completely different person, 100 percent. I'm completely at ease with it. At the moment, I don't think medication seems to be the answer. It's just a short-term resolution. For me, I'd rather live the way I live—unmedicated."

CHAPTER 5

Carrying the Torch

WHILE WORLD CUP QUALIFYING ROUNDS TRUDGED ALONG DURING the summer of 2008, a set of top young American prospects were sent packing to the other side of the world for the Beijing Olympics. There was nothing sensible about Olympic soccer, at least on the men's side. While the women used the Summer Games as a complementary showcase alongside their World Cup, the men's tournament was a clumsy compromise between competition and protectionism, a hybrid of nearly random eligibility and qualification rules. The tournament had been molded and twisted in such unfathomable ways so as to pose no great threat to FIFA's golden goose, the men's World Cup. But then every four or eight years, the Americans found themselves at another Summer Games, competing in earnest to steal a medal. And even if the Olympic "football" competition was more novelty than measuring stick, it presented the U.S. program with another high-profile opportunity to capture lightning in a bottle.

According to International Olympic Committee rules, each nation was required to field a roster of Under-23 players, plus three select players of any age. In 2008, this exception provided the International Olympic Committee the cheap thrill that came with the cameo appearance of superstar Ronaldinho of Brazil. He would compete against the brilliant youngster, Lionel Messi of Argentina, already anointed the future king of soccer at the age of twenty-one. Both those players arrived to great fanfare in Beijing, rendering Brazil and Argentina instant co-favorites for a gold medal. Sixteen nations had qualified, and the three African entrants—Nigeria, Ivory Coast, and Cameroon—were also given solid chances, for the most cynical reason. It was a long-held belief among international federations and officials that African-born players were not necessarily the age transcribed on their birth certificates. In many countries on the continent, birth dates were officially first recorded upon parental registration, which might take place at some later time. Fairly or not, teams such as Nigeria, Ghana and Cameroon regularly overachieved in youth competitions—and, by extension, at the Olympics—because of lax age enforcement. At least one American coach argued that bone scans of wrists should be mandated to correctly determine the ages of these African players. By the next year, 2009, FIFA employed magnetic resonance images to test ages of players before the Under-17 championships in Nigeria, and only seven of thirty-six players on the host team's roster passed the preliminary MRI test. Fifteen players on the roster were dropped from Nigeria's squad. But that technology had not yet been embraced by Olympic officials in Beijing, arguably for another cynical reason. Such testing in all sports might have disqualified too-young Chinese gymnasts, not just too-old African soccer athletes.

The U.S. team could hardly feel too self-righteous about this matter, because there remained in international circles some question about the correct age of Freddy Adu, whose birth date in Tema, Ghana, qualified him to play on the 2008 Olympic team. Adu was the closest thing on the U.S. roster to a celebrity athlete. He was forever a teasing, puzzling talent, a misty legend almost from birth. It was generally accepted that Adu's nimble feet came into this world in the soccer-committed nation of Ghana on or around June 2, 1989. He started kicking the ball at age two. When he was just seven years old, Adu was playing pickup soccer games against adults in the port city of Tema. At age eight, his mother won the Green Card Lottery, the Diversity Immigrant Visa program in the United States that allowed some applicants from relatively low-emigration countries to receive a permanent resident card. The Adus settled in Rockville, Maryland, and Freddy would become a U.S. citizen in 2003.

Adu's extraordinary soccer skills immediately set off alarms of all kinds among local coaches. He was the target of both recruitment and gossip. How could such a young, relatively tiny kid be so technically advanced? His athletic career became the family's top priority as he skipped from seventh to ninth grades at the private Heights School in Potomac, primarily so that he could play on the varsity team—which captured the state championship in 2001. He was offered a pro contract at the ridiculous age of ten years old by Inter Milan—a deal that his mother wisely rejected. Instead he was packed off to the Bradenton Academy in Florida, soccer finishing school, at age twelve in January 2002. Everything about his development was accelerated, including expectations, and much of this hype would prove detrimental. Because he was short—Adu never grew beyond 5-feet, 6-inches—he appeared even more of a misfit when he played with older, larger kids.

"I first saw him when he was twelve at a tournament in Chicago," said John Ellinger, his coach with the Under-17 team at Bradenton. "When he was twelve and thirteen, he had to act a lot older. And at Bradenton, he had trouble with the social aspects. He needed attention in the area of social graces. And then when he got to MLS, he had to act older again."

By the time Adu was a teenager, it seemed half the world knew about his exploits and vast potential. His family seemed to welcome much of this fuss. Then his U.S. Olympic Development team won an Under-14 title against top international competition, and he was named the tournament MVP. He signed a six-year, three million dollar contract with D.C. United, which allowed him to remain near home. It also made him the youngest modern-day American athlete to sign a professional deal. Still only fourteen years old in the spring of 2004, Freddy Adu made his debut in Major League Soccer. It was, certainly, more show than substance. The opening day match on April 3 against the San Jose Earthquakes received a great deal of attention and was nationally televised. But Peter Nowak, the D.C. United coach, would not be influenced by the clamor. The coach believed that Adu hadn't yet earned a starting role and wasn't ready for such a challenge. So Nowak made the audience wait. He brought Adu off the bench as a second-half substitute, embarrassing both MLS and television broadcasters. Throughout that first season, Nowak refused to bow to pressures from spectators or networks and remained stubbornly more concerned with winning. "I told [the media] at the beginning of the season, this won't happen overnight," Nowak said. After starting a few matches, getting bounced around a bit, Adu was replaced by midfielder Christian Gomez in the lineup and became the league's most famous reserve. Adu wasn't exactly a bust. He had five goals and three assists in that first year, for a championship side. He was not much help tracking back on defense, but Adu could create space and dangerous chances with explosive, acute-angled moves. He just hadn't lived up to the headlines, that greatest of all sporting sins.

During his second season on the bench, Adu began to grow impatient. He was suspended for one match after complaining about his playing time to the press. By 2006, he was not only starting, Adu was often selected to take both penalty and free kicks, which became something of a specialty. He was traded to Real Salt Lake in December 2006, and was also starring on U.S. youth national teams, named captain of the Under-20 side. His volatile stock was rising again. After some truly promising performances by Adu at the 2007 U-20 World Cup, Benfica of Portugal paid a $2 million transfer fee to Real Salt Lake for his contractual rights. But here was where Adu's momentum sadly stalled again. He appeared in only 11 matches with the team, before the Portuguese powerhouse sent him to second-tier AS Monaco. The Monaco situation was unique. Club president Jerome de Bontin was a French-American who had voiced the desire to bring a U.S. business model to his franchise. De Bontin championed Adu, yet the player again languished on the bench. He was positioned out on the wing, a more traditional spot for such a diminutive player, rather than in the middle where he preferred. De Bontin would soon leave Monaco at the start of 2009, leaving Adu again without a patron. Eventually, he would land in Greece.

The Americans were handicapped in Beijing by the World Cup qualifying schedule that included a difficult opening semifinal round match at Guatemala, which coincidentally was set for the second week of the Olympics. If it hadn't been for this potential conflict, U.S. Soccer most likely would have tabbed Donovan, Howard and Bocanegra to fill the over-23 quota. But those stars were all needed against Guatemala.

Peter Nowak—the same coach entrusted with Adu's early career at D.C. United—was now the Olympic coach. His bonus players were the veteran forward, Brian McBride, thirty-six, goalkeeper Brad Guzan, twenty-three, and center back Michael Parkhurst, twenty-four. Guzan would prove the most useful of the three. In addition, Michael Bradley and Maurice Edu, both under twenty-three, were reluctantly granted leaves of absence by Bob Bradley from the national team camp to join the Olympic squad. There were some delicate negotiations on this front between Michael and his father, before the son eventually prevailed and was granted a furlough.

Previous Olympic performances by the Americans had ranged wildly, which was the nature of youth competitions. In 2000, the U.S. fielded a side of future national team stars that included Donovan, Josh Wolff, Ben Olsen, Jeff Agoos, Frankie Hejduk, Brad Friedel and John O'Brien. The team advanced past Japan on penalty kicks in a quarterfinal, and played for a medal in the semifinal. Despite the time difference, there was considerable interest back home. But the Americans fell decisively in Sydney, 3–1, to Spain, another lost opportunity to drum up some enthusiasm in the States. Then in 2004, the Americans failed to qualify for Athens, defeated emphatically by Mexico in Mexico City.

The U.S. featured a roster in Beijing with great potential. Jozy Altidore, Sacha Kljestan and Adu represented a trio of young, gifted attackers who were not always the best practice players, but rose to the occasion when afforded meaningful minutes. Each brought very different skill sets to the table. Altidore, despite an ankle injury, was a big, tough kid, difficult to handle for any defender in the box. Adu was a mite by comparison, but could create plays off the dribble. He was adept at crossing and set pieces. Kljestan, a lanky, high-gravity player, often found space where there appeared to be none, on the run.

The U.S. was drawn into the difficult but not impossible Group B with the Netherlands, Nigeria and Japan. The Americans opened in Tianjin against the Japanese, considered the weakest team in the group, played them evenly and escaped with a 1–0 victory on a forty-seventh minute goal by midfielder Stuart Holden, another young man tracked for great things. The game was an uninspired effort all around. And then, just as this tournament appeared doomed to the growing scrapheap of unremarkable, so-so efforts, the next match against Holland in Tian-jin proved nothing short of spectacular. Heading into the game, Dutch coach Foppe De Haan labeled the Americans a generally untalented bunch. "Nobody is extremely good," De Haan had said. "They have a good system." This quote made the rounds, as insults generally do, and then the match was everything that soccer ought to be: a rousing, attack-ing, creative and meandering contest of imagination and will. The Dutch dominated the first half, scoring in the sixteenth minute. A different American team came out for the second half, however, one that was hardly recognizable to any fan or journalist who had followed these na-tional teams over the decades. The U.S. went forward with abandon, dom-inating play and possession. The result was two goals—one by Kljestan in the sixty-fourth minute and then a Ping-Pong score by Altidore off a sharp cross from Michael Orozco in the seventy-second. The Americans were suddenly just minutes away from clinching their second victory in the group and automatic advancement into the quarterfinals.

But institutional memory was missing from American soccer on this front. There was simply no experience to fall back upon for these young players, when it came to closing out leads in a big match. They tightened visibly in the final minutes, with desperate stalling and grabbing tactics that only produced yellow cards for Adu and Bradley. Slowly, as the U.S. team retreated into a flimsy shell, the Dutch gained in confidence and field position. There were only two minutes left in added time when Bradley was carded for his failure to move back a full ten yards into the wall during a Dutch free kick. After the paperwork by referee Michael Hester of New Zealand was complete, Gerald Sibon stepped into the ball from 30 yards and kicked it under the leaping wall, past goalkeeper Guzan. The match ended seconds later in an improbable 2–2 draw, and now the Americans required a tie against Nigeria in their final group match in order to advance. Afterward, Nowak defended his players' per-formance in those waning minutes. But Bradley said he should have known, and done, better. That second yellow card meant he would be ineligible for the third game. "The [yellow card] today I should have been a little smarter," Bradley said. "At the end of the game I know the referee is going to be a little bit looking to make that call. So at that point I should know that I need to play the ball, put the ball back in quicker."

The decisive match against Nigeria took place at Workers' Stadium in Beijing, south of the so-called Olympic Green area and in a pleasant neighborhood of restaurants and shops. The weather was horrible, hot and humid, for the 5 p.m. start. The stands filled up quickly with fans, nearly 50,000 strong for a soccer doubleheader. They were there in large part for a sexier meeting that would follow between Argentina and Serbia. Both Nigeria and the U.S. were suffering a bit from suspensions. Adu and Bradley were ineligible because of their foolish yellow cards in the previous match against Holland. Nigeria, which required a victory for advancement, had its own problems on the backline. Two of its starting defenders were disqualified because of previous cards.

Unfortunately, the game proved to be a particularly anticlimactic, disheartening affair. It was over after three minutes, on one stupid act by the American defender, Michael Orozco. Fans and journalists alike were just starting to settle into their seats when Orozco was red-carded for a loose elbow to the chest of Solomon Okoronkwo, while trying to disentangle himself from a brief wrestling match. The Nigerian player fell dramatically backward, like an NBA player trying to sell an offensive charging call. The result was expulsion for Orozco from the aptly named German referee, Wolfgang Stark. McBride, the team captain, approached Stark and unsuccessfully requested an explanation. "I didn't see it," McBride said. "I asked the referee, 'Was it an elbow?' He said, 'Go away, go away.' That's all he told me." The Americans, a dead team walking, were forced to field a 10-man side in draining, oppressive conditions.

Orozco was fortunate that most Americans don't take their soccer quite as seriously as English fans, or he might have been burned at the tabloid stake like David Beckham—whose red card against Argentina at the 1998 World Cup remained an indelible national tragedy. Instead, Orozco simply walked off the field in a snit and the Americans plodded on for eighty-seven minutes, heading toward a 2–1 defeat and elimination. Needing only a draw, Nowak reorganized his side into a 4–4–1 formation, hoping to hang on for a scoreless tie. But the defensive tactics were premature and doomed to failure. Nigeria set up shop in the Americans' half of the field. In the thirty-ninth minute, Chinedu Ogbuke Obasi went end-line on the defender Parkhurst, then crossed the ball to Promise Isaac for the easy finish. After falling behind by two goals, Nowak ordered a more attacking, three-back formation. Kljestan scored on a penalty kick in the eighty-eighth minute, and a U.S. header glanced off the crossbar, a final, desperate chance. But then the final treble-whistle blew, and the only debate was whether Orozco had deserved the red card.

"Of course it changed the whole picture," Nowak said, at a crowded post-match press conference. "The whole mentality goes in the trash. There was a big scene from [Okoronkwo]," Nowak said. "We will look at the tape. This is a learning experience. These are young guys with lots of emotion. I told them before, 'I know German referees.' The players have to be smart. But I didn't know this kind of reaction would come in the third minute. It's unacceptable."

Orozco walked past reporters in the mixed zone after the match, staring straight ahead with headphones over his ears to block out interview requests. It was a lousy way to leave a tournament that had begun with such promise for the 22-year-old defender. Orozco had played solid defense and set up the go-ahead goal against Holland. Considering the chronic shortage of reliable defenders at the highest levels of soccer in America, he was considered a top prospect—a Mexican-American who played professionally for San Luis Football Club in the Mexican First Division. His temper, however, was clearly a problem. During his debut for San Luis at the Apertura tournament in 2006, he had entered as a second-half substitute and was sent off in just two minutes. If these Olympics should have taught the younger Americans one thing, it was that carelessly earned yellow and red cards often proved fatal to a team's chances. This nonsense had happened before, time and again, often to top U.S. stars like John Harkes and Eric Wynalda.

And yet even after Orozco's folly against Nigeria, he was rewarded with his first invitation to the full national camp, before the World Cup qualifying match against Cuba. Nowak wouldn't blast Orozco, or any of his players. He instead compared them dreamily to the 1980 hockey team in Lake Placid. "These guys are my boys," Nowak said. "They played so hard. They won a gold medal tonight."

Meanwhile, as if to underscore a fundamental difference in mental toughness, the U.S. women's soccer team typically overachieved all the way to the gold medal in Beijing—despite losing its top attacking star, Abby Wambach, to a knee injury. Gulati, as the chief representative of U.S. Soccer, remained in Beijing for the extra week to watch the women march to a title. When the U.S. men's national team played its semifinal qualifying match in Guatemala during this span, Gulati invited a select group of officials and reporters to watch the game by special hookup at Beijing's oldest sports bar, Frank's Place. The complicated feed didn't work properly, and before long everybody was huddled around Gulati's laptop for a fuzzy, live feed from his home television set, via Slingbox. The U.S. won that match, 1–0, despite yet another red card.

Players in Beijing like Adu, Altidore and Bradley were already packed up, headed back to their professional teams. The Americans had lost this Olympic tournament twice—once in the last minute against the Netherlands and then again with an early red card against Nigeria. "You can be on an incredible high and it can change around in minutes," McBride said. The draw with the Dutch was particularly heartbreaking. In order to deaden or kill matches, the Americans required more possession players, and clearer heads. They were not yet Italy.

"We need to polish skills," Nowak said. "Coulda, shoulda, woulda… This is a learning experience. We have young guys with lots of emotion. We have twelve, fourteen, nineteen guys who have a bright future. When life will be difficult, they will have someone standing next to them who went through this together."

This next generation of players now moved on in search of its defining moment, ever searching for the sort of great American soccer victory once achieved back in Belo Horizonte, Brazil.

CHAPTER 6

1950 . . .

JOE GAETJENS WAS A STUDENT AT COLUMBIA UNIVERSITY AND part-time dishwasher in New York City when he declared his intention to become a United States citizen. It was a vow that at the time was a sufficient credential to become eligible for the U.S. national team. And so Gaetjens, a Haitian by birth and by all reasonable definition, fatefully joined the Americans in 1950 for their great World Cup adventure in Brazil.

Nobody really cared much about any of this back then in the United States. "The World Cup wasn't that big time," said Walter Bahr, a midfielder on that American team. "In the U.S. newspapers, soccer news was always back by the obituaries." When the Americans left on a two-day connecting flight for Rio in 1950, their sendoff party was miniscule. A few friends and relatives came to the airport, but no media. Dispatches on the matches from wire services were never more than a couple of paragraphs long and the only American newspaper reporter on the trip was a writer with the incomparable name of Dent McSkinny from the soccer hotbed of St. Louis, home to several U.S. players. McSkinny paid his own way.

This was only the fourth World Cup in history, the first in a dozen years due to World War II, and it began as something of a logistical disaster in Brazil. The showcase Maracana Stadium, seating 200,000, wasn't quite completed for opening day. Teams were at times forced to travel as far as 2,000 miles within the expansive country from one match to their next. Not every traditional power was present. Italy's machine-like soccer system had been badly buffeted by the war. The Italians were out, leaving England and Brazil as the favorites to meet in the final.

For preparation, the U.S. team staged only a single match back in the States against a group of second-tier English players who hadn't been selected for their national side. The Americans lost on a late goal, 1–0—not a bad result, but one that didn't augur a spectacular showing at the World Cup. The group that headed down to Brazil included several players who had played a few relatively high-level international matches against touring foreign teams, and a half-dozen who had competed in the 1949 qualifiers in Mexico. They all required other jobs to support themselves, playing soccer mostly on weekends. It was a relatively young group, for the time. The average age was just past twenty-six.

Nearly sixty years later, Bahr could still offer a solid scouting report on his own teammates: Goalkeeper Frank Borghi of St. Louis, a former professional baseball player, "had great hands." The outside fullbacks, Harry Keough of St. Louis and Joe Maca of New York, were skilled possession players. Charlie Columbo of St. Louis was a perfect center back, tough as nails. Clarkie Souza and Eddie Souza, teammates in Fall River, Massachusetts, played along the left side. Clarkie was considered the team's best player. His real job was as machinist in a knitting mill. Gino Pariani and Pee Wee Wallace, teammates in St. Louis, played in the right middle of the field. Gaetjens was the athletic, acrobatic center forward. He might not have participated in this tournament at all if Ben McLaughlin from Philadelphia had been able to take some time off from his job. But McLaughlin didn't make the trip.

The U.S. national team practiced for three days in Rio, before heading to Curitiba for a tough opener against Spain. This was the match that Bahr remembered as the team's best effort at the World Cup. The Americans scored first, but had no idea how to sit on a one-goal lead. Nobody did such a thing back then, really. Instead the U.S. kept pressing and paid the price when Spain countered with three goals in the final ten minutes of the match.

Next up was England, which had won its first match as expected, 2–0, over Chile. England's coach, Walter Winterbottom, scouted that

U.S.–Spain game and warned his players that the patch-quilt Americans were no pushovers. Contrary to some fictional reports, there was no partying going on in the U.S. camp on the night before the big match. "I can't remember us even all being together," Bahr said. "Three or four players wouldn't even touch a drink. We had maybe two that liked that. All the others were in the middle, maybe liked a beer or two—like me, with my German background."

Much has been made of the messy pitch at Belo Horizonte that day, but Bahr remembered mostly that it was better than nearly all the fields he played on in the United States. "Most of our fields were either dirt or cinder," he said. "The big parks were better, but even on those they didn't cover the infields." England, meanwhile, was having its own problems. This team was not as strong as the one that had drubbed Italy, 4–0, two years earlier. Winterbottom decided to bench for this match his prototype winger, Stanley Matthews, who was thirty-five years old. The English wanted little to do with the chaos of Belo Horizonte, so the team stayed at the living quarters of a gold mine in Morro Vehlo. England dressed for the match in a local hotel rather than at the stadium. Bill Jeffrey, the U.S. coach from Scotland, played it coy when he spoke with Winterbottom's staff: "We ain't got a chance against your boys," he told them. "But we'll fight to keep down any cricket score."

Both sides were respectful before their match in the little stadium. The game began as expected, with England dominating the first twenty minutes or so. There would be no rout, however. The U.S. settled down, held its own. The moment of truth and legend occurred in the thirty-seventh minute, an event related this way by Bahr:

> Ed McIlvenney was my midfield partner. He had a throw-in from the right-hand side, thirty-five to forty yards out from the goal. I collected it, moved toward goal, took a shot off the live ball, twenty-five to twenty-eight yards out. I hit it fairly well, going far post. [England goalkeeper] Bert Williams started moving to his right somewhere in there, Gaetjens got a piece of the ball with the back of the head or his ear. Whether it was his plan or an accident, I cannot deny or confirm. He was a free spirit, an athletic guy at center

forward who does the unpredictable thing. Williams would have most likely deflected or caught my shot, or by some miracle it might have slipped in. You can see in the photos he is moving to his right. Harry Keough was our fullback at the time, he had a good view of it on the other side. He said Joe left his feet, full in the air, diving at the ball, four or five feet. Joe didn't get a clean header on it, but enough on the ball to change direction. The photo shows Bert Williams leaning to his right, the ball going to his left. It was typical of the stuff that goes on in the goal mouth. I'm sure Williams was shielded somewhat on it. I've heard the goal called anything from a complete accident to a masterpiece. The truth is probably in-between. In his defense, Joe had been involved in a lot of goals of that variety. He had a nose for the goal.

The Americans grabbed that fragile advantage and held on for their sporting lives. They had blown the 1–0 lead against Spain a few days earlier, and fully expected to do the same against mighty England. "At the time," Keough said, "I didn't think anything about it, because it was so early in the game. I figured we just woke up the sleeping giant." England had several good scoring chances early and late, striking the woodwork twice. On one occasion, a header by Jimmy Mullen may or may not have crossed the line for a goal, but was cleared out and ruled a corner. The Americans triumphed before an appreciative Brazilian crowd that clearly enjoyed the upset. Gaetjens and others were carried off on the shoulders of fans. Tom Finney, one of England's stars, told Bahr as they walked off the field that he felt as if his team could have played all day and never scored. This was just another generous comment from the losers, who were depicted as far less gracious in the 2005 film, *The Game of their Lives*. Jeffrey, caught up in the moment, made the first of many hopeful predictions for soccer in America: "This is all we need to make the game go in the States," he told a sparse collection of reporters, including McSkinny.

Bahr wasn't thrilled with the portrayal of events in *The Game of their Lives*, by director David Anspaugh, who had a long cinematic history of reveling in the melodrama of mouse versus lion. Anspaugh also created *Hoosiers* and *Rudy*. He had a nice touch with inspirational sports movies, though he assumed occasional license when it came to reality on and off the playing field. Bahr, a former Penn State soccer coach, said nobody conferred with him about the project, even though he was available at his long-time home in central Pennsylvania. If a researcher had asked him a few questions, the star midfielder from that 1950 miracle match might have related some intriguing tales. Bahr thought the action scenes in the film were choreographed incorrectly—"the soccer part was terrible," he said—and that a few too many liberties were taken with the facts. The goalkeeper, Borghi, was a quiet fellow, not the vocal leader shown on screen. And there really wasn't much technical stuff being taught back then, by the head coach Jeffrey or by Bahr himself. The main strategy involved just throwing the right guys out on the field at the right time. In the film, Bahr was credited with grand scheming, with installing the dreaded 4–4–2 formation that would doom soccer all over the world to its defensive rut. Bahr insisted he merely led the players in some stretching exercises. "I certainly did not do any coaching," Bahr said. "I ran them through paces. There was very little coaching going on."

England's players were depicted in the film as stiff, regal, and headed for a karmic comeuppance. Bahr found them instead to be excellent sportsmen. Jeffrey's U.S. team, which included three foreign-born players, was shown as gritty, humble, and inspired. "Everybody thinks we're going to be the clown team down there," one American player says to another in the movie, before they head down to Brazil. It's all a bit formulaic, too much good versus arrogant. But the film nonetheless represented a reincarnation of sorts, a reminder about an astounding 1–0 upset that at the time was largely ignored.

England went on at the 1950 World Cup to lose to Spain, 1–0, and to be eliminated in what was considered disgraceful fashion by its fans at home. Brazil failed to capture the title, upset by Uruguay. Meanwhile, the fairy-tale chapter in American soccer dovetailed into a series of conventional and even grim endings, as the epic victory was all but ignored in America. After the U.S. lost, 5–2, to Chile, the team returned home to a welcome again attended by only their friends and family.

No journalist or filmmaker would bother asking Bahr about the England match, or about that winning goal, for more than twenty years. There was still no first-tier professional league in the States, so the players scrambled to make livings again, never capitalizing financially on their success. Bahr played professionally with the Uhrik Truckers, which didn't amount to a big paycheck, and taught high school in Philadelphia to supplement his earnings. Eventually, he coached soccer at Temple and Penn State, where the Nittany Lions earned an NCAA playoff spot a dozen times. His three sons, Matt, Casey, and Chris all played in the North American Soccer League. Bahr lived a soccer life in America, way ahead of his time.

The worst fate by far was suffered by the hero Gaetjens, who never followed through with his promise to obtain U.S. citizenship. After the World Cup, Gaetjens headed to France to play for Troyes, a second-division club team. He then returned to his native Haiti to become a businessman and company spokesman. Gaetjens continued his international soccer career there, playing for Haiti against Mexico in a World Cup qualifying match on December 27, 1953. A decade later, he disappeared. For years his fate was a mystery. Eventually, evidence emerged that he had been arrested on July 8, 1964, by Papa Doc Duvalier's secret police, *Tontons Macoutes*, and murdered by a death squad. There was no obvious motive for this slaughter, other than the fact Gaetjens was a minor celebrity. But the *Tontons Macoutes* did not require cause for their actions. Unfortunately, Gaetjens would never enjoy the sort of opportunity presented to Jozy Altidore, another Haitian-American, half a century later.

CHAPTER 7

Big Man on Campus

DESPITE THE SETBACK AT THE OLYMPICS, THESE WERE HEADY times for Jozy Altidore. He was set to rejoin his professional team, Villar-real, a top professional club in Spain. Altidore was also convinced both he and the national team were heading in the right direction. "We keep proving on different platforms we can play with anyone," he said. Altidore was in ascendency, for certain. Sometimes it seemed that he was born with a man's body, the way that LeBron James had come by his almost unnatural physique at an extraordinary age. For as long as Altidore's mother could remember, Jozy was considerably larger than his peers. In this way, he was the polar opposite of Adu. Altidore didn't look or sound his age, but in this instance there was not even an iota of controversy over the birth certificate.

Josmer Volmy Altidore was born on November 6, 1989, in Livingston, New Jersey, to Joseph and Gisele, Haitian immigrants who met on Bus No. 20 coming home from work in Orange. His parents had arrived in the United States seeking economic opportunities. They didn't have much time to ponder or choreograph their son's athletic activities. Joseph, a deliveryman, and Gisele, a nurse, had four children in New Jersey. Jozy was the youngest, and he took to a soccer ball from the start. When the family moved to Florida, Jozy joined the local club teams and immediately demanded notice. "They came to us and said, 'He might hurt somebody,'" Gisele said. "So they kept moving him up in age groups."

Soon he was playing for national youth teams and enrolled at the Bradenton Academy, a fast-track development program in Florida that was viewed inside U.S. soccer circles as an efficient, essential and somewhat sterile factory for talent. "As vanilla as it gets," Arena said. "It's very artificial." Altidore joined the Adidas elite club. When he was drafted by MLS, his mother wanted him to go to college, as any mother would. Mostly, she was afraid he would get hurt. The son persisted. "This is what he wanted," Gisele said. "I always said no. I said, 'Go to college for two years.' Him and his daddy, this is what they wanted. They wanted it more."

Jozy took the chance and at age sixteen he signed with the MetroStars (soon to become the Red Bulls) as a second round pick, number seventeen overall, in the 2006 MLS Superdraft. He spent most of that season in Florida, working toward a high school degree. But by September he was scoring goals in MLS—three of them in seven matches for the Red Bulls. Before the start of the 2007 season, he accepted a relatively modest salary of $85,000 (if you included a pro-rated signing bonus, it amounted to $108,333). This was becoming a great investment of time and family assets, with no long-term guaranteed return. His mother moved with him to Montclair, New Jersey, to be near the club's training grounds. His father remained in Florida, working for FedEx, because the Altidores had no idea what would happen next with his fledgling sports career.

Jozy just kept growing, getting bigger and better. He wasn't the most consistent player, and his coach, Arena, became extremely impatient with Altidore's uncommitted posture at team practices. Out there on the Montclair State training pitch back in the spring of 2007, he looked like just another raw teenage prospect finding his way. He was big, brawny, but the ball skipped past him awkwardly at times. There was no real fire in evidence, no internal flame. Yet Altidore was pliable and eager. "I pulled him aside in a couple of instances," Arena said, about the practice sins. "He would apologize. Even when he deviates a little bit, you can get him back in line easily. Some kids don't listen. He's a wonderful kid to be around. Most kids his age don't handle it positively. He's just getting better. Will he be what everybody wants him to be? Who knows? A lot of the qualities are there."

Altidore loped about the practice field, driving coaches to distraction. But then there would be an MLS match, the real thing and as the lone striker up top he transformed into something else entirely. Altidore was suddenly not seventeen years old. He was a mature finisher who would not be knocked off his spot. He netted two highlight goals and two assists in the Red Bulls' first four matches of 2007. By then, he had his own shoe endorsement with Adidas, his own TV commercial and there was no stopping the background noise. "He's a beast," said his teammate, Claudio Reyna, after a 2007 practice. The beast was growing, inches at a time. He was 6 feet, 1 1/2 inches, about 180 pounds, having sprouted more than three inches from age sixteen to seventeen. His personal physician predicted a growth spurt of perhaps two more inches. "My strength is my strength," Altidore says. "Big is good. I cause defenders havoc because of my size." He could plant himself and take considerable pounding inside the box. He also owned an explosive first step, and was becoming adept at spinning off a defender.

Because of his new-found stature and all the hype, defenders began to key on Altidore; maul him, trash talk him. "You're not going to be a phenom today," one opponent told him. They were all coming at him, putting him down. "It's hard now, I'm not going to lie," Altidore said, about his initiation into MLS. Altidore was a smart kid, too. He knew about all the Adu ado, about the perils of unwarranted celebrity. Inside U.S. Soccer circles, Adu's stock had plummeted below Altidore's. Few thought Freddy was the next Pelé anymore. "Unfortunately he got in the spotlight so early," Altidore said of Adu. "There was so much on his shoulders. For me it wasn't that quick. I had to gain some respect."

For that very reason, Arena continued to downplay Altidore's talents and potential. The coach was naturally suspicious of instant success, and he still wasn't thrilled with Altidore's work habits. Besides, it was silly to apply such pressure on the kid. As Arena often mentioned, you never knew with these young players. If you had ten such potential talents, maybe one turned out to be a true star in the long run. There also was the danger that Altidore would jump ship, transfer prematurely to an international team. "You've got to be careful," Arena said after one training session. "We don't want him to lose confidence. I'd love to say he's the best 17-year-old in the world. But he's got a long way to go before we crown him."

Arena offered a cautionary tale for consideration. He once saw Ronaldo and another young Brazilian star in a national youth match. He thought they both looked amazing, sure things. Now Arena couldn't even remember the other kid's identity, which was the point of the story. "The other guy might be selling candy or popcorn in the streets now," Arena said. "That's the trouble with U.S. Soccer officials. They get one promising kid, they get real excited. You need a hundred and hope one works out. It's a crapshoot, a numbers game."

Still, important soccer people were watching Altidore every day. He became the youngest player to score a goal in the playoffs, at sixteen years, three hundred thirty-seven days. Then he became the youngest player ever to start in an MLS playoff match, at sixteen years, three hundred forty-nine days. He would score nine goals in twenty-two games in 2007 for the Red Bulls, although his national team obligations were disruptive to his club season. On August 18, 2007, when David Beckham came with the Los Angeles Galaxy to Giants Stadium to face the Red Bulls, Altidore very nearly stole the big show with two goals in a 5–4 victory over Los Angeles. As he continued his strong play on the U-20 World Cup national team and with his MLS club, serious talk surfaced about a transfer to Europe.

At first there were reports he might sign with struggling English Premier League sides Reading or Newcastle United, which might have been good fits and allowed him considerable playing time. The danger of such a commitment, however, was that these bottom-of-the-table teams might be relegated by the very next season to a lower division. Another report had him going to Real Madrid, the traditional La Liga powerhouse in Spain. This would have been particularly shortsighted, because Altidore was not ready to contribute regular minutes on such a fabled franchise. The club was only interested in him as a long-term project or resale investment. Then in June, 2008, a deal was struck with Villarreal of La Liga. The Spanish team paid $10 million in transfer fees to MLS and the Red Bulls, a record amount for an American player. Cladio Reyna had attracted a $5.7 million transfer fee, from Rangers of Glasgow to Sunderland of the Premier League in 2001. The previous MLS mark was less than half Altidore's total—$4 million, by

Fulham for Clint Dempsey. This was a real windfall for the American professional league, but at the same time MLS had waved goodbye to yet another top, domestic prospect. It was not such a good sign that the league was exporting its young talent. The level of play was impacted negatively and the opportunity was lost to develop a viable, domestic gate attraction. The Red Bulls, in particular, had been unable to establish themselves as a draw in New York, and the loss of Altidore just reinforced the perception that the club would forever feature a second-rung, rotating-door roster. Don Garber, the MLS commissioner, insisted that Altidore's transfer represented a positive step for his league, and not a great loss for MLS.

"Jozy was not the best American player," Garber said after the deal went through. "Landon Donovan is. Jozy is a great prospect. He was signed for what he can be, not what he was. And this was the first time we had a transfer at this level just based on a player's performance with his MLS club. Most others were based on the national team. That's a good statement for the league. Players come and go. Fans understand that. Ten million dollars can buy a lot going forward, more to the team than he was able to deliver."

If he was insulted by such talk, Altidore did not react accordingly. He was thrilled to have all the rumors behind him, ecstatic to deposit so much money in the bank.

"There's a lot of relief now because that pressure factor is gone a little bit," Altidore said. "Now you can play without the worry that it's another audition. I want to be in a place to be challenged on a daily basis. When you go to a new league it's not easy to adjust, especially for me going to a bit of a faster pace of a game over there. At a club like Villarreal, which finished second in the league, it might be tough to get in there right away and contribute the way I want to, so that wouldn't be a bad idea. To go to a team where I could get some playing time and develop a little bit more so I'm ready to play those big games that they have."

After negotiating his own personal contract separate from the transfer fees, Altidore debuted with Villarreal on June 11, 2008, during a friendly match against a club team from San Rafael. He scored three goals during the 7–1 rout, and then appeared as a second-half substitute in a league match on September 14, 2008, after his return from Beijing, against Deportivo La Coruna. This was precisely what he had in mind when he signed with Villarreal. The competition and training were challenging and Bob Bradley would not be able to ignore such quality time when he named his next roster for a World Cup qualifier.

Soon, however, it became obvious that Villarreal was not such an accommodating landing place. Altidore wasn't in the lineup or even on the bench for Villarreal's match against Racing de Santander. He was left off Villarreal's roster again for Champions League play, a blow to both his development and ego. The Champions League in Europe was the ultimate showcase for any team and any player. Europe's most prestigious, successful sides competed for the title of best professional club on the continent, and by extension in the world. Altidore was brand new, untested in such important matches. There was also a foreign quota rule to consider. Ever-changing "homegrown" rules required at the time that four players on each Champions League team must be developed by the club, and that four others could be developed by another club in the same European federation. To be classified as homegrown, a player of any nationality had to be developed by the team for three years between the ages of fifteen and twenty-one. If Altidore stuck with Villarreal for three years, he would meet these standards. For the time being, however, he would take up a precious foreigner roster spot. There was always pressure from FIFA to impose this sort of quota system on its member federations and clubs, as a way of maintaining a degree of parity and job opportunities for the locals. The clubs and coaches from top clubs often fought back against such initiatives, while American players were caught in the muddle. The rules provided more reason to ignore the U.S. stars on their teams, who were never quite indispensable.

If Altidore were older, Gulati said, U.S. Soccer would be worried about his lack of playing time. But Altidore still had seasons to burn at this juncture of his career and a series of professional teams in his near future. If he paid his dues overseas, then it might eventually all work out for him. He was still a teenager, after all. There were many professional matches, many World Cup qualifiers in his future.

CHAPTER 8

Cuba Libre

AFTER THE DIFFICULT LOSS AT THE BEIJING OLYMPICS AND THE
tough victory in Guatemala, the U.S. national team assembled in September 2008, to resume its World Cup qualifying schedule. Bob Bradley
had every player available for his roster, recalling them once again from
all over Europe and North America. It would be nice to report some
instant, mystical rapport among this group, but the fact was that the
U.S. national team—like most others in this modern, global sport—did
not often spend enough time together to form either close attachments
or fractious resentments.

This was no longer 1990, when members of that team performed
almost exclusively for the national side. A few of the current players—
Donovan and Beasley, for example—had formed a tight bond years earlier during their time together at the Bradenton Academy. There would
be several other makeshift alliances along the qualifying route, like
Howard and Jonathan Spector, both Premier League players; Clint
Dempsey and Ricardo Clark, both ex-Furman players; and a younger
group of Jozy Altidore, Stuart Holden, Charlie Davies, and Michael
Bradley. Again, some of these players had been teammates on youth
teams, at one stopover or another. For the most part, however, this was
no reunion party. The Americans arrived for a few days of practice together once or twice a month, shared some meals at a training table and
then did their best to mesh on the field. They lived in very different
worlds, and earned very different salaries. Most players overseas were

receiving comfortable six-figure salaries. But then there was someone like Houston Dynamo midfielder Stuart Holden, who would earn $35,728.75 from his MLS club for all of 2009. For what it was worth, this disparate group of athletes genuinely appeared to enjoy each other's company during these brief stints.

If nothing else, the players were often united by common grudges against the world. And that world included the media, ex-stars, and commentators, who in one fashion or another were perceived to have slighted the current team's efforts. The Bradleys were at times annoyed with Alexi Lalas and John Harkes, who were working with ESPN. Donovan would become unhappy when Eric Wynalda labeled him on a Fox Soccer Network show as ineffective in the toughest matches. This sort of inter-generational feuding was now common among Americans, as it was among more accomplished soccer nations. In an odd way, these incestuous grudges probably represented healthy growth.

Now that most of the starters had professional careers abroad, there was less evidence of the established cliques within the team more obvious at the 2002 World Cup in Korea. Back then, there were clearly two social groupings—foreign-based players and MLS players. Donovan's presence alone assured this would no longer be the case in 2008. He was considered both the team's spokesman and leader on the field, yet he had failed at this juncture to hook on permanently with a professional team overseas. None of his teammates would ever view him in condescending fashion. Donovan was just too good and too committed for that.

This next semifinal qualifying assignment for the Americans, on September 6, appeared more a novelty than a challenge. The U.S. had not played a match in Cuba for more than sixty years, in 1947, before Fidel Castro came down from the mountains to install his revolution. Bob Bradley's only connection to the place was a father who had been stationed there as a Marine in the 1950s. "I saw pictures," Bradley said. There were visa problems galore for fans and journalists who wished to attend this match, but for the athletes it figured to be a treat. When they arrived, several players rode a *turista* bus around the island and then climbed aboard a motorized rickshaw for a trip to a flea market. Havana remained frozen in time by the American economic embargo, a still gorgeous, unpainted mosaic of washed-out white mansions and a haven for 1960s automobiles. Great fun, and yet . . . "At the end of the day," Donovan said of the whole experience, "it's still a soccer game."

The match was to take place in *Estadio Pedro Marrero*, which also could have used a considerable makeover. The building was showing its age, a classic victim of Caribbean under-funding. Conditions were exacerbated by a pair of hurricanes, Hanna and Ike, which sandwiched the match. The eighty-year-old stadium honored a mythical everyman, Marrero, a sort-of Daniel Boone figure in Cuban legend. Other than the name, it lacked greatly in charm or hospitality. On the day before the match, Bradley began practice on the grass pitch, only to discover that Cuban officials were leisurely scouting the session from dormitory landings built into the stadium. A protest appeared futile, because no FIFA representative was immediately available. On the evening of the match, the stadium's light system failed miserably. There was brief talk of postponement. Then power was restored. The lights dimmed substantially again with just over five minutes left in the game. By that juncture, everyone figured it was pointless to halt play. ESPN's broadcast appeared on American television screens to be taking place from inside a cave somewhere. Despite an effort by the Cuban government to paper the building with cheap or free tickets, there were still empty seats. Cubans were baseball fans first and foremost. A few U.S. supporters arrived illegally through Mexico, wearing bandanas and sunglasses to hide their identities, just in case U.S. customs officials were watching. Other than that, the American team was on its own again.

"All these places we go to we don't ever have fans there anyway," Donovan told the *Miami Herald*, about the Americans' lonely qualifying tour in CONCACAF. "It's different from our NBA players. When the U.S. team plays in China, tons of people love the U.S. team and want to see them play. I don't think many people know what it's like, what we go through, to get to the World Cup. But I wouldn't change it for anything. It makes us better in the end."

Before the match began, the public address announcer at Marrero Stadium introduced Maurice Edu as Freddy Adu, who had not been included on the roster against Guatemala or Cuba. Bradley ignored young attacking players Adu, Altidore, and Kenny Cooper, instead relying on his own son, Michael, plus Edu in the midfield. These were standard, conservative tactics on the road. And again, nobody could really argue with Bradley's results. In Havana, Dempsey pounced on a lousy Cuban clearance near the penalty spot in the fortieth minute and right-footed the only goal of the game. The U.S. sat on the 1–0 lead effectively, albeit with little elegance. A tropical downpour made accurate passing more difficult. The Americans emerged from their first two away matches in the semifinal round with two victories and six points. They now hadn't allowed a goal in four qualifiers, and were soon to make it five.

The next match, four days later, was at Toyota Park outside Chicago against Trinidad and Tobago, a side with several international stars who played in England's top leagues and who were largely missing from the lineup. Striker Dwight Yorke, the "Smiling Assassin," was away with his English team, Sunderland. Two other stars had inexplicably been left off the roster: midfielder Chris Birchall, a player for Coventry City, and center forward Stern John, the country's leading all-time scorer who played for Southampton. Defender Avery John had been suspended. The so-called Soca Warriors were hardly at their best, another symptom of CONCACAF's qualifying morass.

Trinidad and Tobago was known within the region as a talented team that did not travel well, and that became evident from the start. T&T typically didn't close down opponents quickly enough, giving them too much space and time to create. Michael Bradley scored in the ninth minute, deflecting Donovan's free kick with the outside of his foot. That ended any suspense. Dempsey and Brian Ching added goals for a 3–0 victory. It was looking all too easy. "Even though we're not playing against the best teams in the world, these games are important," Donovan said. "A slip-up here and there, and you find yourself not in the World Cup."

The U.S. had earned the full nine points in three matches and required only one victory in its last three to clinch a spot in the final, hexagonal qualifying tournament. That 6–1 win would come quickly against Cuba at Robert F. Kennedy Stadium on October 11 in Washington. Even by the one-sided standards of CONCACAF qualifying, this was a tough one to watch for anyone with a smidgeon of sporting empathy. For starters, the Cubans were missing their best player, striker Roberto Linares, who was serving a red-card suspension. Then two of the eighteen Cuban players—not a large ratio, actually, by historic standards—defected after bolting from the team's Doubletree Crystal City Hotel. Midfielder Pedro Faife and forward Reynier Alcantara both joined the growing legion of that country's soccer-playing emigrants to America. Their absence became apparent at a Friday practice before the scheduled Saturday match, when Cuba's coach, Reinhold Fanz, first confirmed to reporters their disappearance. "We have security, but you can't handcuff them to their rooms," Fanz told the *Washington Post*. Faife left on Friday afternoon with a maternal aunt and cousins. They drove him directly to Orlando, their home. By Saturday, game day, Faife was shopping for clothes and shoes in his new home. The defection had not been an easy decision for Faife, an only child whose father was ailing back in Cuba. The aunt had not known of his plans, but simply came to watch him play. When he broke the news to her, she helped him flee.

Cuban television immediately ripped the two players on air. "They betrayed the unity of their select team and gave in to the temptations of the empire's money," a newscaster said. "As always, the team will go out to defend the colors of the national flag, rising above the traitors' mud." The Cubans had endured terrible logistical problems fielding full sides whenever they arrived in America to play international matches. In mid-March of 2008, seven members of the Under-23 team fled from the team hotel in Tampa. Since 2002, fifteen Cuban soccer players had defected to America. Not all of them were able to land soccer contracts in MLS or elsewhere. But former Cuban star Maykel Galindo, who defected in 2005, was a solid striker for Chivas USA and earned $79,750 per year—a decent salary that may have inspired a whole new generation of wannabe Cuban-Americans. Immigration law in the U.S. allowed Cuban defectors to remain in America as long as they had placed foot on land. It was often referred to as a "wet foot/dry foot policy." According to the Cuban Adjustment Act, a Cuban immigrant who arrived in this country could receive a permanent resident green card after one year.

So the Cuban team was already badly shorthanded for this qualifier before the opening kickoff. Or, as Fanz put it, "We have many problems." The first half was competitive enough. The U.S. broke through in the tenth minute when Beasley curled a nifty left footer inside the far post on a first touch from a steep angle. The Americans continued to work the field patiently, and eventually Donovan looped a pass to Beasley that beat Cuba's sleepy offside trap. Offside traps were always a dangerous business, relying not only on field positioning but on the hyper-awareness of assistant referees. Beasley found himself all alone, ten yards from the net, and scored again in the thirty-first minute past goalkeeper Odelin Molina. The chemistry was evident between Donovan and Beasley, a good sign. "It's always great to play with Landon," said Beasley, who was hoping to regain his explosive first step after recovering from a knee injury. "We know each other a lot, understand each other a lot."

Beasley's second goal should have withered whatever remained of the Cubans' resolve, but Michael Bradley backed too far off Jenzy Munoz outside the box. Given some space to pivot, Munoz's twenty-four-yard shot caromed down off the crossbar and into the net to beat Howard. Suddenly, tentatively, it was 2–1 and a ballgame again. Then in the forty-first minute, Panamanian referee Roberto Moreno Salazar ejected a Cuban midfielder, Yoel Colome, with a second yellow card. The match after that was neither fair, nor particularly compelling. Colome went off in tears for tripping Donovan. The Cubans finally lost heart. Donovan finished off a pretty left-foot cross from Heath Pearce in front of the net to restore a two-goal margin in the forty-eighth minute. Donovan had now scored nine career goals in qualifiers, second only to Brian McBride's record of ten. It was then just a matter for Bradley of monitoring the play of young substitutes Altidore, Adu, and José Francisco Torres.

There had been a quiet tug of war between the American and Mexican federations over Torres, who was eligible to play for either nation. With his appearance against Cuba, his first cap, Torres decided that argument. He couldn't play for Mexico anymore. This was a personal triumph of sorts for Gulati, the U.S. Soccer president, who had lobbied Torres for some time. Altidore, the promising teenager, finished off the scoring on a well-timed breakaway in the eighty-seventh minute. The victory before a supportive crowd of 20,293 lifted the Americans to a 4–0 record in their semifinal division. They were 6–0 altogether in 2008 qualifying matches, a record winning streak for the team.

Once again, the Americans could thank their lucky stars they were qualifying in CONCACAF, not in Europe. That same day in Constanta, Romania, perennial power France was forced to come back from a two-goal deficit while scrambling for a 2–2 draw in a qualifier against the home side. There had been no such drama or challenge in CONCACAF's Group 1. Instead this round was little more than a testing ground for the ever-evolving U.S. roster.

Altidore was starting to receive some well-earned attention from Bradley, as a complementary striker next to Dempsey. He scored a goal on a breakaway in this match against Cuba. Then Altidore started in the next semifinal qualifier at Port of Spain in Trinidad and Tobago, a game important only to T&T, with mixed results. An Altidore goal was nullified by a wrongful offside call. He set up another goal that tied the match at 1–1. Unfortunately, he also did something very young and foolish. In full view of the referee, Altidore yanked grievously on the jersey of a Trinidadian attacker in the box. T&T received a penalty kick that proved to be the decisive score in a 2–1 defeat for the U.S.—the first time in history that the Americans lost to that island nation in a World Cup qualifier. "Moron," commented one highly-placed U.S. Soccer official, about Altidore. The organization's hierarchy did not take such losses lightly.

Despite the gaffe, the U.S. easily had clinched a spot in the deciding Hexagonal round. Matters would soon grow less certain and significantly more exciting.

CHAPTER 9

The Man Behind the Curtain

THE MODEST ELEVENTH-FLOOR OFFICE OF SUNIL GULATI, AN economics lecturer at Columbia University, was a portal into the central nexus of soccer in America. "The man behind the curtain," MLS commissioner Don Garber called Gulati. Here was the puppet master of the U.S. Soccer Federation, a slight, Indian-American whose name and face were familiar to very few outside the sport. His Wikipedia entry was for years little more than a stub. And yet he was everywhere, pulling important strings for more than two decades, negotiating his way out of disfavor and potential exile on at least two occasions during that span. He was recruiting players for Major League Soccer, bidding for the World Cup in America, negotiating player contracts, selecting coaches for national teams at all levels.

His Columbia office told its share of tales, though not all. A flat-screen TV above his desk was tuned to the latest stock prices, a single visible concession to Gulati's real-life job, when he wasn't attending to his many duties as the non-salaried president of U.S. Soccer. The place brimmed with memorabilia. Gulati posed in one photo with Alexi Lalas, the former American star. There were game balls signed by the U.S. national team, and there was another photo of Gulati's son, Emilio, holding hands during a pre-exhibition ceremony with the great Brazilian player, Ronaldinho. In the picture, Emilio's best buddy is holding Ronaldinho's other hand. This perk was not easy to arrange, Gulati said. But he had certain patriarchal responsibilities. His family was very international, a direct product of his own soccer wanderings. He met his Mexican wife, Marcela, during a blind, arranged date at the Mexico City airport, on his way to Acapulco for the 1995 Mexican League draft. He was introduced to her by Jaime Byrom, who aptly would become CEO of Match, FIFA's ticketing and accommodations arm. The couple had two young children, Emilio and Sofia. Emilio's favorite player was the flashy Cristiano Ronaldo, having moved on from David Beckham. In this way, the kid was no different than most American soccer fans.

Gulati was born July 30, 1959, in Allahabad, India, a beginning which hardly foretold of such far-reaching influence in the sport. Soccer was not particularly popular in India, lagging behind the likes of field hockey and cricket. Gulati's father, Bodh, was studying for his PhD in mathematics. Sunil spent most of his time around New Delhi, and retained only what he called "memories of memories" from that period. His father moved to America in 1960 to finish doctorate studies at the University of Connecticut. Then in 1965, Bodh Gulati sent for his wife, Santosh; for his son, Sunil; and for his daughter, Anita. The family moved for two years to Wayne, Nebraska, then back to Storrs, Connecticut, when Sunil was seven. Finally, the Gulatis settled in Cheshire, Connecticut, where the father taught at Southern Connecticut State University. It was there that the bug bit the boy. Sunil played youth and high school soccer in Cheshire and Storrs, but he was attracted to other facets of the game. At a relatively young age, he earned refereeing and coaching licenses. Soon, he and a close friend with the Cheshire Soccer Club decided they would enter their own team in the Connecticut State Cup tournament.

"There was nobody there to organize it so we took it upon ourselves," Gulati said. "Everything from printing the T-shirts, to registering, to car pooling. I still remember we got an art teacher at the school to put numbers on the backs of the jerseys, except he did it in magic markers and they all ran the first time we played."

Gulati performed all the tasks usually done by parents, mowing and lining the field. He was also well into grassroots recruiting and administration before he turned eighteen, when he headed off to Bucknell University. Gulati played two seasons on the jayvee squad before becoming an assistant coach of the varsity team his senior year. By age twenty-one, he was coaching an Under-16 select team in Connecticut. That summer, in 1981, Gulati enrolled in the U.S. Soccer coaching program, alongside the son of Werner Fricker, who would become president of the Federation just three years later. This was an important contact, another networking coup. When Gulati entered graduate school at Columbia, he also was heavily involved in coaching and administrative duties with the Federation's development program in Connecticut. He became a research assistant for *Kick* magazine, meeting a highly influential group of soccer journalists and officials that included Paul Gardner and Phil Woosnam, commissioner of the North American Soccer League (NASL). Gardner was an irascible, opinionated, and brilliant analyst of the game, later a writer for *World Soccer* and *Soccer America*. Gardner had an oft-stated preference for the technically superior South American game, rather than the sweatier, more physical style of Northern European nations. In his years as a recruiter of talent, Gulati would demonstrate a similar bias. "Paul influenced me on how I thought about the game," Gulati said. *Kick* was an arm of NASL marketing. In 1983, Gulati and others with the American pro league became active in trying to relocate the 1986 World Cup to the States, after it had been abandoned by financially-strapped Colombia. The bid failed, however, and the World Cup went to Mexico. But during this same time, Gulati was asked to run the U-16 national team camp.

"I got out there and it was complete chaos," Gulati said. "Sprinklers going off during sessions, no balls at a national camp. I'm literally cutting grass, lining fields, buying balls."

Gulati met with Fricker. The new president of U.S. Soccer was a man of the world, born in Yugoslavia, raised in Austria, and later a midfielder on the U.S. national team. Fricker, who died in 2001 at the age of sixty-five, had his share of quirks. For one thing, he forbade the American national teams from wearing red on their uniforms—leaving them with only white and blue as options. This policy was the result of two prejudices. Fricker hated Russia and communism with a vengeance. He also viewed Canada as America's chief rival at the time, and the Canadians were always wearing red. But Fricker loved the sport dearly. And in these formative days, he was open to suggestions from practically anyone. "Your national team program is a mess," Gulati told Fricker, presumptuously. He described the sprinklers, the untended grass.

"Send me a note, but don't send me a seventeen-page memo," Fricker told Gulati.

Gulati sent him a seventeen-page memo, anyway. Fricker ordered Gulati to go do something about the mess, so he did. At around the same time, Gulati also became involved with the International Games Committee of U.S. Soccer. He worked to get Fricker reelected as president in 1987 and, as a reward for his loyalty, was named chairman of the committee. This was a big deal, and became even bigger when the committee decided in 1986 to launch a bid for the 1994 World Cup. The campaign this time was better organized than the impromptu bid for the 1986 tournament. A half-dozen organizers worked all diplomatic channels. Gulati was one of them, convincing global skeptics that America would support such an endeavor with large stadiums and enthusiastic crowds. There was proof, he argued: Huge soccer crowds had turned out at the 1984 Los Angeles Olympics.

The U.S. faced its chief competition in the1994 World Cup bid from Morocco and Brazil. Morocco represented a high-risk foray into Africa. Brazil's economy was never a sure thing, but its love of soccer was legendary and the FIFA president at the time, Joao Havelange, was Brazilian. Many FIFA members believed that America was a great untapped financial market, a worthy challenge. The U.S. organizers also promised to create a professional league, which would become MLS. Still, there were skeptics, for good reason, particularly in Europe and South America. This would be the first World Cup staged in a nation that really didn't embrace soccer as its most popular sport. Americans valued their own brand of football, baseball, and basketball above the beautiful game. There were logistical problems, as well. The distance between host cities was great and required expensive airfares for visiting fans. In the end, FIFA took the leap of faith, and accomplished a considerable money grab. Due to the large stadiums and pre-sold tickets, the 1994 World Cup averaged nearly 69,000 fans per match, a new record, while the total attendance of 3.6 million was also a new mark.

The World Cup in America heralded a new, international era, the first real sign of life for soccer in this country outside the recreational and scholastic ranks since the North American Soccer League died prematurely. Back in the late eighties, when plans for this bid were hatched, the sport's trappings in this country on the professional level were still fairly primitive. Foreign teams would come over as novelties to appear in short, lucrative tournaments—like the Miami Cup, aka the Marlboro Cup. American players gathered at camp to prepare for such a tourney and receive a five dollar per diem for "laundry money." Lothar Osiander was the part-time national coach at the time, and Gulati was forced to pose to him a rather embarrassing choice: "You can either pay players five dollars per day or have an extra day of training," Gulati told Osiander. Gulati had done the math: five dollars times eighteen players equaled ninety dollars per day. Osiander ditched the per diem. "It was the right thing to do—at least from our point of view," Gulati said.

As the U.S. national team finally gained some success in the qualifying rounds, Gulati began to multi-task again. The Americans eked out a CONCACAF berth for Italia '90, if only because Mexico was sitting out a suspension for using over-aged players. Suddenly a player revolt erupted in the U.S. ranks. Gulati had been negotiating contracts with individual players since 1988. By January 1990, with a spot in the World Cup assured, the U.S. players demanded greater compensation. This was not an unreasonable position, because many of them had no other source of income and were being asked to devote a great deal of time to training. There was no top-flight professional league in the States, and only a couple of Americans had hooked on overseas. Paul Caligiuri, who scored the berth-clinching goal in Trinidad, became something of a de facto labor leader, speaking militantly about a possible boycott. But then the camp opened and all the players buckled except for backup goalkeeper David Vanole, who thought that Caligiuri and others were also holding out. U.S. Soccer withdrew its contract offer to Vanole, although the next national coach, Bob Gansler, invited him back that spring as the third keeper. Gulati's first labor crisis had been averted.

Gulati was teaching full-time at Columbia, then went to the World Bank in 1991. The new president of U.S. Soccer, Alan Rothenberg, was a lawyer who had become involved in contract negotiations and administrative roles with the National Basketball Association and the NASL. When Rothenberg first met Gulati, the new president figured he would soon remove Gulati from any meaningful role. "He was Werner Fricker's guy," Rothenberg said. "I came in, I didn't know anything, and the people helping me told me I've got to get rid of all of Fricker's guys. So I was going to fire Sunil for sure." But Gulati had an overwhelming passion for this job and a survivor's instinct. He lobbied Rothenberg, sold the new president on his love for the sport, and soon became a trusted adviser. In the end, Rothenberg relied more heavily than Fricker on Gulati for input on international soccer and personnel. He quickly convinced the economist to drop the professional banking track for the World Cup.

"You can always go back to the World Bank later," Rothenberg told Gulati. "We're only going to host the World Cup once in your lifetime." Gulati couldn't argue with that kind of reasoning. And after the World Cup, he became intimately involved with the nascent MLS, along with a handful of founding fathers, including Rothenberg, Mark Abbott, Randy Bernstein, and Marla Messing. MLS was born as a 10-team league, with the Colorado Rapids, Columbus Crew, D.C. United, Dallas Burn, Kansas City Wiz, New England Revolution, New York/New Jersey MetroStars and the Tampa Bay Mutiny. It was organized around the concept of single-entity ownership, meaning the league controlled the signing and assignment of players to all franchises according to a strict salary cap. Gulati was the point man on the soccer end. He recruited players, domestic and international. One of his favorite national team players, Tab Ramos, became his first MLS signing on January 1, 1995. Jorge Campos, the colorful, wandering goalkeeper from Mexico, was the first international star.

Gulati wasn't the most beloved of figures at this stage of his career. "There was a certain youthful arrogance to his step, a unilateral certainty on matters, that he later moderated," said one associate. Among his detractors was Doug Logan, the first commissioner of MLS, who was a laid-back philosopher, relatively new to the sports world and with little patience for Gulati's frantic activities. Several of the original MLS owners didn't like Gulati, either. In 1998, these relationships were strained anew. Gulati and Rothenberg went to Nike and struck a deal with that company to sponsor the new Project 40 at the Bradenton Academy for top American prospects, who would receive guaranteed roster spots in MLS. It was also known as Project 2010, the projected year when the U.S. national team might be truly competitive on an international level. Without cooperation from MLS, without those guaranteed spots, there could be no Project 40. Yet this huge, $50 million deal was done largely between Nike and U.S. Soccer, somehow not with the league. "Here Gulati was working for the league as deputy commissioner, Rothenberg was on the board of the league, which didn't have a pot to pee in," said one MLS official. "That didn't go over well with anybody."

There was also considerable concern among league officials months later about what was viewed as a conflict of interest involving Gulati's relationship with Tab Ramos. Gulati had known Ramos since he was a teenager, and struck a generous deal for the player that assured Ramos would play several more injury-plagued seasons with the MetroStars. Gulati re-signed Ramos with MLS—against the wishes of MetroStars' owner Stuart Subotnick—as the midfielder was entering the option year of a four-year deal at $250,000 per season. Fed up with Gulati's maneuvers, Logan and the league basically fired Gulati. Three months later, Don Garber replaced Logan and Gulati asked to be reinstated. It was too soon. Gulati had antagonized too many people. He would have to rehabilitate his image working at the club level in New England with the Krafts, a father and son who owned the Revolution. He paid his dues as required with the team, while quietly becoming Garber's key advisor on player personnel and other matters.

Gulati came back to U.S. Soccer when he was appointed vice president in 2000 and served for six years under Bob Contiguglia, a former youth association president, a physician, and a relatively quiet, no-ripples administrator. Eventually, Gulati ran for president in 2006 in the middle of his second term as VP. There were still some sneerers among the coaches' and officials' ranks, when it came to the selection process for U.S. Soccer president. Still, the election was a real process, with the vote divided carefully among different blocs. The professional division had roughly twenty-five percent of the vote. The amateur adult division was allotted twenty-five percent, while the youth division received twenty-five percent. Players' representatives were given twenty percent of the vote. The rest, about five percent, was in the hands of super-delegates.

A two-term limit had forced Rothenberg out of his post as president, but that provision no longer existed. Gulati would be up for reelection in 2010, and he appeared to have every intention of running for the office again and again. He enjoyed spreading the gospel. Bruce Arena may have viewed him as too much the micro-manager, but Gulati insisted he was merely good at delegating responsibility. He maintained a close relationship with the media, which didn't hurt. Gulati had a healthy, cynical sense of humor, well appreciated by the press. He also was extremely accessible and accommodating to reporters, working early and often with them to aid in transportation needs for the logistically difficult World Cup in South Africa.

Gulati's ultimate goal as president was both simple and very nearly impossible: To win the World Cup. He knew there were many soccer officials in America who would argue that such a goal was unrealistic, and that the federation ought to concentrate its efforts on expanding the popularity of the sport and of MLS. Gulati thought this was one of those chicken-and-the-egg quandaries. "They're directly linked," he said. "You have to be rational about it. I understand how few teams have done that. France won one and then didn't get out of the first round in the next one. Turkey got to the semifinals and then didn't qualify for the next one. So we're realistic. But Clint Mathis had it right when we were going to Korea/Japan in 2002. He said, 'I want to win the World Cup.' Why else would we go? Nobody talks about it in the bravado sense. Everybody goes just hoping, praying to get out of the first round and then see what happens. With the exception of Brazil, they expect to win it. But I don't know why our goal would be the quarterfinals. We've done that."

He had engaged in this debate about priorities before, nearly a decade ago. Gulati was at a meeting with the Krafts when the father, Bob Kraft, asked him about his ultimate aim. Gulati replied, "To win the World Cup." Kraft looked at Gulati quizzically. "Shouldn't it be to make

MLS a very successful and powerful league?" he asked. At that point the younger Kraft stepped in and spoke the words on Gulati's lips. "Dad," Jonathan Kraft said, "Sunil believes those two are absolutely linked. Unless we have a top-level domestic league, we won't win the World Cup."

Gulati intuitively felt that soccer required the occasional external boost in America. Many people still viewed the defunct NASL as a failure, but Gulati remembered it very differently. Gulati saw Pelé and the Cosmos in East Rutherford, New Jersey, as great catalysts for the kind of youth movement that occurred nearby in Kearny, resulting in the likes of John Harkes, Tony Meola, and Tab Ramos. He believed the dramatic increase in girls' participation was linked to the 1999 Women's World Cup in America. And he believed the very existence of MLS had increased participation and viewership on television for everything from the Premier League to the Champions League. He saw David Beckham's volatile stint with the Los Angeles Galaxy as a grand public relations coup, as an attention-getter. Gulati always sought awareness for his favorite sport. From his little office at Columbia, he saw the whole ball of wax, spinning and spinning, moving forward slowly and steadily at the same time.

CHAPTER 10

Breaking the Hex

BOB BRADLEY TRAVELED DOWN TO JOHANNESBURG IN MID-
November 2008, on one of those multipurpose trips that national
coaches love to navigate. Here was an opportunity to scout the facilities in South Africa, to make tentative commitments for a training
site in 2010, and to witness the official draws for the final Hexagonal
World Cup qualifying round in CONCACAF—and for the Confederations Cup in South Africa that would take place in June 2009. It
was also a chance for soccer officials from around the world to trade
stories and gossip, to speak of Beckham and Ronaldinho, even if
Bradley was hardly a renowned schmoozer. Of all these matters, the
schedule of matches for the so-called Hex was the most pressing. The
other stuff, by comparison, was just fanciful window dressing. The
Confederations Cup would surely be a blast, an opportunity for the
Americans to face some of the top teams in the world. They had
earned that right by capturing the CONCACAF regional tourney, the
Gold Cup, two years earlier. The Confederations Cup was yet another
pet project of Sepp Blatter, president of FIFA. Club coaches from
around the world were required to release their players, yet again, in
order for them to participate in a tournament that involved considerable time and travel. The U.S. was drawn into a group with both Italy
and Brazil, the last two World Cup champions. Bradley gave a brief,
sardonic nod. A tougher one-two combination of opponents could
hardly be imagined.

Little was expected from the Americans at the Confederations Cup. The Hex was different, however. It was a tournament with extensive ramifications. Six teams—the U.S., Mexico, Costa Rica, Honduras, El Salvador, and Trinidad and Tobago—had qualified through the CON-CACAF semifinal round and would next play a round-robin, home-and-home series of ten games apiece, competing for three or possibly four berths at the 2010 World Cup.

The Hex draw might easily have proved uneventful, like most such matters, except that the U.S. caught what appeared to be an enormous break. The Americans were slotted as the home team in the first match on February 11, 2009, against Mexico, their chief rivals. This was a significant advantage. The Mexicans had struggled terribly of late, barely creeping out of the semifinal round. It was good to play them early in the Hex, before they found their footing under head coach Sven-Göran Eriksson, or before some new coach was likely hired to revive them. In the semifinal round, the Mexicans had gained only one point in their final three matches on the road against Jamaica (0–1), Canada (2–2), and Honduras (0–1), finishing in a second-place tie with Jamaica that was broken by a three-goal differential in the standings. Bradley, understandably, would not acknowledge Mexico's considerable slide. "We would disregard that," he said. "We have great familiarity with their players. Road games and qualifying can be difficult. They certainly showed like anybody, if you go on the road and don't play your best it isn't going to be easy."

There was another factor, even more important and advantageous, about this early date with Mexico. It would allow the U.S. to place the match in some freezing cold venue that would effectively destroy the will and the legs of Mexico's warm-blooded athletes. This had happened before, back on Februrary 28, 2001, when the U.S. whipped Mexico, 2-0, in Columbus in a qualifier that took place at night, just for added displeasure. Crew Stadium that evening felt like a giant meat locker in the middle of Ohio, during the rugged Midwest winter. Tired of being dragged for World Cup qualifiers through the jungles of Guatemala, to the heights of Azteca Stadium in Mexico City, to the bare, sun-baked fields of Jamaica, U.S. Soccer had scheduled that game as close to the sweeping, high-pressure Canadian cold fronts as inhumanely possible. "The colder the better," said Chris Armas, a U.S. midfielder. As temperatures fell through the twenties that night in 2001, the Mexican players remained in their heated locker room until the very last minute. When the second half started, however, Mexico's defense locked up and committed egregious marking errors. The Mexicans were careful back then not to complain too loudly about conditions, acknowledging that the Americans had finally caught on to the wicked ways of the world. "We make them play at *Azteca*," said Enrique Meza, the beleaguered, lame-duck coach of Mexico in 2001. "It is their right to choose a venue they feel favors them." What goes around, comes around—from high altitude to low temperatures.

The Hex draw in Johannesburg afforded the Americans yet another chance to freeze-dry the Mexicans in midwinter. And from the U.S. standpoint, it seemed almost certain that Columbus would be chosen again as the torture chamber of choice. Bradley wouldn't gloat about the opportunity presented by this draw. Gulati was typically more forthcoming. He quipped that the Americans might consider playing that first match in Texas or Southern California, if only the Mexicans agreed to stage their home return match on August 12 at sea level in Monterey, rather than in Mexico City. "Half-joking, half-serious," Gulati said. "Playing at Azteca Stadium has been a big plus for Mexico. We're going, in very strong likelihood, to play in a place where the temperature is lower."

The selection of venues for World Cup qualifiers traditionally is considered one of the most crucial decisions for a coach and for U.S. Soccer officials. Gulati and Bradley already had agreed in principle on certain requirements for qualifying sites. These matches would not be played on artificial turf, even though FIFA had recently ruled this was allowable. They would not be played on temporary grass surfaces, a sadly common situation at American football stadiums. They also would not be staged in ethnic hotbeds, where the fans of El Salvador, Honduras, or Mexico might badly outnumber the U.S. supporters. This ruled out places like New York, Dallas, and Los Angeles. Qualifiers generally were staged in remote outposts like Salt Lake City, Birmingham, East

Hartford, and Columbus in order to assure a favorable balance of fans. There had been charges in the past of discrimination against would-be supporters with Latino names, who felt they'd been systematically denied tickets by screeners when they applied for advance mail orders.

There was a strong argument to be made on behalf of more conventional, East Coast matches, regardless of the fan ratio. The national team trained in California, but many of these qualifiers were fit clumsily between club fixtures overseas. Most of the American roster was now comprised of European-based players, and it was far easier for them to fly into New York for a nearby match than it was to connect on flights to the Rocky Mountain or Pacific time zones. Gulati sat down with advisers to consider all these factors in collecting what he termed "a matrix" of places available. Among the venues discussed were some familiar ones: Columbus; Salt Lake; Washington, D.C.; and Hartford.

The Hexagonal tournament was an enduring test of both resources and resolve. Each of the six nations played ten matches, five of them on the road, spread over a seemingly interminable period of more than eight months. In that span, many unpleasant things could happen to sabotage a national team. Players might be injured or suspended by the accumulation of yellow and red cards. For smaller nations, funding might dry up and player mutinies could fester. A coach for an overseas professional team might hint at retribution if a top player deserted his side for a World Cup qualifier. And all five of those away games were certain to be staged at sites and altitudes that would make the visitors' stay extremely uncomfortable. The 2009 Hex would be no different, offering a fresh assortment of trials and tribulations. The six nations participating represented a wide range of culture, geography, and wealth.

If nothing else, U.S. Soccer now knew the dates and matchups for the upcoming Hexagonal tournament. The Americans would begin and end this 2009 odyssey at home, against what they considered their two toughest opponents, Mexico and Costa Rica.

The U.S. and Mexico were heavily favored to finish among the top three and receive an automatic World Cup bid. But there was some danger posed by those down below. After years of decline, Costa Rica was at the moment on the upswing and had been the only team to sweep all six group matches in the semifinal round. This rebirth had occurred after some typical panic. The *Ticos* were pushed to the limits by the tiny nation of Grenada in a first-round qualifying series, which led to the immediate firing of head coach Hernán Medford, who was replaced by Rodrigo Kenton, a former assistant to Bora Milutinovic at two World Cups. The *Ticos'* top player was Bryan Ruiz, a 23-year-old attacker who played professionally for KAA Gent in Belgium. The Americans historically had a difficult time at matches in the capital city of San Jose, losing there five straight times. *Estadio Saprissa* was arguably the single most intimidating venue in Central America, particularly during night games. Team buses were rocked ominously by fans upon arrival. Bags of urine had been tossed at visitors. And now the pitch was fitted with a turf field. That would surely make things even more difficult.

Honduras was considered the next greatest threat. The *Catrachos* were CONCACAF's most chronic underachievers, but they did not suffer from a shortage of talent. The national team came into the Hex on a high, having emerged as the winner of the toughest semifinal group that included Mexico, Jamaica and Canada. Honduras was led by forward David Suazo, twenty-nine, a star with true world-class credentials. Suazo had played in Serie A of the Italian league for nine years, then signed with Benfica of Portugal. A former MLS player, Ramon Nunez, was the top playmaker. The U.S. had very limited history playing against Honduras in qualifiers and could not truly know what to expect.

Trinidad and Tobago had survived a player rebellion over 2006 World Cup bonuses, then narrowly sneaked into this Hex when Guatemala was upset by Cuba in the final match of the semifinal round. Trinidad and Tobago's soccer federation reportedly was at long last throwing some money behind the Soca Warriors, expecting results. The team's top player arguably was still Dwight Yorke, thirty-eight years young and playing for Sunderland in England. Yorke had been scoring goals for two decades with T&T, and was still scoring them: He had slotted the winning penalty kick against the Americans in the semifinal round. The coach,

Francisco Maturana, was also a veteran of the qualifying wars. He'd led Colombia to the World Cup in 1990 and 1994. Counting that recent semifinal loss, the Americans still held a dominant mark against T&T of 14–2–3.

El Salvador, considered the weakest link in the Hex, had not qualified for the World Cup since 1982, but continued to nurture a great passion for this sport. If there were any doubt about that commitment, the country's history screamed otherwise. This Hex would offer unfortunate reminders of the 1969 Soccer War catalyzed by a pair of World Cup qualifiers between El Salvador and Honduras. There were other issues back then, involving Salvadoran immigrants in sparsely populated Honduras. But the tension came to a head in June of that year, first during a match in Tegucigalpa, Honduras, and then at a second game in San Salvador. Many Honduran fans were beaten, and the country's national anthem was jeered. Back home, Honduran citizens took out their anger on Salvadoran residents and officials, killing an unknown number. Salvadorans fled Honduras. Honduras broke off diplomatic relations with El Salvador, which then launched air force strikes inside Honduras and began a land-force invasion of Honduran islands. Relations were considerably more congenial now. War was not likely to break out when the two teams met at Honduras in June, although Honduras' internal political situation was extremely unstable.

El Salvador was relying on a fresh cast of young stars, a golden generation led by striker Rodolfo Zelaya, twenty, who had scored a hat trick against Haiti and a single goal against Suriname; and on midfielder Eliseo Quintanilla, twenty-six, an enormous talent. Carlos de los Cobos, the coach, had been a member of Mexico's World Cup team in 1998. Despite some promise, it was hard to take El Salvador too seriously. The *Cuscatlecos* were 0–10–1 against the Americans over the past fifteen years.

In the end, U.S. officials could draw up at least three scenarios for successful World Cup qualification. The first was ideal, and perhaps overly optimistic. The Americans would win all five home matches, draw with Mexico and Costa Rica on the road, and capture the three remaining away games for a final record of 8–0–2. The second projection was the expected one: The U.S. team would win its five home matches, lose in Mexico and Costa Rica, draw in Honduras, and beat both El Salvador and Trinidad on the road for a mark of 7–2–1. This was the same record the U.S. posted during the final qualifying round in 2005. Finally, there was a third, scarier route: A draw in one home match against Mexico, Costa Rica, or Honduras; a draw at El Salvador or Trinidad; and losses at Honduras, Costa Rica, and Mexico for a 5–3–2 record that might not get the job done. Nobody wanted to go down that path. Bradley surely had enough veterans, enough talent, to avoid such drama. And his greatest talent of all, his flagship star, was Landon Donovan.

CHAPTER 11

The Golden Child

THE BOY WAS A STRIVER FROM THE START, UNDETERRED BY circumstance or surroundings. Landon Donovan was a preternaturally focused and ambitious child. Like so many key members of the U.S. national team, he grew up in unprivileged fashion, nothing like the stereotypical suburban soccer brat. His parents separated when he was two. The father, Timothy, a former semi-pro hockey player from Canada, soon moved to Nebraska and remarried. Landon stayed behind in Redlands, California, with his mother, Donna; with his beloved twin sister, Tristan; and older brother, Josh, who taught him how to dribble and shoot the spotted ball. Redlands was a relatively happy place for him, the self-proclaimed "Navel Orange Capital of the World." Donna Kenney-Cash, a special education teacher, sent her kids to good schools and made certain they sampled a variety of life's offerings. Landon took up the violin, and was a straight-A student. The family was not nearly as affluent as many neighbors, so when Landon started playing soccer for a local team at the age of five, he wore discount sneakers, not expensive cleats and relied on mini-soccer scholarships throughout his club career. He was an immediate standout nonetheless, playing up in age from the start with the six and seven year olds. Landon starred for the club team Cal Heat in Rancho Cucamonga, then was recruited into the U.S. Youth Soccer's Olympic Develop Program. He traveled to Montana to attend a high-level soccer camp, and to anywhere he might find a world-class game. Landon reconnected with his father, and with his dad's new family. Timothy Donovan would grow closer to his son through their common athletic experiences, a great joy to both.

By the time he was fifteen years old and a sophomore at East Valley High School, Landon had been identified as America's brightest young star. All his soccer experiences had served him well, in one fashion or another. While playing for Cal Heat, he took on a second language by necessity. "The team had a bunch of Latino kids on it—Mexicans, Costa Ricans, Hondurans—and I had to learn Spanish if I wanted to get the ball," Donovan said. He learned what he called "soccer Spanish"— phrases for "I'm open," and "Let me take this corner." In high school, Donovan figured out how to put together Spanish clauses into complete sentences, compliments, and insults. By then, he was the Chosen One, in any language. He toured with John Ellinger's Under-17 team around the world, beating powerhouse European sides that didn't expect nearly this much talent from such American upstarts. Donovan was tabbed to become a member of the small, inaugural Bradenton Academy class down in Florida, part of Project 2010. He was already scouted and soon signed as a teenage prospect by Bayer Leverkusen of the German Bundesliga, his financial future virtually assured as a teenage phenom.

"Landon was the best of the bunch, just as he still is," Ellinger said. "He was focused on what he wanted from the start." He wasn't an automaton, however. Landon got down to Bradenton, dyed his already-receding hair blond, made the Sunday night trips to Walmart with his teammates, and had a good time. But Donovan never lost sight of the goal, which was to become an international soccer star. He was forever planning, acquiring his GED in advance so that he wouldn't have to return to high school after Bradenton, and therefore could head straight to Germany. This ambition nearly cost him, indirectly, one or both of his precious feet. Donovan earned his degree and was done with classes before his teammates, so the coaches took him out to a local course one day for a round of golf. He was walking toward an errant ball and heading straight for a four-foot alligator before his golfing partners finally screamed a warning. Donovan jumped away, startled, rescuing the extremities that would make his fortune.

Donovan was prideful to a fault, born with a global vision. He desperately wished to succeed overseas, to gain the sort of respect from an international audience that was so elusive for American players on domestic clubs. "Unfortunately, it's at the point where if a guy like Landon only makes it in MLS, he isn't viewed as a real success," Tab Ramos said. Landon fully grasped that concept. But anybody who has played this sport in more than a single uniform knows of its greatest puzzle: A player can appear a fluid, comfortable star on one team, and then a clumsy, ineffective clod on another. This transformation has very little to do with individual form and a lot to do with the very intricate nature of soccer. It is a game of shared space, exquisite timing, and alternating pace. If one's own playing rhythms are a poor match with teammates, or a coach's vision, then failure is certain to follow. To exacerbate matters, soccer offers few objective measures of success. Other than goals scored, statistics are virtually nonexistent or just plain silly. It is all too easy to be dismissed as extraneous by a coaching staff or journalists, without definitive proof. And this seemed to be the case with Donovan, whenever he ventured across the ocean to ply his wares in Germany.

On paper, his disappointing performances there made little sense. Donovan was a fleet, imaginative open-field athlete. As a withdrawn forward or attacking midfielder, he would be named in 2009 U.S. Soccer Male Athlete of the Year for the third time and Honda Player of the Year for the sixth time, an unprecedented achievement. He had graced the covers of both *Sports Illustrated* and *ESPN Magazine*, essentially accepting the role of cover boy for U.S. soccer. On the Los Angeles Galaxy, with the aid of David Beckham's through balls and seeing-eye crosses, Donovan scored twenty goals during the 2008 season, then led the team to the MLS Cup final the next year. Arena was the Galaxy's coach, with considerable history between the two men. There had been some tense moments earlier when Arena was the national coach, prodding Donovan, announcing publicly that Donovan wasn't fit enough to play ninety good minutes in any match. "It isn't his fault," Arena would say of the player, but that was always meant as a criticism. Arena felt Donovan simply didn't have the strength or training to perform consistently. And in parts of the soccer-blogging world,

Donovan was dubbed, "Landycakes," for a perceived softness that allegedly derived from an imaginary California lifestyle.

That lack of training or toughness was not what doomed Donovan to chronic failure in the Bundesliga. It was lousy chemistry, more than anything. America's great, hot soccer property would enroll three times in the *fussball* institution of higher learning and basically flunk out on all three occasions. Almost straight out of Bradenton Academy, he signed his first contract with Bayer Leverkusen in 1999, far too young at seventeen. Donovan couldn't crack the first team. He fled back to the MLS two years later. His stock rose dramatically at the 2002 World Cup in Korea, where he scored two goals and then drove the Germans crazy during a tight quarterfinal defeat, outracing defenders, scooting along the wing. He tried Germany again in 2004. Donovan played a starting role for Leverkusen in a Champions League match against Liverpool, but generally received limited playing minutes. He returned to the States again by the next year, for a second time. Germany hadn't been a total waste of time, Donovan said. He learned to be more independent, less reliant on friends. He absorbed important lessons about professionalism. He remembered watching Jens Nowotny at Leverkusen, how the stalwart sweeper from the German national team would slide-tackle some young reserve during a meaningless morning practice on Monday. "If he was doing it, then maybe I should be, too," Donovan thought.

The world shrugged at his disappointing appearances, figured that was about all you could expect from an American attacker. There were plenty of other disappointing examples in the past. Ramos was arguably the most effective midfielder ever on the U.S. national team. He had eighty-one caps for the Americans, from 1988 to 2000, and was a superb, creative player with an explosive first step. He also was named U.S. Soccer Player of the Year. Yet despite Ramos's unique talents, he was simply not as effective in a professional career that took him to Spain and Mexico, in addition to a seven-season stint on the MetroStars. At the peak of his career with Real Betis in La Liga, from 1992 to 1995, Ramos appeared in fifty-nine matches and scored only one goal. This was what often happened to the very best American stars, who instantly turned into support-role players in the top leagues. The British soccer magazine *FourFourTwo* published in 2008 a list of the hundred greatest foreign stars ever to play in England, and only four Americans cracked the group. Two of them, Brad Friedel at number thirty-nine and Kasey Keller, number one hundred, were goalkeepers. The only two field players were Roy Wegerle at number forty-two and John Harkes at number ninety-nine. Wegerle was a multi-citizenship player, hardly an American at all. Harkes was the rare success story, crafting a lengthy career at Sheffield Wednesday, Derby County, West Ham United, and Nottingham Forest from 1990 to 1999. "The fans embraced me when I proved I could play the game," Harkes told the *New York Times*. "Before that some said, "Yank go home,' or 'Where's your baseball bat?' But it was hard, long, and lonely and at times you question whether you made the right move." If you polled the experts, especially the European experts, they were unlikely to place a single U.S. player in their list of the top one hundred current players in the world, unless he was a goalkeeper. Donovan was ranked right on the cusp of that elite corps for a few months, after the 2002 World Cup. Then he wasn't.

"It's on me to perform," Donovan said, of his erratic international resume. "Do circumstances help? Does coaching help? Do teammates help? Of course. But Germany doesn't work well for me. It's hard for me to be successful there. I think I'd do OK in England, in Spain."

For one reason or another, Germany seemed the most intrigued with Donovan during the qualifying runup to South Africa. The lack of outside interest didn't make much sense, really, because there were numerous examples of successful Donovan-style athletes in the Spanish top division and in England's Premier League. Spain was filled with light-framed prototypes. The players generally were larger and rougher in England, true, but slight, swift open-field swoopers had flourished while chasing down balls for years—from Ryan Giggs at Manchester United to the young Theo Walcott at Arsenal. But back in autumn 2008 it was evident that prestigious Bayern Munich, coached by Klinsmann, was his hottest overseas suitor. Klinsmann still remembered Donovan's strong performance during the quarterfinal against Germany at the

2002 World Cup. The German coach also lived part-time on the West Coast and was plugged into the soccer scene there.

Donovan at this juncture was settled comfortably into Los Angeles, married to the actress Bianca Kajlich since January 2007. He had dogs, too. He insisted on finishing the season with the Galaxy, an exciting but terribly flawed club—even by MLS standards—that scored many goals and yielded even more. He spent ten days on a trial run with Bayern in November 2008. He then agreed during the holiday transfer window to a seventy-five-day loan arrangement with the German club, his third career shot in the Bundesliga at the prime-time age of twenty-six years old. Donovan's desire was to stay on a more permanent basis this time, if things worked out and MLS agreed to a transfer fee. If not, he would return to the Galaxy for the start of the 2009 season.

Donovan arrived in Dubai in January 2009, to join the team's mid-season camp. This was clearly not going to be easy, because Bayern Munich was brimming with star attacking players: Luca Toni from Italy, plus the two starting strikers from Germany's 2006 World Cup team, Miroslav Klose and Lukas Podolski. The team posted on its website interviews with Donovan and Klinsmann, in which Donovan swore his third time in Germany would be the charm. "I've grown up, especially mentally," he said. "I'm more experienced and mentally stronger, and I know what to expect here. Back then in Leverkusen, I wasn't ready for Germany and the Bundesliga. I thought for many months about the decision to come back, and spoke to lots of people. I know I'm ready for it now. I can learn lots from them. At the same time, I do believe I can bring qualities of my own to the team. I'm a different type of player compared to Luca, Miro, and Lukas. I do a lot of work off the ball and at a high pace."

He had been impressed during his brief November stay. "It was all wonderful—the coaching staff, the players, the medical unit, the performance center, the training conditions, the whole club, the city." Asked to compare soccer in America and Germany, Donovan was typically honest: "The people in Germany have much greater passion for soccer. Soccer is in their blood, as soccer has such a long history in Germany, but we've only had MLS for thirteen years. Bundesliga matches are obviously very high quality. Every player at a club like Bayern has class, which is different from America. The playing styles are different too. You get more one-on-one situations in the Bundesliga. The players are technically strong and good on the ball. MLS is faster and more physical."

One thing was clear: Klinsmann very badly wanted Donovan to succeed in Germany this time and was staking his own reputation on this pet project. Donovan started immediately in two friendlies against truly odd competition during a winter tour by Bayern Munich of the Middle East. His first match, bizarrely enough, was against the Al Jazeera Sports Club in the United Arab Emirates. He was credited with an assist and drew a foul that led to the winning set piece during a 3–2 victory. Then against Al Wehda of Saudi Arabia, Donovan scored during the 3–1 win. "His goal was beautiful, with ball control, the first touch, and a shot on the run," Klinsmann told the German magazine *Bild*, which dubbed Donovan, *"Klinsi's Liebling."* Klinsmann immediately promoted Donovan to the status of third striker, behind only Miloslav Klose and Luca Toni; ahead of injury-addled Lukas Podolski, who was headed for a transfer to FC Cologne in the summer. Klinsmann raved over Donovan's performance. "To fit in overnight at Bayern Munich is no mean task. The impression he makes, in my opinion, is very positive. Not just in the two exhibition games, but how he has fit in with the group. How he communicates with teammates. How he stays longer at the table. How he wants to find his way. Now he needs to really prove himself. If something happens up front, he's the first choice."

Donovan scored again on January 19 in his first friendly against a German opponent, Kaiserlautern, before 42,604 fans. This time it was a header, not exactly Donovan's specialty. He entered the match in the sixty-third minute, which seemed to be his assigned substitute role leading up to the start of the season's second half. On the same day, Podolski's transfer to Cologne was finalized for a $13 million transfer fee. "For me, everyday is a countdown," Donovan said. "I have to show something everyday. In practice, on the bus, on the plane. It's all important. This is a once in a lifetime chance." He scored yet another two goals in a friendly against second division Mainz, coming off the bench again in the sixtieth minute. Four goals in five friendlies made Donovan the leading scorer during Bayern's midseason break. Asked again by German reporters about returning to the Galaxy, Donovan said, "That would be sad. . . . I want to stay here a few years."

This arrangement was uncomfortable on a number of levels. Back in Los Angeles, the Galaxy coach, Arena, kept telling people he fully expected Donovan to return when the loan deal ended on March 8. Officials at MLS were feeling the heat, now that it was becoming apparent both Donovan and Beckham wanted to escape. At Bayern Munich, Donovan's situation was viewed with some suspicion by at least one star, Luca Toni. Nobody likes the teacher's pet, and Donovan was seen in most quarters as Klinsmann's guy. But it was more than that. It came down to something real and tangible, namely playing minutes. Toni was visibly steamed when he was replaced in the seventy-second minute by Donovan, with the score tied, 1–1, against Borussia Dortmund. Although Donovan didn't score in those final minutes, Bayern went on to win, 3–1, with two goals from Klose. The club president, Franz Beckenbauer—like Klinsmann, something of an American-phile— commented on live television that the victory was in part because of Donovan's appearance. "Luca Toni is a typical Italian striker, who sees only himself, the ball and the goal," Beckenbauer said. "Klose suffers because of that. After Toni left, Klose had more space."

Everything looked so promising, so hopeful, and then it all came crashing down again on Donovan when the Bundesliga resumed its regular season. It was as if a switch had been flipped somewhere, and the player was suddenly, completely out of place again. Donovan was still getting into matches with enough time to impress people in the second halves. But now his impact was so slight as to appear irrelevant. Stranded out on the right wing, Donovan was utterly lost, not part of any pattern of play. His teammates weren't quite freezing him out, yet he was incapable of reading the play and moving to a constructive position. He was positively un-Landon-like. Donovan appeared in five league matches and a Cup match after the winter break as a reserve, scoring in none of them. His only worthy contribution was clearing the ball off his own goal line in one desperate moment during a 2–0 loss to FC Cologne. "Offensively he showed nothing," reported the *Suddeutsche*

Zeitung. Suddenly the little guy was a huge target for the German press. The *Rheinische Post* sneered, "Klinsmann's darling made it clear why club chairman Karl-Heinz Rummenigge wants to get rid of him."

Klinsmann, it turned out, had done himself no favors with this Donovan experiment. When Bayern sagged in early spring, he was fired. Klinsmann might have been happily coaching Donovan and the U.S. national team through qualification. Instead his own star had fallen considerably back home. Donovan, for his part, became resigned to another humbling exit. He tried to put a happy face on things, declaring this more a homecoming in Los Angeles than an exile. "My wife is there, my dogs, and my team of the last four years with many friends," he told the German publication *Mercur.* "I love the Galaxy. My heart belongs to it. I have always said that I want to play in Europe. If not now, then maybe next year. My contract with MLS runs through 2011. That means in 2010, when the contract end nears, the stars might align so that it makes sense for the Galaxy and for me."

And so Donovan returned to open arms again in defeat, to a coach, Arena, who now embraced him as the best player in MLS. For the time being there was no Beckham, who had drifted away to Italy, a much happier European transplant story. If Donovan was depressed about any of this, he hid it well. He had tried his best, auditioned again. Southern California really wasn't such a terrible purgatory. The Galaxy had been revived with Arena's revamped defensive line. "I had a good time in Germany," he told reporters, at his first practice at the Home Depot Center. "It was a very interesting experience for a lot of reasons. Some good, some bad. You always wonder if you're capable of playing on that level, and it quickly became apparent that I was and that I enjoyed it. But there's something distinctly different about the environment here." Back in his number ten jersey and seventy-degree comfort zone, Donovan prospered immediately. Down two goals in an MLS home opener against DC United, Donovan scored on a penalty kick in the eightieth minute and demonstrated his uncanny ability to anticipate passes and time a scoring run. He neatly beat United's backline with an onsides spurt, then headed a long centering pass from Kyle Patterson past goalkeeper Josh Wicks from six yards out. Back home in America, Donovan was no longer invisible, as he had been in those regular season Bundesliga matches. He was essential once again. He more than earned his $900,000 per year salary, on and off the field. "The most important player in the league," commissioner Don Garber called him, soon after his return.

There was another advantage to playing here. Donovan required no trans-Atlantic flight to join Bradley and his teammates on the national team. Bradley soon moved his senior star to a right midfield position, where the player could have more room to work in open space and create chances for others. Donovan would start every meaningful national team match. He was now the old pro, calmly assessing things out on the wing, taking more time with the ball before making decisions. Life had its perks, including a black Maserati and just the right amount of public attention. "I think actually we're lucky, as soccer players," Donovan told Paul Oberjuerge, a Los Angeles–based reporter. "We kind of fall right in between those lines where you're not so famous that *paparazzi* are following you around, but you also get a lot of benefits of being an athlete. People have been respectful."

When he showed up at the Miami camp, Donovan declared his experience overseas just another building block. "It was very instructive watching the other guys on the team—how Franck gets the ball, how Klose moves into space to get the ball, how Toni would look to receive, those things will help me a lot. With Bayern, opponents tend to sit in and defend in numbers. There wasn't a ton of space. It was about trying to make little advantages without having much space. That was good for me, makes me brighter and sharper."

Donovan would have more chances overseas, another trial in 2010 with Everton in the Premier League. But for now, international soccer presented a humbling road to self-discovery. In Europe, Donovan remained a relative nonentity. In Mexico, however, he was something much bigger and more menacing: the devil incarnate.

CHAPTER 12

The Rival

IT MUST BE SAID FROM THE OUTSET, ABOUT AMERICA'S FAMOUS soccer rival: The greatness of Mexican soccer has been, at times, greatly exaggerated. The country's beloved national team, *El Tri* (the three national colors are green, red and white), has never emerged as much more than a regional power capable of scaring some very good international sides. Other than drubbing the United States for many decades, Mexico's accomplishments have fallen into the relatively modest category.

There is, admittedly, an admirable consistency to the side's competitiveness. During the past four World Cup tournaments, Mexico advanced each time out of its preliminary group—no mean feat—but then was immediately defeated in the Round of 16. Mexico reached the quarterfinals of the two World Cups staged on its home soil in 1970 and 1986. It captured five Gold Cups, and before that three CONCACAF titles and three North American Nations Cups. As an invited guest, Mexico twice reached the final of the Copa America, the South American championship. The country's professional leagues are rock solid, financially and artistically superior to MLS, fueled by fat television contracts. This is a solid resumé, but hardly worth the sort of haughty, expectant attitude demonstrated by the local press and populace in run-ups to major matches. If Mexico is not Canada, then it is also not Brazil.

Soccer in Mexico began in much the same way it started in America, imported there by European workers in the early twentieth century. There had been ancient Mayan games in some ways vaguely similar to the sport. But English miners from Cornwall were the first to teach the modern game to the locals. By the 1920s the Mexicans were playing organized matches against neighbors from Central America. The *Federacion Mexicana de Futbol* was formed on August 23, 1927, to found, promote, and fund a national team. The squad itself was still a bit wobbly, losing at the 1928 Summer Olympics, 7–1, to Spain and then finishing dead last in the 1930 World Cup after defeats to France, Chile, and Argentina. A friendly draw at their own World Cup in 1970 allowed the Mexicans to advance to the quarterfinals, where they were drubbed by Italy, 4–1. They failed to qualify in 1974, then were humiliated during three losses in 1978, including a 6–0 loss to West Germany. This was hardly a juggernaut.

The 1986 World Cup became Mexico's true debutante ball. The tournament was originally awarded to Colombia, but that country's officials backed out in 1982, pleading poverty. Mexico was chosen by FIFA as the substitute host over bids by the U.S. and Canada. A devastating earthquake struck Mexico in September, 1985, yet officials persisted with preparations for what would be called, *El Mundo Unido por Un Balon*—"The World United by a Ball." Coached by the opportunistic Serbian Bora Milutinovic, Mexico avoided all the top powers in the first round through careful seeding. It defeated Bulgaria in the Round of 16 and performed quite well during a scoreless quarterfinal match against West Germany. But in the end, the Mexicans were undone by the penalty kick tiebreaker, 4–1.

By the mid-nineties, Mexico had gained considerable respect with solid showings in Copa America. And then the team won the Group of Death at the 1994 World Cup, finishing ahead of Italy, Ireland, and Norway before losing again in a second-round penalty tiebreaker to Bulgaria. Germany, a regular tormentor, put out Mexico in the second round at France in 1998. Mexico, however, had proved consistently capable of advancing past the group stage at the World Cup. This was more than could be said of the Americans, who were often overwhelmed when they traveled to Europe. At the 2006 World Cup in Germany, the U.S. was knocked out early again while Mexico put on a brilliant show before losing in the second round to Argentina, arguably the match of the tournament. Mexico was respected internationally, if not quite feared. The Americans were still viewed only as erratic upstarts. Yet in head-to-head matchups, the U.S. had gained considerable footing against Mexico. It was something of a mystery, a rock-paper-scissors kind of thing. The U.S. could beat Mexico at home and on neutral ground. Mexico could beat the rest of the world, or at least play competitively with top opponents. Meanwhile, the rest of the world was still thumping the U.S., on most notable occasions.

One thing was a constant: All of Mexico despised the U.S. national soccer team—even if that passionate loathing went unrequited and unrecognized by Americans. The anger had been stoked by harsh words, by the occasional elbow, and at times by urine flying from both sides. The resentment was no great mystery. Mexico was the older brother, eclipsed suddenly by a younger sibling at his favorite sport by way of sheer size and athleticism.

"The last ten years, it's a bit insulting to them," said Claudio Reyna, the veteran U.S. midfielder. "Soccer is their one and only sport." While the recent decade had been difficult for the Mexicans, the Round of 16 match at the 2002 World Cup in Korea stood above all other soccer events as a national humiliation. "It was the biggest game we ever had against them and it might be for the next 100 years," Reyna said. That 2–0 victory by the Americans forced Mexico to reevaluate its comfortable superiority complex. The win was decisive, no fluke. The Americans accomplished the feat with speed, stamina, and counter-attacking imagination. And to make matters more insulting, Donovan scored one of the goals.

Donovan was forever the point man in this rivalry, if only because he spoke the language. He had never played for clubs in Spain's La Liga, in Mexico, or in South America, yet could exchange trash talk in Spanish whenever required. Television and radio crews from Mexico therefore would seek him out and ask Donovan questions about an upcoming match, and he would answer them in a frank way. It was a comical sight, because at times Donovan was doing this within clear earshot of his coaches, who would have been horrified to know what kind of bulletin-board material he was providing—if only they spoke

Spanish. While these quotes were rarely picked up by American news outlets, they made large headlines in Mexico and were often distorted in wild ways. Somehow, inevitably, Donovan was predicting a crushing victory by the Americans.

With few exceptions, Donovan was up for the battle. He had over the years insulted the Mexicans in Spanish, English, and body language. He had called the Mexican crowds "ignorant," and after that famous 2002 World Cup victory, Donovan was so incensed by a head-butt to teammate Cobi Jones that he said of the opponents, "They're dirty and they're nasty and they spit on you and grab you where they shouldn't." Then there was the unfortunate exchange of urine at the 2004 Olympic qualifying match for U-23s in Guadalajara. During a practice session on the day before the match, a security camera caught sight of Donovan, who thought he was unseen, urinating into a shrub. The incident was viewed as the ultimate display of disrespect by an American. When the match was played, fans in Guadalajara hurled limes, batteries, and baggies filled with their own urine as retribution. The crowd chanted, "Osama, Osama" at the Americans during a 4–0 victory for Mexico that eliminated the U.S. from the 2004 Athens Olympics. "It was a little humiliating, a little degrading," Donovan said. "At one point it is surprising. At another point, you come to expect it. Fans are fans. But I wish they saw players as human beings on the field. Players don't have anything to do with what happens politically in our country." Donovan was later able to play off his own villainous image on Mexican television, appearing disguised in a hilarious commercial during which he purchased a national lottery ticket, claiming, "It's easier to win in Mexico."

For many years, U.S. vs. Mexico had dredged up none of this emotion. It was anything but a real soccer rivalry. The Americans beat Mexico, 4–2, during a 1934 World Cup qualifier in Rome. After that, however, the Mexicans enjoyed a one-sided dominance spanning more than four decades. From 1937 until 1980, Mexico went on a 21–0–3 streak against the U.S.; many of those victories were posted in key World Cup qualifiers, as Mexico became the concrete wall blocking American passage into big-time international adventures. There were some truly demoralizing routs, like the back-to-back qualifying losses by the U.S. in 1957, a 6–0 defeat at Mexico City followed by a 7–2 rout at Long Branch, CA. By the 1980s, the results and scores were far more respectable. Then in the 1990s, the U.S. took ownership of practically every home match. Going into their World Cup qualifier at Columbus in February 2009, the U.S. was 8–0–2 against Mexico over the previous ten matches played on American soil.

In Mexico City, however, it always has been a different story. *Estadio Azteca*, Aztec Stadium, is Mexico's not-so-secret weapon. An enormous building that seats 105,000, *Azteca* is no great beauty. It is sometimes called *Coloso de Santa Ursula*, the Colossus of Saint Ursula, referring to its Mexico City neighborhood. Before the stadium fills for a match with color and drama, it is merely a harsh concrete bowl dropped into a labyrinth of parking lots. The playing surface is separated from the masses by unsightly fencing and moatwork. Still, the place has seen its share of history. Built in 1966 for the 1968 Summer Olympics, *Azteca* was the stage for the World Cup final in 1970 and 1986. It was the site of Diego Maradona's "Hand of God" goal, a not-so-miraculous feat during a quarterfinal match that was never quite forgiven or forgotten in England.

Most important for Mexico, *Azteca* stands 1.4 miles above sea level, often drowning in air pollution from the sprawling city to the north. This environment creates an enormous problem for opponents, who often huff, puff, and cough their way to defeat with familiar futility. The Mexican national team had dropped only one qualifying match at *Azteca* ever, to Costa Rica. The Americans managed just one draw there in November 1997, during the qualifying run under coach Steve Sampson. More often than not they were forced to play in the worst summer weather, fading badly in the second half. The Mexicans were merciless in this regard. They preferred to play these World Cup qualifiers in mid-afternoon, under the hottest sun.

"It's not that you worry about these things, so much as these are realistic issues," Donovan said. "You just walk around Mexico City, you get tired." Over the years, opponents had learned there were only two ways to approach the match: arrive weeks beforehand, leaving enough time to adjust to high altitude; or show up in the last minute, leaving bodies little time to become adversely affected by the thin oxygen. Coaches discovered the worst results occurred when their teams traveled to Mexico City four or five days before the game.

"You're not playing on a level field," Arena said. "At sea level, I'd favor the U.S. But it's hard, an awesome challenge. The elevation, the sight-lines are difficult. It's twenty yards from the touchlines to the dugouts. The massive field looks like it's out in the country. You have the heat. It all gets to your head. We tried oxygen at halftime. We tried a lot of things."

First, though, came a meeting in Columbus. And a wicked storm was brewing to the west.

CHAPTER 13

Riding Out the Storm

SOMETIMES YOU WONDERED WHY HE BOTHERED. BOB BRADLEY called twenty-five players into the national team camp at the Home Depot Center in Carson, California, on January 4, 2009, to begin preparations for a friendly against Sweden and then for the key, final-round qualifying match against Mexico in Columbus on February 11. If this had been twenty years earlier, Bradley would have been able to gather virtually his entire first squad together for weeks, run them through scrimmages, and work on timing drills. But now there were just the off-season MLS guys available for this early camp, and only a precious few had more than an outside chance of playing quality minutes against Mexico or to make the final roster for South Africa. This was more a matter of numbers, of plumbing the depths of the player pool in search of an unpolished gem. The calendar year 2009 figured to be an extremely busy time for the U.S. team. In addition to all-important qualifiers and tune-ups, the Americans were scheduled to participate in both the Gold Cup, which was the CONCACAF championship; and in the Confederations Cup in South Africa, which was a reward for winning the previous Gold Cup. Bradley would need to stretch his roster, if the stars were going to survive the long international campaign in addition to their pro seasons.

There were a few MLS-based players worth watching. Ching, thirty-two, the veteran forward from the Houston Dynamo, had been a starter for Bradley by default on occasion. He offered a solid physical presence.

Kenny Cooper, twenty-four, an effective striker from FC Dallas, was definitely on the radar. Marvel Wynne, twenty-two, from Toronto FC and Jonathan Bornstein, twenty-four, from Chivas were at this time somewhere between eighth and twelfth on the depth chart of national team defenders. It was easy to move up in a hurry on the back line, however. At midfield, developing stars Sacha Kljestan, twenty-three, from Chivas USA and Ricardo Clark, twenty-five, of the Houston Dynamo were promising. Kljestan was particularly intriguing, occasionally demonstrating real flashes of brilliance. Like most creative players, Kljestan might disappear for an entire half, only to create a goal later from nothing or a half-step advantage. He was not the most dependable two-way midfielder. He rarely tracked back to make the rough tackles. Kljestan had been up and down at the Olympics, but his gorgeous shot against the Netherlands was cited as Best Goal of 2008 by readers of *Soccer America*. He had played briefly for Bradley at Chivas, and returned to this camp after spending some training time with Glasgow Celtic, which had offered MLS a $2.9 million transfer fee. And then during a friendly in California against Sweden, the first U.S. match of 2009, Kljestan exploded for three goals—only the eleventh hat-trick in the national team's history. His first score, in particular, was impressive: a searing, curling free kick from nearly thirty-five yards out. Nobody had scored his first three goals for the national team in the same game since Buff Donelli, during a World Cup qualifier against Mexico in 1934. Kljestan said he'd never heard of the guy, "But he's my *amigo* now."

Kljestan was a player caught between generations and continents. He was five years older than Altidore, and could no longer afford to sit around on the bench at Glasgow Celtic or anywhere else, if he coveted a significant role on the national team. Yet if he stuck around and succeeded in Europe, his financial future was secure. Stories of success and failure abounded for Americans abroad. In theory, Clint Dempsey, Jozy Altidore, Eddie Johnson, Pablo Mastroeni, DaMarcus Beasley, Michael Bradley, Oguchi Onyewu, Maurice Edu, Carlos Bocanegra, and Tim Howard were all gaining invaluable experience against the highest-level competition possible overseas. But that wasn't necessarily the case. Johnson was having a tough time breaking into the lineup at Cardiff, on loan from Fulham. Freddy Adu wasn't playing at all in Monaco and Altidore was viewed as a long-term project at Villarreal. Most disturbing: Beasley, hanging by a jersey thread to his starting role on the national team, was struggling with injuries and rarely played for Glasgow Rangers. His teammate there, Maurice Edu, was also buried on the bench. Edu had gone to Glasgow after the Rangers paid MLS and its Toronto franchise a $5 million transfer fee. But he was about to turn twenty-three, and was not helping himself with Bradley. Edu would have been better off in this regard sticking with MLS, or joining a growing legion of Americans invading the less-prestigious Scandinavian leagues.

The U.S. national team was no different in this regard than the other patch-quilt sides from the CONCACAF qualifying round. That included Mexico, which was missing a handful of top players due to injury or suspension for this match against the Americans. Rafael Marquez, the team's star central defender, had suffered a calf injury while playing with Barcelona and would be less than fully fit for the qualifier. Marquez was the most successful Mexican playing in Europe since Hugo Sanchez. Another Spanish League starter, Andrés Guardado from Deportivo Coruna, was expected to miss the match because of injury. Three players—Gerardo Torrado, Fernando Arce, and Carlos Vela—were suspended for infractions in the semifinal round. Coach Sven-Göran Eriksson had some difficult decisions to make. Several other starting candidates were not getting much playing time in Europe and might be judged off form. Then in a disturbing tune-up match, Mexico was defeated, 3–2, by the same touring team from Sweden that lost to the Americans.

It had now been a decade since the Mexicans beat the U.S. national side in America. Things appeared rather desperate, and a Mexican newspaper, *Record,* began giving out coupons to be exchanged by the locals for voodoo dolls of generic U.S. soccer players. A customer needed only bring the coupon with him during a purchase at a local RadioShack affliate in Mexico, and he would receive a free doll. Accompanying illustrations demonstrated how the owner of this voodoo creation could then cut off its legs with a pair of scissors. The offer did not last long, because RadioShack also did business in the States. When the doll promotion began making international headlines, the corporation withdrew from the whole deal. One Mexican journalist brought a voodoo doll to Columbus and asked Donovan to pose with it. Donovan politely demurred. Eriksson also declared he wanted nothing to do with such matters. "I'm Swedish," he said.

Eriksson was portrayed at this time by the Mexican media as a befuddled coach on the brink of dismissal, after his team's desultory performance in the semifinal round of CONCACAF qualifying. By the time Eriksson stepped off a bus for practice at Crew Stadium on Tuesday, one day before the match, wistful rumors were flying that he would soon leave the Mexican team to take a position as head coach at Portsmouth or even Chelsea of the Premier League. Once again, American coaches everywhere were left to wonder how failed peers from overseas appeared to have limitless career options. As Eriksson said, "It's not bad to be linked with such good jobs. It's worse if they never mention your name." Eriksson insisted his status would not be a distraction for Mexico, and that he had every intention of winning this match and defusing the issue. But his task was a difficult one, frustrated further by the relatively remote location. Mexico found it nearly impossible to line up a training site in the area. In most other nations these big matches were played in large stadiums, not in pseudo-Erector Sets like Columbus Crew Stadium. The weather on Wednesday was on the warm side—much warmer than the Americans would have liked—but there were forecasts of rain and wind. Eriksson briefly complained, always with a smile.

The art of choosing a favorable soccer venue for a World Cup qualifier is fraught with danger, unexpected climatic spins, and odd fan migrations. You never know what to expect until the gates or the heavens open. Crew Stadium, which always had served Americans well with its inclement surprises, suddenly turned on match day into a vengeful, howling wind tunnel. There were terrible storms leading up to kickoff, with winds gusting up to sixty-six miles per hour. Fans were ordered back to their cars by a public address announcement for their own safety and peace of mind, as the sky veered from gray to pitch black. "The wind is something you don't really know how to prepare for," Bob Bradley said. "You can't make the coin flip that much of a big deal, because you don't know if you're going to win it." It was, in fact, a very important coin toss. The Americans won the flip, allowing them to play with the ungodly winds howling at their backs in the first half. Their clearances and shots would carry hard and long, while the Mexicans battled desperately to keep the ball on the ground.

Bradley's starting lineup for this showcase match included eight foreign-based players and just three MLS stars—aging, scraggly, ever-enthusiastic Frankie Hejduk on the back line, Kljestan at midfield, and Ching up front. Donovan and Beasley were attacking midfielders, out on the wings. Ching and Dempsey, with his reliable first touches, were at forward. Michael Bradley started at central midfield next to Kljestan. Carlos Bocanegra and Oguchi Onyewu were the central defenders. Hejduk and Heath Pearce played the wing backs. Howard, as usual, was in the net and promised to monitor carefully his own emotions. Too much passion might mean too many fouls or marking errors. "We have to be aggressive, but I need to make sure we play intelligently," Howard said.

Bob Bradley gave one more locker-room speech beforehand about how the team needed to be even more careful than usual about spacing, due to poor conditions. There could be no gaps out there, because the ball was likely to carry anywhere at any moment. He told them, too, to keep the ball low if they expected any semblance of control or possession. Then the Americans took the field and the wind was stronger than anybody expected. Sitting behind the goal in the only protected stands, Uncle Sam's Army of fans attempted in vain to wave oversized flags, that were buffeted by the currents and only wanted to point straight back into the faces of their holders. Paper and plastic garbage flew throughout the stadium.

Howard rescued the nervous Americans in the third minute with a kick save off a point blank shot from Giovanni dos Santos, Mexico's brilliant young attacker. This superb save allowed the Americans time to settle down, and then Michael Bradley scored the critical first goal in the forty-third minute after a mischief-making, lefty corner kick from

Beasley. The in-swinging ball was flicked back into the goal mouth from the far post by a Donovan header, booted into the Mexican goalkeeper by Onyewu, and finally kicked high into the net by Bradley off the re-bound, past Oswaldo Sanchez. "It bounced loose for me," said Michael Bradley, a two-way midfielder who rarely strung together more than five words for reporters when speaking about his own exploits. The lead was all very nice, but the Americans still needed to kill off forty-five minutes against the wind in the second half. They managed this with disciplined marking and precise offside traps, defending the swift Mex-icans with care, and occasional rescues again from Howard. Mexico's best chance to tie the match transformed into its final undoing, after the ball somehow scooted harmlessly across the U.S. goal mouth amid a bundle of bodies. Marquez flew spikes-first in frustration into Howard's thigh and was red-carded by Guatemalan referee Carlos Ba-tres. The man advantage for the Americans neutralized the stiff breezes against them in the second half.

The match ended with Bradley's second goal, a sharp right-footer off a pass from Donovan in the second minute of extra time—against a Mexican defense stretched both by numbers and urgency. Altidore, a substitute in the eighty-third minute, started the scoring play when he was pulled down in flight. The ball found its way in any case to Dono-van, who made the pass to Bradley. The Mexicans then headed unhap-pily toward their locker room, where an international incident broke out. Like many such matters, it was based on a linguistic misunder-standing. Hejduk, celebrating the victory as he walked toward the U.S. clubhouse, screamed, "Fuck, yeah!" An assistant coach for Mexico, Paco Ramirez, heard it as, "Fuck you." Ramirez slapped Hejduk's face in the area between the U.S. and Mexico locker rooms, precipitating a shoving match with security guards that was quickly posted on YouTube. Pretty goals are not the only thing you can watch on the Internet. "I think they may have been a tad upset about the result," chuckled Gulati, inside a rattling, wind-whipped media tent after the match. The qualifying sys-tem in CONCACAF was complicated, but it was also simple: If you beat Mexico like this to lead off the final round, then the path to a World Cup was considerably easier.

And so Crew Stadium became the sacred burial ground for yet another Mexican national team. This had been the third straight 2–0 victory in Columbus for the U.S. over Mexico, which was now 0–9–2 in its last eleven matches on American soil. Marquez found himself apologizing for his red card—although soon after the match he would argue that the entire nation and its media were at fault. "If you ask me, Mexican football has a deep-rooted problem and that's the cause of the bad patch we've been going through," Marquez said in an interview posted on FIFA.com. "Our football is stagnating and with everything that's happened, it's time to come right out and say it. If we carry on like this we're all going to pay for it. There are a lot of things that are going on and we need to analyze them closely to find out why they're happening. It's almost like we're trying to shoot ourselves in the foot. I'm talking about everyone on the outside of Mexican football. Not everyone, of course, but sometimes the press seems to be trying to outdo each other and publish the most trashy stories to sell more papers. That doesn't help the national team."

Not everything had gone well in this match for the Americans, either. Ching was ineffective. Beasley showed his rust. Kljestens, too, gave away the ball too easily, and somehow his creativity didn't translate. The team attacked almost exclusively from the wings, limiting Dempsey's potential clout. When Hejduk started limping after a mid-game collision, Bradley didn't replace him for good reason. There really wasn't another proven defender on the bench. Worst of all, Howard was shown a yellow card by Batres for delay of game in the sixty-seventh minute. The card did not seem deserved, because Howard was shaking off a minor injury, not just stalling. It was his second yellow of qualifying, which meant he would be suspended for the next match in El Salvador. Still, all told, a victory over Mexico was not to be dismissed casually. The U.S. was tied for first with Costa Rica in the Hex with three quick points. People noticed, too. The match was watched in the U.S. by nearly seven million viewers, on Univision and ESPN2—twice the number that saw the North Carolina-Duke basketball game on ESPN during the same time slot.

The Bradley family should have been ecstatic about the whole performance. How often does a twenty-one-year-old midfielder score two goals against his country's nemesis? How often is he the son of the coach? But the Bradleys were practiced in the fine art of understatement. Bob and Michael sat next to each other in that wind-blown media tent afterward, and neither of them so much as cracked a smile. When the coach was asked directly how it felt to be the father of this night's hero, Bob Bradley refused to assume that viewpoint, even for a moment. "You have an environment you want to create, a high level of being a pro," Bradley said. "I have three children, and I've got to tell you I'm proud of all my kids. I have a great family and I'm a lucky man."

CHAPTER 14

Late Bloomers

A.C. MILAN IS ESTABLISHED SOCCER ROYALTY IN ITALY'S
Serie A, forever assured of important championship trophies and fabu-
lously expensive athletes. The club is owned by Silvio Berlusconi, the
center-right prime minister of Italy and an industrialist with a bound-
less fortune. Over the decades since he purchased this expensive hobby
in 1986, Berlusconi has populated his roster with superstars such as
George Weah, Marco van Basten, Frank Rijkaard, Ruud Gullit, Roberto
Baggio, Franco Baresi, Roberto Donadoni, and—more recently—Kaká,
Ronaldinho, and Andriy Shevchenko. While he was coaching at Princeton, Bob Bradley would at times view tapes of Milan's matches with his
players in order to better understand how this formidable club controlled play and distributed the ball. His son, Michael, couldn't help but
learn about the famous side, by sheer osmosis. "He'd hear me talk, see
the way they played," Bob Bradley said.

When Michael went as a first grader in 1994 with his father and the
Princeton team to a couple of A.C. Milan matches in Italy, he might
have been expected to form a cosmic attachment to one of the club's
gaudy goal scorers. Instead, the young boy couldn't take his eyes off
Demetrio Albertini, a solid two-way midfielder who performed no
fancy ball tricks but instead held his ground stubbornly and stymied the
runs of opponents with remarkable efficiency. Albertini, who played a
strong supporting role at Milan for fourteen seasons, would become
Michael's role model, and that attachment would serve him well. In

addition to his contributions on the national team, Michael grew into one of the most successful American field players overseas. His seventeen goals for Heerenveen in the Netherlands during the 2007–2008 season stood as a record scoring binge for any U.S. player abroad. He later became the starting midfielder for Borussia Mönchengladbach of the Bundesliga, playing a more attacking role than he did for his own father in World Cup qualifiers.

Considering such positive results, you would think that Bob Bradley might wax proudly about his son's accomplishments. It never worked that way. The father was terribly uncomfortable speaking about Michael in any context other than how he might discuss Donovan or Dempsey. Bob Bradley was painfully self-conscious about potential charges of nepotism, even though any educated observer could see that Michael had earned his spot many times over in the lineup. And Michael was just as guarded about discussing his father. It was a puzzling, protective pact of silence, devised, it seemed, to avoid a string of feel-good media features on a solid, heartwarming familial relationship in sports.

It had been this way for quite some time. When the teen-aged Michael played a key role in a winning goal for his dad's team, the MetroStars, he left the stadium in New Jersey quickly so that he could travel back to a Chicago suburb to attend the high school prom with his girlfriend. The team's public relations staff informed the media about this, because reporters were annoyed that a star of the match was unavailable for an interview. Instead of embracing this cuddly revelation, Bob Bradley was displeased by his staff's openness. "All the players are teasing him on the field," he complained to the public relations director, Nick DiBenedetto.

What happened with the Bradleys, stayed with the Bradleys. DiBenedetto remembered walking in on a typical father-son moment at their home in north Jersey, during the MetroStar years. "Bob and Michael were sitting there with the TiVo, breaking down a game," DiBenedetto said. Boxes of match films were transported from one city to another, whenever Bob Bradley relocated with his wife, Lindsay, to yet another job. This would be the very nearly compulsive environment that nurtured Michael, and a far more comfortable suburban setting than those experienced by most national teammates. When he was finished with his season in Germany, or enjoyed an extensive break from the Bundesliga, Michael still returned to stay in the extra bedroom in his parents' house at Manhattan Beach, a few blocks from the ocean.

To fully understand this soccer-bonded relationship, one first needed to learn some history about the Bradley family; how the process of striving was held precious within the household. Bob was the oldest of three sons born to Jerry and Mary Bradley, to a family ruled by work ethic and practicality, and to nothing fancy. His father was raised by foster parents and began life with limited resources. Jerry Bradley joined the Marines at the age of eighteen, right out of high school, rather than sign a minor league contract with the Chicago Cubs. Korea was the more direct route to a college scholarship on the G.I. Bill, a surer bet. He earned a purple heart, then headed to Upsala College in East Orange, NJ, where he was a solid baseball and football player, later elected to the Hall of Fame of that now-defunct school. Jerry married his sweetheart from Caldwell High School at age twenty-four and earned a living by selling heating and ventilating systems on building projects. He loved baseball more than football. Soccer was not on the radar back then, hardly a thread in the fabric of mainstream America. Jerry Bradley never kicked a soccer ball.

Bob, the first son, was a natural athlete. "I grew up playing all sports," Bob Bradley said. "I was lucky I lived across the street from a field and from basketball courts. The only thing we did all day was go out on those fields and compete and play." He was a Pop Warner quarterback right through eighth grade in Essex Fells, New Jersey, then began playing soccer with some older Germans in town. His youngest brother, Jeff, remembers that Bob was "mesmerized" at his first sight of a game.

West Essex High School was a soccer school at a time when only a dozen or so others around the area took the sport seriously. The coach, Ralph Dugan, had come from the hotbeds of Kearny and Harrison to establish a top program that competed regularly for state championships in the 1970s. An assistant coach spotted Bob Bradley when he was still in junior high and invited him to practice with the varsity. He was then promoted to the varsity as a freshman, playing right wing for four years and capturing a Group III title. When he graduated in 1976, Bob Bradley was considered one of the better players in the state. But again, this was a different time, and most of the area universities didn't excel at the sport. Rutgers wasn't very good. He could go to Bucknell or Princeton, which offered no athletic scholarships. The Ivy League was considered a soccer mecca then, and Princeton was a Top Ten program on the rise. Bob felt guilty about the financial stress on the family, but Jerry Bradley wouldn't hear about such nonsense. His son had been admitted to Princeton, to the Ivy League. "You go, we'll make it happen," he told Bob.

When he was a sophomore, suddenly, it appeared Bob's soccer career was done. He planted his foot in the grass during a match, an opponent knocked him the wrong way, and he suffered an ugly compound leg fracture. His bone stuck out so far from the skin that only a doctor wanted to look. Team members figured that was the end. He was a Princeton student, after all. Surely he would just give up this dead-end sport and return to classes, which represented his future. But soccer was illogically important to Bradley. He rehabbed religiously on his own time, and somehow returned to the field by the summer leading to his junior year. "I had an injury. A lot of athletes have injuries," Bradley said. "From my standpoint, I was working hard to come back and not worrying about what anybody else said. There was never a moment I was thinking of not doing it."

In his first game back that fall for Princeton, he scored four goals and was converted into a striker. Here was a guy who had legs like tree trunks and the speed of a stalled locomotive. Yet Bradley prevailed, modeling himself after the prolific German scorer, Gerd Müller. Bradley had studied Müller religiously, watching scratchy Super 8 footage of the player scoring goals during the 1970 World Cup. Bradley learned where and how to finish a play. Upon graduation he was given the team's most dedicated player award and sent out into a world where there were almost no opportunities for a solid American college player. If this had been 2010, Bob Bradley might have hooked on with a second division team in Norway, or elsewhere. Not in 1980.

"Right or wrong, I felt I was still improving," Bob Bradley said. "I was a late bloomer. Was I good enough? I don't know. When I was done playing in college I still felt I was getting better, that I had something to offer. Yet there wasn't any place to try it out. Yes, there were reserve teams with the NASL, but there weren't that many opportunities for Americans. They held open tryouts. You played games where you play against a reserve team. You played in men's leagues, but nonetheless it was not that easy to find good ways to continue to play. You chased the game."

Bob watched his younger brother, Scott, set out on a professional baseball career that would eventually land him a spot with the Seattle Mariners, playing with both Ken Griffey Jr. and Ken Griffey Sr. Bob reluctantly accepted a job with Procter and Gamble. He had college loans to pay, a career to think about. It was an unhappy corporate post, and it was killing him. He would receive work calls at all hours, get hazed by executives who told him to make certain a display of cookies was just right. The company often hired former athletes, and then the firm's employees made a real effort to break these new hires so they would conform to future tasks. Jeff was still in high school at the time, playing soccer. Bob would show up at his brother's practices, wanting so badly still to be out there on the field. He would drive his little company car to the workout, watch, then cross the street to kick a soccer ball into a wall of the elementary school. He'd bang and bang the ball, wishing his job would go away and he could just be playing soccer again.

"It was a frustrating year, no two ways about it," Bradley said. "When you're leaving a place like Princeton you feel good that academically it was a challenge. I wasn't super smart. When you're done, you've come up to that challenge. But for me, you find the answers once you get out. Not when you're in that sheltered world. I learned what was important for me."

Bradley could take no more of the suit-and-tie world and enrolled at Ohio University to major in sports administration, becoming a graduate assistant in the athletics department. His timing was impeccable. The school lacked a soccer coach, so he submitted a resume and was hired in the fall of 1984. He was just twenty-three. Many members of the team were older than he was, some of them foreign-born. Bradley loved his new job immediately, coaching the team for a couple of seasons and to one particularly sweet victory over Ohio State. He then migrated to the University of Virginia to become Bruce Arena's graduate assistant. He didn't always agree with Arena's methods, but Bradley was learning the ropes.

"Bruce and I probably argued about everything," Bradley said. "Both of us always thought we were right. We didn't and still don't see things the same way, or do things the same way. But he had a good feel for how to set a tone for being successful." Sitting in his own office for the U.S. national team at the Home Depot Center in Carson, CA, Bradley remembered how the soccer office in Charlottesville was uniquely situated right next to the visitors' locker room for basketball. Coaches and assistant coaches from different sports at Virginia would gather together inside his office for some secret communal notes-taking as Atlantic Coast Conference rivals came to visit. "We sat in there at halftime, not to spy for information, but to hear how these guys went about their business," Bradley said. "We could hear Dean Smith, Mike Krzyzewski, Jim Valvano, Lefty Dreisell . . . you could pretty much hear what they were saying. They all had very different personalities."

Bradley also met his wife at the University of Virginia, the greatest perk of all. Lindsay Sheehan was a top athlete in both field hockey and lacrosse, on the way to becoming the all-time NCAA leading scorer in lacrosse. Her genes, arguably, would have more to do than Bob's DNA with their children's future athletic talents. Her unselfish willingness to live the life of a coach's wife was equally valuable. UVA went to the soccer Final Four during Bradley's final season there. At the still tender age of twenty-six, he got a call from Princeton asking him to return as the full-time soccer coach. He transformed that job into a full-year commitment by joining with a local soccer institution and mentor, Manny Schellscheidt, to guide a New Jersey amateur club team, the Union Lancers. The Lancers captured back-to-back national championships. The two men would climb into Schellscheidt's diesel-engine Rabbit Volkswagen, drive around to matches, and talk endlessly about the game. These early relationships with Arena and Schellscheidt would stick with Bradley his whole life, shaping his thoughts about the sport. He maintained regular phone contact with them, soliciting feedback whenever possible. After the funeral of cherished assistant U.S. coach Glenn "Mooch" Myernick, who died of a heart attack at age fifty-one while jogging in 2006, Bradley described to the *Boston Globe* a sense of the intense pride he shared with this small circle of friends. "You couldn't have had a better gathering of soccer people," Bradley said. "All of us in this room, it makes you feel there are roots in this country, there is history, and we don't always do the best job of putting that story out there. That story involves the coaches, players, administrators, referees, writers, all people who have been hooked by this game. When everyone is together, even for a very, very sad reason, something happens and it makes you realize why you are still doing it."

Bradley threw himself hard into his extended stint at Princeton, from 1984 to 1995, a period of time when college soccer was still the primary destination for America's top players. The Tigers won a couple of Ivy League titles and reached the NCAA Final Four in 1993. But after a while he found that this university job was incapable of adequately supporting his obsession. There were inconvenient limits on the number of games and practices. The season was far too short. When it ended, Bradley felt an emptiness. He didn't always know what to do with himself. The Lancers helped—Bradley later coached a Princeton-based amateur club, the Union—but even they weren't enough. If he could, Bradley might have held training sessions 365 days a year.

That driving passion brought him to the professional ranks, once MLS was formed. He hooked on with Arena again as an assistant with D.C. United before becoming head coach with the expansion Chicago Fire and winning the MLS Cup in 1998. He had less success with the MetroStars, a club that had a history of dragging down some of the finest, most famous coaches from all over the globe. "Managers around the world know this: You don't become a coach until you know what failure is," Bradley said, about that tenure in north Jersey. "Humility is important." When an American coach has such problems, however, it is always harder to come back.

Michael Bradley was born in Princeton, while his father coached the university team there. He grew up, mostly, in Palatine, IL, after Bob accepted the head coaching position of the Chicago Fire. After his amateur team, Sockers FC, advanced to the 2002 national championships, Michael was quickly singled out as an exceptional talent. His parents then reluctantly agreed to send him off for two years to the Bradenton Academy in Florida. This was no easy decision for the family.

"One of the things we've tried to instill in our kids in order to be good at anything, is you have to put heart and soul into what you do, not be afraid to live out your dreams," Bob Bradley said. "We always tried with our children to do that. My oldest daughter, her passion was ballet. My wife was not a dancer. I was not a dancer. But this was something from a young age you could see she loved. In the U.S., when you have kids you think they'll be home with you until the time they're eighteen years old. And so when all of a sudden, there's this idea that Michael might leave at fifteen, that's different. But you can't talk about having dreams and working hard for dreams and then all of a sudden when the day comes, you say, 'No,' at that moment. It sounds selfish. The day comes, he says, 'I want to go.' You talk about it. You try to make certain points: 'Family is important. I'm not going to be there every day. Stay in touch with your mother, sister and grandparents. That's important. You've been a good student, that's important. You have certain habits how you compete and play, that can't change.'"

At Bradenton, Michael played for John Ellinger and the Under-17 national team that trained there. Bob would come and visit his son for a week at a time, just to keep tabs and watch Michael grow in both skill and physical stature. "He always had the tactical brain and the technical ability," Ellinger said, of Michael. "But when he first came, he was small. There were some naysayers who said he was only there because of his dad, but there aren't any naysayers now."

After Bradenton, Michael made a career commitment to soccer, a risky gamble. Rather than take the Ivy League route pursued by his father, Michael signed a contract with Project 40 and MLS. He was a professional by the age of sixteen, ineligible for an athletic scholarship at the University of North Carolina or any of the other schools eagerly willing to throw money at him. The choice to follow a professional path so early in life was a considerable shocker for the extended family. It seemed an odd decision by Michael and Bob, because education always had been the top priority with the Bradleys. Bob's father, Jerry, made certain that his three sons attended the best schools available to get their degrees. When Scott Bradley, the middle brother, was tearing it up with an American Legion baseball team in North Carolina, a Minnesota Twins' scout asked the father how much money it would take to change his mind and allow the teenager to sign with the pros out of high school. "I'm not giving you a number," Jerry Bradley said. "He's not signing." Bob Bradley always had been schooled on the value of school. Yet in this matter he would turn his back on family tradition, because Bob understood his son's single-mindedness and perhaps because he was never afforded the same opportunity. This was a different time from when Bob played at Princeton, when there was really nowhere to go for a solid American soccer player. "We are a conservative family, but not Bob," his brother Jeff said. "Bob felt, 'If it's in your heart, try it. Your life's not a dress rehearsal for another one.'"

Bob Bradley gave the okay again to his son, after another debate.

"Now the time comes to discuss pro versus college, and again there's a conversation about the plusses and the minuses, what you're giving up," Bob Bradley said. "I can remember saying, 'If you turn pro and in a couple of years it doesn't work out, you're a good student you can go back. When you do that, you won't be able to play soccer in college. That's a risk you'll be taking.' He understood that. You cover that stuff. You want your kids to have goals and dreams. The only part is you have to professionally still be able to assess whether the goals he has are realistic. I was comfortable enough he could do that. The one thing I also remember saying is that, 'Look, as a player you are not going to be a prodigy, not somebody who is going to shoot to the top.' Physically, he'd started to grow. I said the starting points are good. But you probably are going to be a late bloomer. He understood that, too."

Michael turned pro and never harbored regrets about skipping college. Several former academy-mates at Bradenton would call him from one college or another to reinforce his perception that he'd made the right decision. They were having a great time, but they knew Michael could not abide the softer work ethic of a university athletic program. "While you're busy hydrating for the next match, everybody here is out drinking," one friend told him. The friend was not referring to Gatorade.

Michael wasn't one of the top picks in the 2004 MLS SuperDraft. He went thirty-sixth overall, falling all the way to his father and the MetroStars. This was in part a gentleman's agreement to allow the son to play for his father. But it also represented some skepticism on the part of the other MLS franchise officials, who did not feel that Michael was a sure thing. He wasn't fast. He wasn't flashy. He had endured several growth-related injuries while at Bradenton to his neck and knees, after sprouting to six-feet, one-inch from five-feet, seven-inches in just over a year. Michael would spend much of his rookie MLS season in a boot from a foot injury. But his father saw immediately what other coaches didn't necessarily spot at first. His son had vision and purpose, if not pure world-class athleticism. These attributes appeared to come to him naturally, passed on not only by his father but his mother, Lindsay, the two-sport college star. Bob firmly believed his son was a very good player, and that he would only become better because of his unequaled dedication. When there were rare moments of doubt, or self-consciousness, Bob found reassurance from close associates. He would turn to assistant Mo Johnson with the MetroStars, and ask, "Is it time to give Michael a rest?" Johnson would answer, "Why him? He's not the weak link." There were awkward occasions whenever the MetroStars slumped, which was often, or when Michael sat out with an injury. A segment of the media questioned the wisdom of this draft pick and Bob Bradley was very sensitive to that. But the MetroStars were not the Yankees in the New York market, so there was no great, public uproar. While murmurings of nepotism could be heard in some places, they soon were proven foolish enough. By 2005, Michael had earned a regular spot in the lineup. He played thirty matches for the MetroStars that season, finally scoring his first goal in the very last game of 2005 on a header against Chivas USA.

By then, nobody could say he was playing because of his father. Bob Bradley had been fired from the coaching post nearly two weeks earlier. That dismissal had been a very nasty story, the beginnings of an unfortunate feud between two of America's most visible and entrenched soccer personalities:Bradley and Alexi Lalas. It was a generational battle, as much as anything, and a terrible shame. Lalas was something of a New Age thinker, a pioneer player overseas for Padova of the Italian Serie A. Bradley was an old-school, work-rate kind of guy. When Lalas was hired as general manager of the MetroStars, Bradley quickly and correctly became convinced that Lalas would dump him shortly. The two men met for hours upon Lalas's arrival as Bradley basically argued for his job. But from day one, Lalas appeared to be planning for Bradley's release. He bounced the idea off some newspaper beat writers, gauging potential media reaction. And there were other signs: Lalas canned Bradley's trainer, the way George Steinbrenner would fire Billy Martin's pitching coach, as a precursor to the inevitable dismissal. Lalas also demanded that Bradley discard his informal team sweatsuit attire and wear a jacket and tie along the sideline—a fashion conceit imported from the Italian league.

In Lalas's defense, the MetroStars were struggling badly on the field. They still had a decent shot at the playoffs, but Bradley's success in New Jersey was definitely open to legitimate question. When the MetroStars lost in embarrassing fashion, 4–1, to D.C. United before the home fans at Giants Stadium, everyone on the team understood that Lalas was about to pull the trigger—including Michael Bradley, who was near tears during that match. Three days later, on October 4, 2005, Lalas fired Bradley. "Regardless of the work behind the scenes, the results were not acceptable from a MetroStars perspective," Lalas said. The traditionally pathetic Metros had been 36–35–28 under Bradley for three seasons. They were just three points behind Kansas City at the time in the race for the final playoff spot, with a game in hand. Bradley returned to Giants Stadium one more time, worked out and packed his things. He wouldn't say anything publicly about Lalas, but the dismissal was considered both a personal and professional slap. This was a man still confident in his own methods, still hoping to find a place coaching at the national and even the international level.

Bradley would fight his way back with Chivas, then with the national team. The feud with Lalas, however, would always play out in the background. Michael shared that resentment. If anybody worried about Michael playing for his dad—with the MetroStars, and later with the national team—it was only that he would become alienated when his father inevitably was fired or moved to another job. As a rule, the shelf life of coaches was rarely as long as that of promising young stars.

CHAPTER 15

Frankie Goes to Nashville

THE HEX TOURNAMENT ROLLED ALONG. ON MARCH 28, 2009, the U.S. faced a road qualifier at El Salvador, a country with a chaotic soccer tradition all too familiar in CONCACAF. The nation's pro teams had resisted releasing some of their players for national matches, and there was almost constant friction about pay among Salvadoran players. The Americans harbored some harsh memories about games there. DaMarcus Beasley, during his first journey to San Salvador in 1999, was famously the target of a flying chicken's head while he was taking a corner kick with the U-17 team. The crowd laughed. Beasley, being Beasley, took the chicken head in stride. There also had been more recent, nastier incidents involving the *Cuscatlecos*. In a qualifying Gold Cup match against Costa Rica in January, 2009, two El Salvadorans were ejected during the first twenty-five minutes. The coach, De los Cobos, clearly incensed, quickly made his two allowed substitutions. Then three more Salvadoran players insisted they were injured and unable to play. Because El Salvador was down to just six players, below the FIFA minimum, the match was suspended. Costa Rica was eventually declared the winner, while the El Salvador federation was fined $20,000. The three injured players were suspended for two matches and the Salvadoran team doctor was suspended for a year. In addition, FIFA had fined the federation $25,000 for crowd misbehavior at a qualifier against Trinidad and Tobago.

Estadio Cuscatlan in San Salvador was a tough place to visit, but the host team was still considered the weakest in the Hex. The Americans owned a 10–0–1 record against El Salvador since 1993, with a 16–0 aggregate score in the most recent six games, so a victory was fully anticipated. El Salvador had tied its first Hex qualifier at home against T&T, and did not appear formidable. But you never know, as events would soon prove. The city of San Salvador was energized for the match. More than 53,000 fans poured into the brightly-colored stadium five hours before an evening match—standard practice in Central America, where few seats are actually reserved. Spectators wore blue en masse, and decibel levels increased right up through the opening whistle. ESPN commentator John Harkes, hobbling on crutches after hip surgery, was greeted with good-natured taunts as he made his way up steep, cement steps to the overhanging telecast booth. The crowd was boisterous, not angry. Passionate, not edgy. The fans had come for a good show and would get one.

Bob Bradley chose an aggressive lineup with some obvious and necessary weaknesses in the back, a shortcoming that would haunt the Americans throughout this qualifying run. Ching and Donovan played up top, even if Donovan tended to trail the plays at times while Dempsey moved forward. From left to right, Beasley, Michael Bradley, Kljestan, and Dempsey comprised the midfield. Onyewu was out with a minor injury and Howard was serving his suspension, leaving the U.S. vulnerable at critical defensive positions. Pearce, Bocanegra, Danny Califf, and Frankie Hejduk were the shaky back line. Brad Guzan, arguably America's third- or fourth-best keeper, was given the start in goal. The idea of calling up Brad Friedel from Aston Villa for an emergency appearance was never discussed by Gulati or Bob Bradley. "When Brad told us he was retiring from the team, he said it was time to move on and for the younger players to take over," Gulati said.

The Americans came out strong, creating a couple of decent early chances. Kljestan produced a terrible first touch on one dangerous ball from Donovan. Then Beasley gave the ball away to Eliseo Quintanilla, beginning a quick series of nifty short passes to Osael Romero, Rodolfo Zelaya, back to Quintanilla, over to Romero, and finally an angled touch to Quintanilla for a clear shot past Guzan in the fifteenth minute. There had been a series of errors from the back line that allowed such a lengthy combination. Pearce and Bocanegra wandered too wide. Beasley made only a half-hearted tackle. The goal was an unpleasant surprise, the first time the Americans had given one up to El Salvador since 1997. The crowd grew emboldened and loud as the U.S. lost its way late in the first half. Bradley attempted to calm things down in the locker room at the break, recasting a few assignments, but again nothing worked. In the seventy-second minute, El Salvador scored a second goal when Cristian Castillo timed a running header over Hejduk from six yards out past Guzan. Howard or Friedel might have made this save. To be fair, Guzan had executed an impressive fingertip save earlier on Romero that might have beaten the others. It was pointless to hypothesize. Guzan had been known to get down on himself after allowing such a semi-soft goal. He showed no sign of a letdown after this one. But as Bradley would mention later—without pointing a finger at Guzan—Howard's assertive organization of the backline was a major plus in any match.

The Americans were now down two goals with fifteen minutes to play on the road. Their only hope, really, was the heartfelt belief that El Salvador was not fit for a full, ninety-minute match. "We knew they were going to die," Donovan said. "We just had to press the game." And so they did, buzzing around the box, throwing numbers at the chase. Altidore, who had come on as a substitute for Pearce in the sixty-first minute, headed home a cross from Hejduk in the seventy-seventh minute to cut the deficit by half. The crowd quieted, bit its collective lip. The *Cuscatlecos* stalled desperately, falling to the ground and grasping their knees at the slightest excuse. Benito Archundia, the Mexican referee, ordered the Salvadorans to rise and play. A full seven minutes would be added to injury time. In the eighty-eighth minute, a header flicked sloppily by a Salvadoran defender found its way to the left side of the goal mouth where Altidore and Hejduk were both waiting. Nobody was going to stop Hejduk, a bit of a crazy man, from finishing this rare chance. He shoved aside Altidore and nodded the ball into the net for the draw. "I saw Jozy in the periphery," Hejduk said. "Luckily, he let me in there." At the close of the day the Americans were 1–0–1 and still led the Hex table with four points after two matches.

Hejduk, America's least elegant player, hair matted and flying about at the same time, had rescued his more glamorous teammates. The surfer dude was king for a day.

Frankie Hejduk identified his strengths and weaknesses at an early age, while attending San Dieguito High School. "I don't take people one-on-one or create any fancy moves," he said. "I'm a runner." And so he ran. He was much smaller than his father, who had been a basketball player and coach back in New York and once coached Lew Alcindor, the future Kareem Abdul-Jabbar. Hejduk ran on the beaches of Southern California. He ran so hard, so fast, and for so long, coaches all over the world fell in love with him—or more accurately, with his work ethic. He was always moving or playing at something, never at rest. Put him on a field, his feet would start churning even before his brain issued commands. He was only a second-team All-American at UCLA, and yet Hejduk would play for the U.S. two years later in 1996, scoring a goal in his first international start against Guatemala in a World Cup qualifier. He was considered no more than a token end-of-the-roster player, yet he somehow impressed Steve Sampson enough to start in two of the three matches at France in '98. This was in part because Hejduk always understood his unflattering role. "You never have an entire team of super-skilled players," he said. "You need a couple of hard-asses. One of my things is trying to take people out."

Hejduk idealized the mean, harsh soccer of Argentina, of Boca Juniors, not the sweet technical game of Barcelona, where a perfect, thoughtful outlet pass was preferred to a harsh tackle and clearance. On his own clubs, he would be the enforcer. He flung himself at soccer matches the way he threw himself at those large Pacific waves, during his favorite pastime of surfing. Hejduk might be anywhere on the field, at any given moment. He was a throwback to the U.S. national teams of the 1930s, a "shotputter." Hejduk was a character, besides. Before every match, he would write a Bob Marley quote on the locker room grease-board for inspiration. Then he would go out and do crazy, reckless things, getting opponents upset, earning some yellow cards, and turning beautiful matches into ugly scrapes with his fast and scarily fearless play.

Considering his limitations, Hejduk managed a remarkably success-ful international career. He played four seasons with Bayer Leverkusen in the Bundesliga, working his way up from that club's developmental third division team, always proving himself. He was named Man of the Match twice during five Champions League games. A broken shoul-der blade slowed his career in 2001. He returned to the States and MLS in 2003, signing with the Columbus Crew. There was a bittersweet ac-complishment in the spring of 2006: Hejduk was named to the World Cup team, his third, but he tore an ACL in his knee the same weekend as the announcement. He was nearly thirty-two years old then, married with children, and it figured that Hejduk would walk off into the sun-set, surfboard tucked under his armpit. There were always new names, fresh-faced American defenders who were supposed to be the next great defensive markers, the heirs to Eddie Pope and Thomas Dooley. Michael Parkhurst, for example, was viewed as a tremendous positional player when he was named MLS defender of the year in 2007, a very different sort of backline player than Hejduk. Parkhurst never needed to foul anybody and was awarded the league's Fair Play award two seasons in a row. But then Parkhurst went off to play in Denmark. Not partic-ularly impressive in his U.S. auditions, his star faded. Hejduk was still playing, just as he had vowed to his son, Nesta, when the pair attended the 2006 World Cup in Germany as spectators.

"I made a promise," Hejduk said. "I set a goal for myself when I tore the ACL that I would make the 2010 World Cup team. It was a bit of a longshot at the time, but it was a goal." The knee healed, he started to run again, and then Steve Cherundolo was injured. Sure enough there was still an open spot at right back for a hard-ass, for somebody who could ramp up the energy level just when hope was fading. That's what he had done against El Salvador, on the road. He assisted on one goal, scoring another. His head never dropped and his cleats never stopped kicking shins. "That's part of my job, to pump everyone up," he said. "I get people energized with a hard tackle. That part of it is second nature to me. This is not rocket science. I'm into the game. You know what you're getting from me every single minute. No trash talk, though. I let my tackling do the talking."

He fueled this hyperactivity with still more training, more running, and six or more espressos a day. In many ways, Hejduk epitomized how the rest of the world stereotyped American players. He was ninety-nine percent desire and resolve, one percent technical sophistication. He would play soccer as long as they let him and nobody was pushing him out at the moment. Hejduk was captain of the Columbus Crew and starting right back for his beloved national team.

"Why would I want to retire?" he asked. The question was rhetorical.

There was no use fooling themselves about the standings, despite their top-dog position. The Americans were now behind schedule in this final qualifying run, having thrown away two points in El Salvador with a sub-par performance. "We're pretty aggrieved at not winning that game," Donovan said. "A tough day like that is a reminder. If we didn't know before, we certainly know now it isn't easy to go any-where." Gulati and Bradley conferred about the missteps on the field in San Salvador, but really what could anyone do? Gulati was not about to start screaming. "I don't get in Bob's face. We don't have that kind of a relationship," Gulati said. "We had a bad game." Gulati, a physically slight and reasonable fellow, was no bully. He lacked a hot temper, which was surely a good thing considering the vagaries of soc-cer. About the worst Gulati did was slump his shoulders a bit. "For one thing, I don't own the team," Gulati said. Bradley, too, demon-strated patience and hoped for a quick rebound. The very best news was that the next match in Nashville was against Trinidad and To-bago, a team known for its poor road record and one that was missing its veteran scorer, Dwight Yorke, due to a suspension. This was surely a gimme. Even T&T's coach, Francisco Maturana, appeared concilia-tory before the match, after a practice on the pristine LP Stadium pitch. The Colombian spoke almost ruefully about the softer attitude of his adopted team, and its nation. "Football is an extension of the people," Maturana said. "There's a big difference in the culture. There's much more pressure in Latin America. You go to a game in Trinidad, it's a party. In Latin America, that's impossible." There were other dif-ferences in style, he said. The South Americans preferred to "work around the ball a little more," Maturano said. "We don't have the power that the Caribbean players have." More power at T&T, less finesse. He looked at the U.S. team that was walking past in a tunnel, preparing for its own training session. "The Americans have a great mental capacity," Maturano said.

That collective will would be tested only briefly during a 3-0 rout of Trinidad, which performed down to its reputation on the road. Bradley made several lineup changes, dropping Beasley back to the black hole that was left back, benching Kljestan and starting Altidore, who had a strong practice week. Despite Altidore's inactivity overseas, Bradley never forgot the striker's natural strength on the ball or his nose for the goal. Howard returned to his goalkeeping duties, aggressively organizing the back four. The field in Nashville was immaculate, the weather perfect. The attendance of 27,959 was described by the public address announcer, without a trace of irony, as "the largest soccer crowd in the history of Tennessee." The Americans controlled this game from start to finish—with an unwanted hiccup here or there. Probably the scariest moment arrived early on in the sixth minute, when the usually reliable Howard booted a simple clearance onto the feet of Trinidad's surprised striker, Stern John. The ball bounced harmlessly away for a goal kick, when it might have deflected straight back into the American net and changed everything.

Given the most important start of his young career, Altidore responded with a stunning hat trick. At age nineteen, he was still a big, galloping bruiser out there. His first touches were often an adventure, but Altidore was quite capable of holding a ball, once he settled it, with his back to the goal and with a large defender pressing hard from behind. He was also more than a mere target player, as he demonstrated again. Given a well-timed pass above the box, he could make effective runs. He seemed intuitively to know where to go, and when. McBride and Wynalda had required much longer to learn the positional play that Altidore understood by sheer instinct. If only those Spaniards who stubbornly assigned him to the bench would appreciate his assets. . . . "In Europe, anywhere, you have to earn it," Altidore said. "It's a tough lesson for everyone, myself included."

His first goal against T&T, in the thirteenth minute, began with a long pass from Carlos Bocanegra, then a timely, backward head flick in traffic from the workhorse Ching to Donovan, who crossed the ball into the box for an in-stride run by Altidore. His second score was even prettier. Donovan beat one defender on the left side, then cut back a pass to Altidore in space above the box. Altidore beat one defender, then pushed the ball past goalkeeper Clayton Ince. The third one in the eighty-ninth minute was a gift from the wide-open Donovan, who easily might have scored himself. There was a message attached to that assist. "He deserved it," Donovan said. "He worked hard all week, now he needs to do it on a consistent basis. It was clearly Jozy's night."

The hat trick was the first for an American in a World Cup qualifier since Eddie Johnson accomplished the same feat against Panama in 2004. Several of the Americans were careful to cite that experience as a cautionary tale. Johnson was with the team in Nashville, but he was not getting minutes and his star had been badly tarnished since that spurt in 2004. The same could happen to Altidore, they warned. Everyone worried that Altidore would fall back into lazy training habits, after his six goals in nine U.S. national team appearances. "Let's not get carried away," Donovan said. "This was one game. There are guys who have been doing this for a long time." Gulati said the same thing. So did Bradley, who appeared more impressed with the way Altidore had chased after opponents whenever he lost the ball. "Sometimes in the past he might not have done as much," Bradley said.

Howard would make his one and only save off Keon Daniel from twenty-five yards in the sixty-third minute. It had been a good day at the office for the U.S. team after a very bad one in San Salvador. The Americans now owned a 15–2–3 record overall against Trinidad and Tobago and remained atop the Hex standings at 2–0–1 with seven points. They were still two points behind where they had hoped to be at this juncture, and facing an extremely difficult match next at the hellhole that was *Estadio Saprissa* in San Jose, Costa Rica.

CHAPTER 16

1989 . . .

FROM A HISTORICAL STANDPOINT, THESE CRITICAL QUALIFYING victories were not to be taken for granted by the Americans. Thirty-nine dreary years once had passed between memorable goals for the U.S national team, from 1950 to 1989. The demoralizing drought doomed the sport to second-class citizenship—or was it the second-class status that created the drought? There already had been an earlier Dark Age, following the 1934 World Cup. Now came a second, even more damaging and unforgivable, lacking the alibi of a World War. The goal by Gaetjens against England took place on June 29, 1950. For decades after that, the national soccer scene was wholly demoralizing.

It wasn't as if the sport completely died in America. Youth soccer was taking root at the high school level in various locales, from north Jersey to St. Louis. Top foreign clubs toured the U.S. or played in the International Soccer League (ISL) on Randall's Island in New York until 1965—when the U.S. Soccer Federation feuded with ISL organizer Bill Cox over the right to import such teams. Underfinanced leagues such as the United Soccer Association and the National Professional Soccer League jockeyed for support and competed for talent, never quite succeeding. The North American Soccer League popped up in 1968 and soon attracted some of the greatest foreign players and biggest crowds ever on the continent, fielding the likes of Pelé, Johan Cruyff, and Franz Beckenbauer. Pelé's magic and allure was incomparable, even in his mid-thirties. In 1977, a crowd of 77,691 fans at Giants Stadium saw the

Pelé–led Cosmos beat the Fort Lauderdale Strikers in the playoffs by an outrageous score of 8–3. At the close of that season in October, Pelé was featured in a celebratory retirement exhibition between the Cosmos and his old team, Santos. Again Giants Stadium was sold out, and the match was televised by ABC on the *Wide World of Sports.*

But despite this exposure for the sport, the U.S. national team was consistently horrible, even irrelevant. It was no wonder, really, considering the lack of competition. After the Americans returned from the 1950 World Cup, they didn't play their next match for nearly two years, when their rag-tag squad fell to Scotland, 6–0. The U.S. scheduled only that one match in 1952, then one more, a 6–3 loss to England, in 1953. Unless there was a World Cup qualifier on the docket, the Americans were unlikely to gather together at all. It was too expensive, and there was no public demand for the games. From 1951 through 1964, the U.S. national side played a grand total of fifteen international matches, averaging just over one game per year, posting a record of 1–13–1. The results were beyond embarrassing. The Americans were eliminated from the 1954 World Cup by little Haiti, after a 3–0 drubbing in Port-au-Prince. They lost to Iceland. They were shut out, 6–0, by Mexico. They fell to England twice in the sixties, by the scores of 8–1 and 10–0. Before long, that 1–0 upset over England in Belo Horizonte appeared even more surreal in retrospect. After that one flirtation with international success, the U.S. team had been destroyed by sheer entropy, while the rest of the world poured its passion and resources into the sport.

Then, finally, the door opened a bit. Twenty-four nations were to qualify for the 1990 World Cup in Italy, two from CONCACAF. With the notable exception of 1982, when El Salvador and Honduras both advanced, Mexico appeared forever assured of one spot in the tournament. That left only the second CONCACAF berth up for grabs. But the Mexicans were disqualified by FIFA from the 1990 World Cup for fielding overage players in an Under-20 competition, a sloppy infraction that provided minimal glory and created unthinkable repercussions for that country. This left regional qualifying wide open, and at last the Americans were taking a more serious approach under U.S. Soccer president Werner Fricker and head coach Bob Gansler. A training camp was established and actual tune-up matches were scheduled for the spring and summer of 1988, leading up to the first qualifiers. Gansler was a quiet, Austrian-born fellow with deep roots in U.S. Soccer. He had twenty-five caps for the national team between 1963 and 1969, and was captain of two Olympic teams. Hired full-time on January 16, 1989, to replace Lothar Osiander, he immediately began to assemble a young amateur national team while ignoring more seasoned professionals such as Hugo Perez and Rick Davis. Rather than select some veterans from a professional indoor league after the North American Soccer League collapsed, Gansler built toward the future with college kids. He assembled a team that would include a core of players who anchored the nation's World Cup teams over the next eight years.

That meant considerable learning on the job, a perilous adventure. The defense was at times vulnerable, even if the goals-against average wasn't awful. Steve Trittschuh was young and made mistakes. Mike Windischmann was a steady sweeper, but a tad slow. Up front, Bruce Murray was the only veteran striker who seemed capable of finishing chances. He was strong in the air, but not too graceful. John Harkes and Tab Ramos transformed the midfield play into the team's greatest strength, while Tony Meola offered considerable heft and confidence in goal.

With Mexico eliminated, the qualifying run should have been a cinch. But an early loss at San Jose, Costa Rica, a draw at home against Trinidad and Tobago, then scoreless draws at Guatemala and at St. Louis Soccer Park against El Salvador left the Americans vulnerable, with a 3–1–3 record. Costa Rica (5–1–2) already had clinched a spot. The U.S. had scored only five goals in its seven qualifying matches during this phase, hardly a good omen. The Americans would require a victory at Port of Spain in Trinidad to earn that second berth, their first trip to a World Cup in forty years.

That Sunday in Port of Spain, November 19, 1989, became an engraved memory for any participant or spectator. It was a gorgeous, cloudless day, a climatic blessing that would tilt the final result. The entire island of Trinidad was prepared for an epic celebration, that country's first World Cup qualification in history. All that was required of the adored "Strike Squad" was a draw at home against a nation that couldn't score goals. Grudges were dug up against the U.S. side, as if the Americans had been long-time archrivals. T&T coach Gally Cummings claimed the U.S. had bugged his bench electronically during a match the previous May in Torrance, California. "A microphone was taped to the bottom," Cummings insisted. "Lots of tricks, lots of games they play. They try to win the match before the match." There had been charges by U.S. players that T&T officials bribed Guatemala and El Salvador to play hard against the Americans in regional qualifiers. "Can you imagine the nonsense, to bribe a team to do what they are supposed to do anyway?" Cummings said. There was some water tossed at the Trinidad players in Torrance, after the 1–1 draw. There were a dozen other things, Cummings said, and the U.S. soccer team was now going to pay. "A tie?" Cummings said. "Trinidad and Tobago might need only a tie, but it doesn't play for a tie. We are too proud. My players eat and sleep America. America is better than us in nuclear weapons. We are better in football."

A "Winners' Week" was declared on the islands. Wednesday was "Never Say Never Day." Thursday was "Unity Day." Friday was "Red Day." Calypso music rang out all week long from steel drums in every corner of the city. CD recordings were sold or handed out for free, featuring sing-along ditties celebrating the team. "We want it," one song went. "We want a goal. . . ." It was difficult to find any citizen who was not garbed in the team's colors, a bright crimson. One might have thought this was an island nation united forever in a single purpose. Yet when a journalist left the upside-down Hilton hotel (the floor numbers went up as you descended by elevator into the hill) to jog around the green, he spotted a wounded soldier limping with the aid of a compatriot from a helicopter, returning from the island's interior. There, the government was battling a rebel group called the *Jamaat al Muslimeen*, which would hold the government hostage the next year for nearly a week.

Such background noise was not a consideration for the U.S. team as it took the field for this decisive match at the National Stadium—later to be renamed Hasely Crawford Stadium, for the country's Olympic sprint champion. The Americans had practiced together during a final week of secluded preparations in Florida, where they played an odd, closed-door match against Bermuda and claimed to have put aside petty grievances. "That week we became a team of not just eleven, but twenty-five, with all the players and coaches coming together," Harkes said. Then they got another big break: The field inside National Stadium dried out beneath a warming sun. The pitch had been a mucky mire, an almost impossible tableau for attacking soccer. It still wasn't sodden Old Trafford in Manchester, England, but there was footing to be had. About 30,000 packed the stadium early on the day of the match. It was a joyful crowd, not the sort of edgy mob seen during night matches in places like Costa Rica or Mexico. There were red shirts and black umbrellas for shade, as far as the eye could see. It was an overwhelming sight. Yet as they exited the little hut that passed for their dressing room, the Americans believed they had considerable reason for optimism. "The main thing I remember about that game was how scared the Trinidad players were when we walked out on the field," Ramos said. "I couldn't believe it. How crazy is that? Here we were, twenty, twenty-one years old, but I think there was so much pressure on those guys. And all they needed was a tie. And they were going to fold."

Whether or not the T&T players were tight, the Americans still needed to score a goal. This would be no easy task for the U.S. side, which entered the match having played 208 minutes without knocking the ball into the net over a two-month period. Gansler made some desperate, aggressive changes in his lineup, but told the Americans before the match to be patient. "Simple things," he said. The play began evenly enough. The Americans were pressing, kept honest by T&T's countering speed. One goal by the home side would have ensured a bad fate for the Americans, who were wholly incapable of scoring twice. There were few real opportunities. This was just fine with the T&T crowd, which smelled a successful scoreless draw. But in the thirty-first minute, center midfielder Paul Caligiuri received a square pass from Brian Bliss forty yards out. His first touch was a right-foot chip past a defender to himself. Moving to his left, the wind blowing in his face, Caligiuri looped a left-footed volley from twenty-five yards that was perfectly placed on the high, far side of Michael Maurice. The T&T goalkeeper lost sight of the shot momentarily in that blessed sun. The ball curled just inside the right post.

"We knew we needed a shot," Caligiuri said. "I knew I had the space. You have to take what they give you." Caligiuri was an enigma on that team, a labor leader of sorts who hadn't exactly endeared himself to U.S. Soccer when he organized and then aborted a work stoppage for national team members. Among officials around the team, he was considered a bit of a troublemaker. But he was also quick and level-headed under pressure, and Gansler knew Caligiuri was that rarity, an American with a left foot. "I can shoot with the left foot," Caligiuri said. "The left or the right. Doesn't matter." This was his first start during the final qualifying phase, inserted into a more aggressive lineup and formation, ahead of the slower, more defensive John Stollmeyer—whose great claim to fame was his long throw-ins. Years later from his California home, Caligiuri would be more analytical and appreciative about his own accomplishment.

"The actual shot was instinctive, an initiative that came out of a feeling of frustration," he said. "I don't think I realized how far out I was, and then after I shot with my left foot I was thinking, 'Wait, this has a chance to go in.' It's definitely been an incredible moment in the history of soccer. It propelled us to the level where we've been ever since. We were the ones who defied the odds, who were told we couldn't play soccer, who had lower living standards. The financial rewards weren't there. But we literally refused to lose."

When Caligiuri scored that goal back in Port of Spain, the calypso music stopped and the mourning began in that nation of 1.2 million. "The other side seemed to lose something after that," Trittschuh said. "They seemed to give up a little." The Americans were unaccustomed to sitting on leads, yet they managed. They dropped back, and Mike Windischmann in particular effectively cleared the ball from trouble whenever necessary. Trinidad picked up the attacking pace very late in the match, for now all the pressure to score had been shifted. Meola made two difficult saves in the eighty-fifth and eighty-sixth minutes, while screened by bodies in the box. When the whistle blew, the Americans were headed to Italy. They gathered in their little locker room, popped an odd assortment of both beer cans and champagne bottles and chanted, "I-tah-lee." They did what twenty-three-year-olds are supposed to do. They celebrated. They dined with the U.S. ambassador in his white house overlooking the city, then prowled the hallways of the Port of Spain Hilton and partied into Monday morning. Harkes and his teammates found themselves recognized in a local bar later that night, and he worried for their lives. Instead, the Trinidadians forgave them and joined the fun. It was good to be young, American, and heading to the World Cup.

Caligiuri's goal put about ten million dollars in the coffers of U.S. Soccer, its share of FIFA's World Cup broadcast, attendance and licensing rights. As for the player, Caligiuri's watershed moment did little for his own wallet. When he arrived home in Los Angeles on November 20, he was courted by magazine writers and television networks. "I was on the *Pat Sajak Show*. I was an American hero," Caligiuri said. Then trouble began in January, when U.S. Soccer mailed out nonnegotiable contract offers to a select group of players that Gansler wanted to be part of his World Cup training camp. Caligiuri did not like the terms of his deal, a two-year commitment to the national team. He wanted the option of returning overseas following the World Cup. So he joined the U.S. team camp in 1990 on a volunteer basis, receiving only the $40 per diem. He was having trouble making payments on his condo in Los Angeles. A few teammates offered to give him their per diems as well. Eventually, Caligiuri signed that exclusive contract with U.S. Soccer and went on to play in 1994 with second-division SC Freiburg in Germany, then signed with MLS. There, once again, Caligiuri found himself bucking authority. He successfully forced the league to let him play for the Los Angeles Galaxy, rather than for his assigned club, the Columbus Crew. Considering what Caligiuri had done for American soccer, it was not too much to ask.

CHAPTER 17

The Kearny Boys

NOT MUCH IS THE SAME AT KEARNY HIGH SCHOOL IN NORTH
Jersey these days except for the soccer, and even that doesn't quite re-
semble past glories. The second-generation Scottish- and Italian-Amer-
ican players have largely been replaced by talented Portuguese or
Central American immigrants. The roster is filled with names like
Franco Gamero, Eduardo Silva, and Jesus Olivares. "The last five or ten
years, it's changed," said John Millar, the long-time head coach of the
old super-teams at Kearny. "I'd say that 2004 was the last group we had
where the team had gone through the entire community experience.
Those were kids who would come out and watch our games when they
were six or eight years old, then grow up in the program."

The best athletes no longer play their club soccer with Kearny Thistle, where they once perfected together a passing game and set plays
that would carry into the high school season. Instead the golden
prospects are now culled early from the herd, recruited by elite regional
teams, part of the Player Development Academy system. Millar's role
changed, too. In 2005, he accepted a job as athletic director at the high
school, and reluctantly resigned from the coaching position he first took
in 1975. Millar's legacy was assured: His teams made the state final on
fourteen occasions in those thirty years, nearly half the time. Now he
stalks the sidelines during matches, still squawking at referees and shaking his head at futile attacks. Kearny is no longer a dominant force. It
won its sixteenth state championship in 2004, but now it is just another

solid team, ranked in the Top Ten among the largest north Jersey state public schools. The Kardinals were knocked out in the very first round of the state tournament in 2009.

Soccer is still the crown jewel at Kearny, however. Not enough students even bother to try out for the football squad, which only dresses about thirty players for its games. The soccer team is brimming with candidates—twenty-five on the freshman team, twenty-five on junior varsity, and twenty-five on varsity. Almost nobody is cut, according to school policy. The games are played on a perfect turf field constructed five years earlier directly behind the school, built into a hill below concrete stands that seat as many as 4,000 fans. Millar mumbles along the sidelines, remembering better days on a much worse field. When John Harkes and Tony Meola were starring for his side, Kearny played a couple of blocks from here on a baseball field. The rutted grass gave way to a dirt infield on one end, sabotaging many a dribble, yet those teams rarely seemed to stumble.

Back then in the mid-eighties, Harkes, Meola, and Tab Ramos from nearby Hillside played together for Kearny recreation clubs coached at times by John's father, James Harkes. In many ways, the road to World Cup Italia '90 started in the dank basement of the Scots-American Club on Patterson Street, on the south side of this ambitious textile town. There were white and red soccer jerseys strewn about the cellar floor, with leaky showers in the back, and with nets and balls stuffed into sagging wooden shelves. Players from the Thistle F.C. junior team pulled on their uniforms there, in what they dubbed "the dungeon." Harkes, Ramos, and Meola once played four matches in a single day at the nearby Gunnel Oval. Charlie McEwen coached the three players through the ranks. "It's not exactly Giants Stadium," he would say, giving a reporter a tour back in 1990. "But the parents would come and stuff the kids in the car and they would play and play."

It was quite amazing, really: three World Cup players nurtured by one working class community—the very same community where soccer first took hold in America. "It was like a boom, like a baby boom," Harkes said. "There were just so many good players here." The early Scottish immigrants working at the Coats and Clark thread mill had been joined much later by more immigrants from Scotland, Poland, and Lithuania. Even, in Ramos's case, from Montivideo. "In Uruguay, I was number one in my profession," said his father, Julian Ramos, a dye maker and former soccer pro. "But I saw the country was going down. I saw the future of the kid was somewhere else." In 1977, the family settled in Harrison, a few short miles from Kearny. Less than two years later, at age twelve, Tab Ramos met John Harkes. They dressed together in the dungeon and played on the champion Thistle youth teams at the Oval. "Tab was so far ahead of the others when he came here," McEwen said. "He could turn it on and take over a game whenever he felt like it."

John Harkes was one of those kids that Millar talks about now, who grew up watching the older boys winning soccer games at the high school. At age four, he sneaked into a league for six-year-olds, playing for Thistle. "He grabbed his big brother's boots and stuffed newspapers in the front of them to make them fit," McEwen recalled. "He was always such an eager, aggressive boy." When the three Thistle kids went to Italy for the World Cup, the brick library on Kearny Avenue put together a soccer exhibit celebrating their accomplishment. Harkes was always the little guy with the long hair in the front row of team photos. His teammates called him "Mickey Mouse," because that's what he sounded like when he called for the ball. Harkes's father and mother emigrated separately from Scotland in 1966, then met at a dance in the Scots-American Club. Although Harkes's mother, Jessie, arrived with a different date that night, she left with James, the future father of a World Cup midfielder. Harkes's first job was at the Thistle Fish and Chips shop, sponsor of the youth teams; Harkes was always a natural, like Ramos.

It was different with Meola, at least early on. "Tony was too small and fat, the coaches said he couldn't run, so they put him in goal," said his father, Vincent, who ran a barber shop in East Rutherford. Meola didn't look then like a kid destined to drive his Porsche down Kearny Avenue, or own an endorsement deal with Reusch-USA worth about $1 million, before the 1990 World Cup even began. Still, he always had potential. "We spotted him playing under the lights when he was eight," McEwen said. "I remember looking at the baby fat and thinking, 'I don't know.'" Meola's parents traveled to America from two different provinces in Italy to meet in their teens in north Jersey. This city of two-story homes and abandoned factories was a matchmaker for them, too, just as it was for the Harkes family. When it was time for Meola and Harkes to leave for Italy, about five hundred fans came to the Scots-American Club to stage a goodbye party. But even as they celebrated back then, they worried their soccer tradition was eroding. After school, there were no longer pickup games at Gunnel Oval. A steady influx of white-collar workers and commuters didn't seem to instill the same sort of competitive fire in their children. The high school team suffered through a losing season for the first time in memory. "It's devastating to me when I don't see kids kicking the ball anymore," Harkes said then, about his hometown. "There's been a drop-off."

Millar coached some of those glorious club teams at Thistle and his high school teams were virtually untouchable, reaching the state final four times in a row. Meola became such a spectacular athlete that he played only half the time in the goal, so that the Kardinals could use him in the field as the team's top scorer. Kearny advanced to the state final at Princeton in 1983, only to be upset, 3–2, by Toms River on a fluky two-on-zero breakaway against goalkeeper Sal Rosamilia, a future All-American at Columbia University. Rosamilia is now an assistant coach at Kearny, and that goal still bothers him. "That was probably our strongest team," Rosamilia said. The following year, in 1984, Harkes was a senior and the team rolled to a 24–0 record and a state title—his third championship in four years. The Kardinals absolutely destroyed everybody, scoring more than a hundred goals that season while giving up fewer than ten.

There are very few routs anymore for Kearny High. "Everybody has players now," Millar says. "Every team can play." The legacy and lore of those one-sided seasons are still made available to today's players. Trophies, photos, and newspaper clippings from the glory days are scattered about the working class town. Meola drops in occasionally to watch a match or speak to an assembly. Harkes lives in Virginia, but a student needed only to turn on ESPN to hear the former midfielder's thoughts on the game. Bill Galka, the head coach, was yet another star for those teams in the 1980s. Soccer at Kearny High can be traced back to the 1930s, and it is a glorious thing for any player or student who wishes to explore its history. The terrain has changed dramatically, however. Just a few miles away in Newark, St. Benedict's Prep School is now an international magnet for some of the best young players in the world. It wasn't just Ramos who played there. Claudio Reyna and Gregg Berhalter, two future U.S. national players, became teammates on St. Benedict's in the late eighties. The school established in the nineties a pipeline from the Tahuichi Soccer Academy in Bolivia. Ambitious and talented teens from South America who wished to sample life in America accepted scholarships at the private school. Other area public high schools became resentful, and resisted scheduling St. Benedict's. "They play by completely different rules," Millar said, referring to the scope of recruiting. There were so many available private schools, clubs, and academies that it was sometimes hard to figure which ladder led to which landing.

One thing seemed clear, and a bit sad: Even as more American kids became involved, high school soccer was increasingly irrelevant as a pathway to future success in the sport. Soccer wasn't football. A stellar high school career alone did not often guarantee college scholarships and certainly did not lead inexorably to the pro draft. The golden children no longer played with their community teams. There was now a feeder system in place more similar to Europe. The process was no doubt more efficient in producing national players, and was important for the success of the U.S. teams. But it also cheated many kids of the good feelings produced by star turns at their local high schools. What was good for the World Cup was not necessarily good for the vast majority of prospects who would never earn a living from the sport.

Tab Ramos was now a part of this youth development process. In fact, he made his living from it. He had been a key member of three U.S. World Cup teams, then the first player to sign with MLS. Ramos was a stud with those World Cup squads, before injuries, age, and an entirely different set of teammates sabotaged his career with the MetroStars. Some players just seemed to blossom on national teams. Ramos was one of them, a midfielder who could change the pace of an entire international match with a first-step dribble into open space and a quick through pass. "Guys like me, John Harkes, Eric Wynalda, Alexi Lalas, Cobi Jones, we were guys who made it for a long time," Ramos said. "We were guys who really didn't care who we played against. We weren't intimidated by playing other countries, playing name players. You just played. Maybe that was the difference. I couldn't pinpoint anything else."

His office in Aberdeen, New Jersey, is filled with photos of those glory years, with pictures of teammates and life-long friends Harkes and Meola. Ramos was the CONCACAF Player of the Year back in 1994. He was also a smart guy. If his past successes had been accomplished with almost any other national team, he would be immersed in offers to coach club teams in MLS and abroad. He'd also be a major celebrity with significant endorsement opportunities. But that wasn't the case and Ramos always knew those were the rules. High-paying soccer jobs in America were rare, and many of the coaching positions in MLS went to foreigners. There was no point in even thinking about coaching or working overseas, because Americans didn't get hired. They just got disrespected. "When I was playing in Spain," Ramos said, "it worked like this: If I was playing great, I was called the Uruguayan-born standout. If I was playing poorly, I was the U.S. national team midfielder."

Ramos proudly offers a tour of his Sports Center in Aberdeen, a sparse suburb in central Jersey. There is a roller hockey rink at one end, an indoor soccer field at the other. Parents can climb to the glassed-in bar above, looking down on the matches going on below. Ramos's first love, however, is the center's academy soccer program. For a significant fee, the kids play outdoors, two or three nights a week under the lights, even in winter. There are players here from Connecticut, from New York, from Pennsylvania. Ramos is now part of the system that uncovers future stars much like himself. He coached the center's Under-14 team, the Gunners, to a national championship in 2008. "You go from travel teams to recreation teams and then the phenomenal kids do the whole academy scene and practice all-year round, except for Christmas to New Years," Ramos said. "That part is different. I played up in my days, when I was fifteen, with the twenty year-olds. Now you have U-16s, U-17s, they want you to go through the process. Then the best of these go to the Bradenton Academy. These exceptional players, we can only screw them up. A lot more players have the chance to succeed. It's harder to hide now." There are other differences from when he played with Kearny Thistle, Ramos said. Like the parents.

"In those days, there wasn't the involvement of parents that there is now. I remember my parents saying, 'When is your next practice?' And I'd say on Thursday. And then they'd say, 'OK.' Then you just got there. I'd get myself there. Not like now with the parents looking for the best coaching you can have. If it's two hours away, they're still going. My parents would never have driven fifteen minutes to take me to practice. It was just, 'Where is it? Good. Go.' Whatever the local club was. There were one or two kids even back then who drove one hour to play with us, but my parents would never have made that trip."

So the parental commitment has increased, and the opportunities have grown in bounds. And yet . . . Ramos knows the next question, has heard it a million times. Where are the American stars? "We're still years away from an offensive guy making a difference on a major club. Our goalies are world class, but field players, I don't know if you can name one who will make it. We're still working on that."

There are candidates. There are always candidates, even at his own academy. One player from nearby Holmdel, Sean Davis, had already entered Bradenton Academy. Another one, Markhus "Duke" LaCroix, was arguably the very best talent in the country for his age group, but Ramos thought his parents were not likely to ship him down to Florida and disrupt family life. Back in December 2008, Ramos was anxiously awaiting word from a U.S. Soccer committee, hoping his Aberdeen center might gain national academy status. There were seventy-four academies in the program at the time, with plans to expand to about eighty. This was a feeder system of elite talent that might lead to Bradenton and further recognition. Ramos had been told by the four-member committee—including Jay Berhalter, deputy executive director of coaching education for the Federation—that his academy was on the short list for inclusion. If it was not selected, Ramos unselfishly planned to send his best players elsewhere. There was little point in retaining a star youth player in a relatively dead-end program.

Ramos was not enamored with the whole process. For one thing, nobody in the national soccer hierarchy ever bothered to contact him to find out if he knew of any potential stars. "It's an iffy process," he said. "Unless I call someone, no one calls me to ask what players there are in New Jersey. Which they should be doing. That's the best voice you can have here. But some of the bigger clubs through their connection, through Nike and Adidas, maybe they're getting their guys in. Bradenton doesn't end up getting our best players. I'm on the Federation technical board. Can you fix it? For that, you need manpower, you need money, and right now it's going to take a little bit at a time."

By the spring of 2009, Ramos's club had been accepted as part of the academy system. There was a little less to complain about.

CHAPTER 18

Inside the Monster's Cave

THERE WERE SEVERAL OMINOUS SIGNALS THAT THE NEXT HEX match on June 3, 2009, would not end well. The Americans had scampered home from various parts of the world, only to arrive at the portals of CONCACAF's most hellish venue. Costa Rica might be that rare land of relative serenity and political stability in Central America, but there is rebellion fomenting inside every soccer fan. The U.S. teams had a history of problems in San Jose, losing five straight matches at *Estadio Saprissa*. The dilapidated building, also known as *La Cueva del Monstruo*, or the Monster's Cave, represented a great home advantage for the Ticos. A more modern, civilized national stadium was being reconstructed downtown, and would be ready for the next qualifying cycle. In the meantime, *Saprissa* would suffice as a visiting team's nightmare. The place was hardly a work of art—a rectangular bandbox with 23,000 seats, stuck in the hills of a perimeter San Jose neighborhood, Tibas, on the north side. It was also the home of the country's top club, *Saprissa*, and that team's purple colors were everywhere. The press facilities were absurd by international standards. For years, a tiny press room served as the work center where journalists would fend off roaming spectators and attempt to transmit their stories on one or two scratchy, shared phone lines. Now the media were moved to the upper deck, where a new crisis confounded reporters: There were no power outlets for laptops.

Fans always arrived early and stayed late to celebrate, rocking and taunting the busloads of visiting teams and officials as they entered and left the stadium compound. The building had no substantial moat or running track encircling the pitch, so spectators were seated right up against wire fencing and the field on all four sides, perhaps 10 yards from a throw-in or corner kick—an intimidating sight and sound. They chanted, sang and were known to hurl the occasional flare, bottle or smoke bomb. The field itself had been converted to old-school artificial turf—matted green material which played hard and fast, or slow and slick, depending on the timing of precipitation. This was not the kind of modern turf familiar to many MLS players, which might soften a bounce or a body tumble. Players would be punished severely for sloppy first touches.

Several of the Americans, such as Beasley and Altidore, were now growing rustier from lack of playing time on their European teams. Ching, the workhorse forward capable of holding a ball for a few precious seconds inside the box, was suffering from a strained hamstring and was scratched. A series of injuries had sapped the Americans of whatever little depth they once mustered on the defensive line. Hejduk and Cherundolo were unavailable. The left back position, in particular, was becoming an open wound during this qualifying run. Beasley might suffice there against weaker teams, but Costa Rica had rolled to a 9–1 record in qualifying and was arguably the hottest side in CONCACAF. The Ticos' talent, technique and chemistry belied a No. 41 FIFA computer ranking. Beasley preferred to move forward and hardly demonstrated the mentality of a defender. Such attacking inclinations would again sabotage his performance.

The Hex schedule had been fairly generous early on to the U.S. team, but now turned with a vengeance. Because of their requisite participation in the Confederations Cup at South Africa in mid-June, the Americans' match against Costa Rica was moved ahead to June 3, while their game against Honduras in Chicago would follow shortly on June 6. This created a logistical problem for many players. Tim Howard appeared for Everton against Chelsea in a losing cause at the FA Cup final in Wembley Stadium on May 30, then caught a flight home for a brief visit to Memphis, then traveled to Miami to join the U.S. team, then to Costa Rica. He admitted to a degree of mental fatigue. Yet another blow: Affable Peter Nowak, the one and only coworker known to put a smile on the face of Bob Bradley, had resigned his post as assistant with the national team in order to become head coach of the new Philadelphia Union franchise of MLS. Nowak's light touch would be greatly missed along the sideline and in the locker room.

There was a bitter distraction, too, for the Americans' most stalwart defender, Oguchi "Gooch" Onyewu. Playing for Standard Liege in a match to decide the Belgian League title in May, Onyewu complained to the referee that an opponent, Jelle Van Damme, had called him a monkey, among other racist remarks. The official did nothing about it. Onyewu considered quitting the match, then thought better after discussions with teammates. Later, he filed suit against Van Damme in a Belgian court seeking no punitive awards but rather something amounting to moral compensation—Onyewu was demanding an apology. He didn't get one from Van Damme, a white player who continued to deny he had violated Belgium's laws against public defamation. In unscientific newspaper polls, most Belgians backed Onyewu, a perennial All-Star and solid citizen. "There are certain boundaries that shouldn't be crossed," Onyewu told *The New York Times*, while training later in South Africa. "Race is not a topic to make fun of. From what I gathered, [Van Damme] was just trying to provoke me. There's other means of provoking a player without crossing that threshold." FIFA carelessly did nothing about the incident, despite its mostly symbolic stand against racism at European venues. Sepp Blatter, president of FIFA, merely urged Onyewu to drop his legal action. In contrast, when the Italian defender, Marco Materazzi, uttered a sexual slur at the 2006 World Cup aimed at the sister of Zinedine Zidane, he was suspended for two matches. Materazzi had admitted his guilt in the affair, which was a factor. He also vehemently denied early reports that falsely claimed he had taunted Zidane about his Arabic background.

Anybody who knew anything about Onyewu immediately understood he was telling the truth. A quiet, thoughtful giant at 6-foot-4 and 210 pounds, Onyewu was never one to seek controversy or publicity. He did, however, hold strong to his opinions and sought explanations from authorities—even Bob Bradley—when he felt that he was being dealt with unfairly. Onyewu was the prideful son of Nigerian immigrants, who both moved to Washington D.C. to attend Howard University and raise a large, thriving family in a household where education was always the top priority. Onyewu's siblings were anything but jocks. One sister was a doctor. A brother had earned his doctorate in education, while another brother and sister were both engineering majors. Oguchi was on his way to a political science degree at Clemson when he simply became too good at soccer to turn his back on the sport. He starred for two seasons with the Tigers before European sides began to take notice and offer him contracts. He played for Metz in the French League, then was a great triumph at Standard Liege (there was also a less-successful trial with Newcastle United). He figured soon to step up again in class, perhaps to the German Bundesliga, perhaps to the Italian League. At age twenty-seven, Onyewu insisted he wouldn't sign with anyone, unless he was assured of playing major minutes—a vow that did not work out as planned when he later signed with AC Milan. Negotiations were going on in the background with several clubs at this time, along with developments regarding the racial incident that were a far less pleasant diversion.

The Americans arrived in San Jose with considerable, well-warranted trepidation. They practiced for two days inside the stadium to become accustomed to the surface—which several players declared worse than the field at Giants Stadium, the gold standard for professional inadequacy. In the locker room just minutes before the match, Bradley calmly delivered a speech to players explaining how they needed to cautiously manage the early minutes, when the game was at its most volatile. "Nobody wins or loses the match in those first ten minutes," he told them, urging the Americans to think defensively. If they could just survive the opening of this tough game on the road, the crowd would settle down and confidence would grow. At the same time, Bradley started an attack-oriented lineup, with Altidore, Donovan and Dempsey up top and utilizing a surprisingly ambitious 4–3–3 formation that would stretch the field and test defenders on both sides. Beasley was at left back again, by default. The inexperienced Marvell Wynne started at right back.

The match began, and quickly devolved into sheer folly. Costa Rican forward Alvaro Saborio beat defensive midfielder Pablo Mastroeni one-on-one outside the box with embarrassing ease, then curled a perfect shot high and to the left beyond the reach of Howard. Incredibly, the Ticos led after just seventy-nine seconds. The fans, ecstatic, became even more of a force. They rose as one from their lilac seats, substantially hiking decibel and adrenaline levels. Costa Rica continued to attack. The Americans continued to cede far too much space. A second goal followed by Celso Borges, a holding midfielder, at the thirteen-minute mark. It was another case of miscommunication in front of Howard.

By now, it was apparent this would be a long and humiliating night. Bradley stood and scowled along the sideline, while his team failed to muster a sustained passing combination anywhere on the field. The Americans' traps and first touches were far too sloppy on the unforgiving turf. Forget the formations, the injuries, the rust. The U.S. lineup simply couldn't match the technical skills of the Costa Ricans. The ball would run too far away from players like Beasley and even Donovan. Through passes were struck too hard, often rolling over the end line for yet another harmless goal kick. Of all the Americans, only young midfielder José Francisco Torres (unexpectedly benched by Bradley at the half), Michael Bradley and Dempsey appeared on this night technically equipped for such a surface. They could stop the ball on a dime, or at least a dollar bill. Most of the other Americans could not.

Michael Bradley exacerbated matters with a late and clumsy tackle in the fifty-fourth minute, earning his second yellow card and a one-match suspension that would carry over to the critical next home game against Honduras. A third goal by Costa Rica followed in the sixty-ninth minute from Pablo Herrera, another example of too much space and muffed marking. Wynne and Beasley appeared completely lost. Donovan uncharacteristically began lecturing Mastroeni about positioning, right out there on the field and in full view of ESPN's cameras. A marginal penalty whistle in the box eventually rescued the U.S. from a shutout. Donovan stepped up quickly and slotted the ball low and left, which was really the only shot of note on goal for the Americans. "The game got stretched out, and as a result we chased the ball," Bradley would say later. "We didn't fight back for a point. I got the sense we were all shellshocked."

Gulati, misfortunate enough to be on hand for the misshapen, woebegone match, would later call this effort arguably the worst he'd ever seen from the U.S. team. It was so bad, in fact, that for the first time Gulati said he could envision how it would be possible for the Americans to fail in their qualification bid. This was not a nightmare he wished to entertain.

Howard, meanwhile, heaped a great deal of responsibility and blame upon himself. This had been an extremely long week for the fellow. He had recently finalized a five-year contract with Everton, then headed out on his long personal odyssey. Howard was mentally tired, but said he needed to assert control over whatever defenders were placed in front of him. "I can stop shots just by putting people in the right position," Howard said. "There's nothing behind me. I can see everything. If I can be an extra set of eyes and a voice, that's important." Howard couldn't trap the ball for his midfielders or heal his injured teammates, however. And the Americans didn't have much time to come up with a solution for this crisis of confidence.

They headed immediately for Chicago and a swing match against Honduras.

The U.S. Soccer Federation is headquartered in a grand limestone and slate mansion, the former Kimball House in the Historical District of Chicago. The U.S. Soccer House, as it is now called, moved into this millionaire's row in 1991, when the Prairie Avenue homes were still in some disrepair and not fully restored to the glories of their early-1800 roots. The federation was nomadic for decades, moving from New York to Colorado Springs, where it was afforded free rent from the U.S. Olympic Committee. U.S. Soccer was looking for a more central location, however. Its secretary general, Hank Steinbrecher, was a native of the Chicago area. The lease on this place was cheap, with one catch: The mahogany-and-oak-lined walls and ceilings of the Kimball House (William Wallace Kimball had been the founder of Kimball pianos) could not be altered, because they were protected by their historical status. If the federation wished to project the image of a modern, growth-oriented agency, this might not exactly be the right setting. But it was a gorgeous building, and the organization's home base might have swayed Gulati and Bradley in their decision to locate such a key match in a major city—and at cavernous Soldier Field, which was merely the length of one pedestrian bridge in distance from the Soccer House.

The Americans planned to entertain FIFA officials there at the Soccer House before the Saturday match, as part of their ongoing campaign to win the right to host the 2018 or 2022 World Cup. Since the headquarters was so close to Soldier Field, hometown fans would walk past the building and chant, "U-S-A," conveniently demonstrating to FIFA ambassadors that the country had its share of passionate supporters. Still, this venue was a risky enterprise for such a pivotal qualifier. As a rule, the Americans carefully selected remote venues for high-profile matches. Soldier Field would surely afford the federation a huge pay day, but it would not create the benign home-field advantage of Columbus or Nashville. Chicago was known for its large Mexican population and the city also was certain to attract a substantial number of Hondurans and Honduran-Americans for this match. Federation officials insisted the ratio of Honduran fans to U.S. fans would not be overwhelming, yet the city became a blue-and-white festival in the days leading up to the game. Like it or not, this match would be played before a crowd of staunch Central American partisans.

Everyone understood the significance of this qualifier, both in the Hex standings and for the mental well-being of the American team. The U.S. now stood at 2–1–1 with seven points, sitting in second place. This was the third of five home games, and a loss would place the Americans at .500 going into a meeting with Mexico at Mexico City in August. Before that game, there were scheduled Confederations Cup matches in South Africa against Brazil, Italy and Egypt. It was possible that the U.S. could run up a significant losing streak against such tough competition, reversing years of progress and self-confidence.

The Soccer House became the cozy scene for Bob Bradley's press conference, one day before the match. He was properly humbled after the team's horrendous performance in Costa Rica. Months later, Bradley would admit the disaster in Costa Rica was "the low point" of the qualifying cycle, though at the time he was more focused on this next Honduras game. Appearing next to Howard and Bocanegra in a small, elegant room no doubt devised once upon a time for tea service, Bradley did not single out any player for criticism. His disapproval, as usual, would remain "inside the team" and become apparent only via his starting lineup. Bradley pointed out optimistically that since his reign officially began in January 2007, the national team had rebounded well from important defeats. Yet he faced some major obstacles.

His son, who had evolved into the team's most dependable midfielder, was suspended because of two yellow cards. There was therefore a question of whether the Americans could maintain possession and build from the back. The entire concept of the holding midfielder was testimony to the slow disintegration of creative, attacking soccer over the previous two or three decades. It wasn't so long ago that coaches were more concerned with acquiring a playmaking midfielder, a pure, No. 10 jersey wearer, to act as general on the team and distribute the ball on the run. Now this position had somehow been bastardized and nuanced into something quite different. The central holding midfielder was valued most for his ability to retain possession of the ball against pressure, to slow the pace of a match when preferred, and to track back when necessary to re-take the ball. He wasn't really expected to explode forward and make the brilliant pass, as Michel Platini or Pelé once did. His main purpose was to calm matters, not propel them.

Given the Americans' propensity for panic, a sense of serenity at midfield was not to be underestimated. Michael Bradley would be badly missed. Other troubles persisted. Hejduk and Ching were still unavailable due to injury. Honduras was an athletic and experienced side and it would enter the match after full rest and preparation in South Florida. In 2001, the *Catrachos* had been the last team to beat the Americans on U.S. soil in a World Cup qualifier. They were led in part by Amado Guevara, the former top scorer with the MetroStars who knew Bradley's methods and defensive trends all too well.

It was a formula for considerable anxiety. Gulati stood nearby during the Friday conference at the Soccer House, as curious as any reporter about Bradley's answers. Gulati quietly wondered about Torres's fate. The federation president had worked hard to convince Torres to play with the U.S. side, and not with Mexico. The U.S. team clearly required another midfielder with decent technical skills. But Bradley didn't quite trust Torres yet, looking in other directions to replace his son at midfield. Strapped by this combination of injuries, rust, yellow cards and fatigue, Bradley tightened his formation and made four lineup changes. He went with two forwards, Altidore and the bulldog Conor Casey, dropping Donovan back to midfield, which would become a long-term shift. Beasley and Wynn were benched to start the match. In their place on the defensive line were Jonathan Spector from West Ham United and Jonathan Bornstein of Chivas USA. Bradley also tried Ricardo Clark of the Houston Dynamo in place of Michael.

The starting lineup against Honduras on June 6 included five players from MLS and four with fewer than twenty caps. This was hardly the side envisioned by officials when the qualifying cycle began in 2007 with such great depth and glowing credentials. It was becoming clear that Bradley had reached his limit with Beasley, once viewed as an untouchable core player and still in his footballing prime at age twenty-seven. There were at least three reasons for this gradual souring: Beasley was considered too adventuresome, particularly when assigned to the back line. He also hadn't played any minutes recently with Glasgow Rangers, and therefore was considered well out of top form. Lastly, Beasley had been labeled with the same sort of reputation once assigned to Clint Mathis. Fairly or not, he was viewed as a bit of a party guy, not seriously committed to training. After this match was done, Bradley would state directly that Beasley had better start playing professionally if he intended to fill a meaningful role on the national team. That role, as it turned out, would be drastically reduced. "It's one thing if it happens for three or four months," Bradley said. "If it happens one year after another, then, guess what? It's trouble." This was more than Bradley liked to divulge about any given player, but on very rare occasions he sent such messages to players via the media. He'd already done it to Altidore following the victory over Trinidad and Tobago, basically warning the teenager he was on thin ice if his former bad practice habits resurfaced.

When the Americans came out for the anthems at Soldier Field, they were mercilessly jeered by an overwhelming sea of blue-clad Honduran supporters. It was a reminder the U.S. can never really muster the sort of home-field advantage enjoyed by the Central American teams, and that the Federation had woefully miscalculated the partisan factor in scheduling this key match for a major city. "You can only control what you can control," Bradley said. "It is what it is." The game then began in dismaying fashion, all too similar to the previous match in Costa Rica. The ball was thumped around for a few minutes, before Dempsey got too fancy and was stripped in a dangerous part of central midfield. Wilson Palacios found Carlos Costly at the top of the box, where Costly drilled a left footed shot into the lower left corner past Tim Howard from twenty-three yards. Five minutes into the match, the Americans were chasing the game again. "It was a little bit of, 'Crap, here we go again,'" Bocanegra said. "But we regrouped." The Americans attacked earnestly, albeit clumsily at times. Some ugly first touches from Bocanegra and Casey sabotaged solid chances. Finally, the U.S. was literally handed a break. Mario Beata, the Honduran defender, slapped at a looping pass from Onyewu in the box with the side of his hand as Donovan drifted dangerously behind him.

Mexican referee Mauricio Morales whistled a penalty kick, and Donovan stepped forward courageously again to take the shot. He squatted down momentarily, performed the requisite Holy Trinity gesture on his chest, then calmly converted the chance with a hard, rising boot into the upper right side of the net in the forty-third minute. The Americans carried play for most of the second half, holding the ball with greater command. Ricardo Clark cleared one ball off the line and smothered another attack on a delicate sliding tackle. The other newcomers were less impressive. Finally, in the sixty-eighth minute, the U.S. scored its biggest goal of the tournament. Bocanegra followed the fickle, bouncing soccer ball as it traveled from Donovan's corner kick on the left, to Dempsey's head at the far post and off a Honduran defender in front of the net. "I was just being busy in the box," Bocanegra said. He dived low for the loose ball, struck the winning header, and put the U.S. national team squarely back on track toward a berth at the 2010 World

Cup. The defender's goal gave the Americans a narrow 2–1 victory over plucky Honduras, a successful comeback after four very difficult days of frustration.

The Americans had played sloppily at times and very nearly gave the match back in the closing minutes. There was evidence again that precious few players on this team were capable of technically setting a pace and settling the team. When it was time to stall and sit on the lead in those final minutes against Honduras, only Dempsey dribbled out the clock on his own effectively. In the end, however, the U.S. had earned some breathing room at the halfway mark of the tournament. The victory made the hand wringers and teeth gnashers in the media appear too jittery. At 3–1–1 the U.S. was situated safely again in the Hex table. Observers could take what they wanted from the victory. The Americans continued to struggle against weaker, less resourceful competition in CONCACAF, a depressing notion. Yet the team had rebounded from a nasty loss days earlier in Costa Rica and then another early goal by Honduras, demonstrating a degree of resilience. "The most important thing was the response of the team after giving up the first goal," Bob Bradley insisted. "The response was strong."

That response had disappointed the majority of the crowd at Soldier Field, but not all of it. Sam's Army was elated.

CHAPTER 19

Uncle Sam Wants You

AN AMERICAN SOCCER FAN MIGHT BE IN CHICAGO, IN NASHVILLE, in Salt Lake City, or in San Jose, Costa Rica. He might be swallowed whole by the sheer mass of boosters from Guatemala or El Salvador. And then suddenly the trumpets will blare John Philip Sousa's, "Stars and Stripes Forever," and the red-clad Uncle Sam's Army appears, cavalry-like, marching to the rescue down a hill and around a parking lot outside the stadium. The Army does not represent all American soccer fans, not even close, but it has over the years become the most visible and persistent group of supporters.

The idea of the Army was really born from the World Cup on our own shores in 1994, when founding fathers Mark Spacone and John Wright first realized there was a void that badly required filling. The seats at the U.S.-based tournament were practically sold out, but not many of them were filled with American fans rooting for the American team, even at home. This was particularly evident at the match against Colombia in the Rose Bowl and then, most embarrassing, during a desultory 1–0 defeat by Brazil at Stanford on the Fourth of July. Scattered boos greeted the Star-Spangled Banner. The sad truth was that there were at least as many fans cheering for the other guys as were rooting for the U.S. team, even at a home World Cup. This lack of support was more understandable back at World Cup Italia '90, when the tournament was a well-kept secret in the States. By 1994 there had been plenty of publicity, and the Americans were evolved enough in the game to advance into the second round. European journalists commenting on the proceedings praised the facilities and organization of this World Cup, while condemning the general lack of home-cooked emotion.

It was always difficult being an American soccer fan. Such dedication required considerable initiative. The scores weren't often relayed on talk radio's 20-20 updates, or on the TV sportscasts. The local paper didn't always include the latest MLS rumors. The mentality of the U.S. soccer fan had historically been investigatory and semi-covert. Soccer was a guilty pleasure, shared with a precious few others who were in on this great secret. To admit one's sporting preference was to risk incredulity, even open mockery, by a neighbor or relative. Because of such adversity, the American fan didn't really know how to celebrate in public. He lacked soul, by international standards. His straight-laced chants were dull, not worth repeating. There was no cheer quite as biting as the taunts by victorious spectators at one-sided English Premier League matches, "Can we play you every week?" In the face of probable defeat, the rah-rah stuff from U.S. supporters sometimes just sounded stupid. How could you cheer a 5–1 loss to Czechoslovakia? A 2–0 hammering from Germany?

Having witnessed this appalling absence of passion first-hand, Spacone and Wright went about the tough job of organizing a fan club for the team, a group of traveling supporters based on the European models—with generous amounts of partying, minus the hooliganism. They settled on the name Sam's Army, in honor of Uncle Sam's famous visage. And in their debut game at a 1995 friendly, the group managed to gather together about twenty-five fans, who tailgated briefly before the match and cheered loudly after the kickoff. By the second game, there were fifty of them. Word spread quickly over the Internet, and there were one hundred fifty in the stands by the end of the year, many in full red-white-and-blue costume. As the phenomenon grew exponentially, Spacone thought this was all pretty cool. "Soccer is such a niche market," said Spacone, a high school social studies teacher living in Buffalo. "We've only tapped the tip of the market, the hard-core followers. We're just starting to attract the casual fans."

Spacone and his brother, Chris, took over from Wright when he joined the military. The Spacones organized road trips while Mark Wheeler set up the club's web site, an essential tool for recruitment and publicity. The U.S. national team had grown accustomed to playing before hostile crowds, even at home during World Cup qualifiers. Now at least there was always one familiar section in the stands sporting that friendly red color, a refuge in the storm. After a goal, typically, an American scorer would run toward Sam's Army to take his bow. The supporters were easy to spot, and not only because of their clothing. In the spirit of international soccer, they were auditioning more imaginative chants and taunts, beyond the standard, "U-S-A" stuff. They sang "Adios, Amigos," to Mexico and crooned patriotic songs slightly off key. They were having more and more fun, as their numbers burgeoned.

At the 1998 World Cup in France, there were still too many empty seats at the U.S. matches against Iran and Yugoslavia, but now there was a noticeable contingent of Sam's Army representatives. This was becoming a very social affair for these soccer crusaders. Wright met his wife through club activities. Trips and parties were planned and executed with pinpoint precision. Monty Rodrigues, a financial analyst from Nashua, New Hampshire, remembered when he first heard the siren call. It was back on April 20, 1997, at Foxboro Stadium, He was sitting with his dad, midfield at the top level, part of a crowd of 57,407 fans for a qualifier against Mexico. Rodrigues recalled two things about that 2–2 draw: Carlos Hermosillo blocked Kasey Keller's clearance back into the net for a shocking goal right at the start; and Sam's Army was partying in the lower bowl, no matter how the match meandered. "I was looking down and I saw this group of people having a blast," Rodrigues said. "I thought, 'I'm never going to sit anywhere else.'" He didn't, either. He joined the group, started going to the parties on the eves of games, to the tailgate parties right before the games, and to the post-match parties after games. "We're bringing in people from all over the country that we get to see only during these games, long-distance friendships," he said. "You talk about what's happening in your life, have some beers, go out, have some more beers." Rodrigues would become what he called "a board member" of Sam's Army, even though there was no such formal position. The demographics of this early group was largely middle class professionals, young adults who might have been called yuppies a couple of decades earlier. It was important to have some disposable income, if you were going to follow the national team all over the globe. Airfare and hotels were not inexpensive.

The 2002 World Cup in Korea and Japan was half a world away, and there were many reasons for Americans not to go, not to care. The team had failed miserably four years earlier in France, finishing dead last among thirty-two teams. The U.S. was stuck in unglamorous Korea, not Japan. The long, expensive flight and the change in time zones all seemed unattractive. And yet Sam's Army was there, still growing.

By 2006 at the World Cup in Germany, everything was different, a new world. U.S. Soccer was allocated 19,000 tickets for the World Cup. It received requests for 60,000. Sam's Army had grown to more than 10,000 unofficial members. Not everyone was paying dues, and so there was no certain way to know the size of the rolls, but there was a rapidly expanding data base. "At some point," Rodrigues said, "we need to make it more official."

It was now quite simple to find others in Sam's Army who were eager to travel and share accommodations. Rodrigues and seventeen other members descended upon Diebach, a Bavarian town not too far by train from the centrally located city of Frankfurt. The group consisted largely of New England Revolution supporters and a few members from the D.C. area. They rented a thirteenth-century mill in the middle of nowhere, for a month. The whole municipality embraced these nutty visitors. Teenagers and young adults would go out drinking with this battalion from Sam's Army. The Americans managed to set up an old-fashioned grill and invited practically the whole town to a barbecue. Diebach had its own semi-professional team that played in Germany's sixth division and a challenge match was arranged. "They kicked our asses," Rodriques said. In order to commute to the games, the group would catch a small train to one location, then transfer to yet another train into Frankfurt. The journey was enlivened by a considerable amount of ale and spirits. On the way to Gelsenkirchen for a match, there was just enough time to run off to a store during one stop in order

Donovan's success on the national team earned him national Player of the Year awards again in 2009, while he starred professionally with the Galaxy and signed on for stints with Bayern Munich and Everton. (Joy Rubenstein)

Landon Donovan and Michael Bradley take issue with the referee during a disheartening, opening-round loss to Brazil at the Confederations Cup in South Africa. The Americans nearly pulled off an upset in the final against the same fabled team. (Joy Rubenstein)

Clint Dempsey's meeting with Bob Bradley during the Confederations Cup resulted in a rejuvenated player, and national side. (Joy Rubenstein)

A rare pose: Frankie Hejduk, the perpetual motion machine, resting just a bit during practice. (Joy Rubenstein)

Bob (left) and Michael Bradley, father and son, chatting at practice. The two men share a passion for soccer and a distaste for discussing their own tight bond. (Joy Rubenstein)

Jozy Altidore is America's great young hope at striker—though he doesn't always impress during training sessions. (Joy Rubenstein)

Sepp Blatter (left) and Sunil Gulati before a 5-0 humiliating U.S. loss to Mexico at the Gold Cup in Giants stadium. Gulati sat next to the FIFA president during the match and admitted to considerable embarrassment. (Joy Rubenstein)

Oguchi Onyewu (middle) takes advantage of a game break to huddle with Tim Howard (left) and Jay DeMerit. (Joy Rubenstein)

The U.S. team, with arguably its strongest lineup before the big upset over Spain at the Confederations Cup: (back row) Spector, DeMerit, Bradley, Howard, Bocanegra, Onyewu, and Dempsey; (front row) Davies, Donovan, Clark, and Altidore. (Joy Rubenstein)

Oguchi Onyewu was a dominant force in the box for the Americans, but faced a tough road to recovery from knee surgery if he was to play at the World Cup. (Joy Rubenstein)

Altidore (left) celebrates after he scores winning goal in key 2-1 victory over El Salvador at *Rio Tinto*, Utah on September 5, 2009. Michael Bradley is trying to catch up to the fun. (John Todd, ISI)

Tim Howard makes another acrobatic save to preserve the tight victory against El Salvador. Howard's exploits rescued several World Cup qualifiers for the Americans. (John Todd, ISI)

Uncle Sam's Army brings its boisterous chants and oversized flags to matches all over the world. (John Todd, ISI)

DaMarcus Beasley during his last qualifying appearance against Honduras at Soldier Field in Chicago on June 6, 2009. Beasley began the qualifying cycle as a national team mainstay, but is struggling to get back in the good graces of Bob Bradley after too much time on the bench with Glasgow Rangers. (John Todd, ISI)

A young John Harkes honed his game in Kearny, the birthplace of soccer, before he enjoyed breakthrough success in England and with the U.S. team. (New York Daily News)

Bruce Arena can be condescending with the media, but his credentials as America's most accomplished soccer coach are impeccable. (New York Daily News)

Tab Ramos (airborne, middle) was a brilliant midfielder for the national team while playing in three World Cups, though injuries short-circuited his professional career with the MetroStars and abroad. (New York Daily News)

Walter Bahr (far right) goes up to challenge for header against England during classic 1-0 upset by the Americans at the 1950 World Cup in Belo Horizonte, Brazil. Bahr assisted on Joe Gaetjen's winning goal. (Getty Images)

Donovan (left) and Beckham reconciled their differences and together led the Los Angeles Galaxy to the MLS Cup final. They were expected to face each other in the World Cup opener, playing for the U.S. and England. (Getty Images)

Jozy Altidore (left) and Charlie Davies made for a formidable pair of young strikers, until Davies was badly injured in an automobile accident that threatened his participation in the World Cup. (Chris Brunskill, ISI)

to carry some twelve-packs of beer aboard. Drinking laws were considerably more liberal in Germany than in America, particularly during the World Cup. When late-night trains out of Gelsenkirchen and Kaiserlautern became too crowded for comfort, the Diebach division of Sam's Army stayed behind and found friendly taverns to keep them occupied. One bar remained open all night for ten Americans. "As long as you guys keep drinking…," they were told, by the proprietor. This was Germany. The beer was very good indeed. The Army endured until six o'clock in the morning, when the trains started running again.

That was 2006, a compact and relatively affordable journey. During the recession that followed, members of Sam's Army were a bit fearful that the upcoming trip to South Africa would be a bit more unwieldy and expensive. "South Africa isn't Europe," Rodrigues said. "It's tougher to travel, the sites are farther apart." Because of the economy, there were second thoughts, even about traveling to the qualifiers. "There are people who do it, and I went to four of the five home games at the last Hex," Rodrigues said. "This time, I'm saving for Mexico City."

The cost of these treks was changing the demographics of Sam's Army. The older fans were largely white-collar, with greater income and vacation time to travel. The newer members of Sam's Army were younger, some of them college and high school kids. They could only afford to attend the matches in their area. A trip to South Africa was outside their means, unless parents were subsidizing the trip. "I don't think there'll be more than a few hundred of us at South Africa," Spacone predicted. "We figured it would cost $6,000 from tour operators just for the U.S. group matches. But we're still busy. We're in the process of organizing brigades across the country."

Meanwhile, Sam's Army did what was necessary to attend as many Hex qualifying matches as possible. Corey Vezina, a thirty-four-year-old Internet travel agent from the Bronx, was in Columbus, Ohio, for the first, storm-plagued match against Mexico. "I went out for supplies for the tailgate party, for hot dogs and buns, but then the tornado came through and it didn't really work out," Vezina said. "Mostly we were trying to eat some cookies and not get water in our beer." He flew out to Chicago for the match at Soldier Field against Honduras, and later he would go to *Azteca* for the showdown in Mexico City. The Mexicans were fun—playful and polite to these visiting Americans dressed in red—until the actual match.

"Everyone not at the stadium is cool, really nice," said Vezina, a co-leader of the Army's New York Brigade and organizer of the Empire Supporters Club that backs the Red Bulls. "During the game it's the complete opposite. You have people throwing bottles on you, lining up to spit on you as you leave the stadium. You have to remember these are just some bad apples, the minority, but somehow you're surrounded by 100,000 of them."

Sam's Army would watch that match in the upper deck of *Azteca*, protected by riot police. During most visits there, the American fans were held inside the stadium after the match until the Mexicans left and were then marched out. In 2009, for some reason, Sam's Army was escorted out first and became easy targets for flying objects of various kinds. Then they were held in a parking lot, until offered rides out of the place in vans. All the while, the fans were singing songs, jumping up and down.

"We got free rides in a Mexican riot van," Vezina said. "That was a treat."

Onward, soccer soldiers. . . .

CHAPTER 20

1990 . . .

AFTER FOUR DECADES OF LOOKING FROM THE OUTSIDE IN AT
the globe's biggest sports extravaganza, the Americans were back at the
World Cup in 1990. Now there was the matter of facing some of the
best teams in the world. This would be a harsh learning process begun
in June, at picturesque *Stadio Artemio Franchi* in Florence, Italy. The
U.S. team had toured Europe in the spring of that year for preparation
purposes, losing at Hungary and at East Germany. There was also a
3–1 victory over Poland in Hershey, PA, that was particularly promising, and a 2–1 defeat at Switzerland a week before the tournament.
The Americans played respectably then, but these were not quite the
European powers thrown into their difficult group at Italia '90. They
would face Czechoslovakia, with its giant striker Tomáš Skuhravý.
Then would come the daunting task of Italy in Rome. Finally, Austria
was the third match, in Florence, with that country's all-time leading
scorer Toni Polster.

Very quickly, the young Americans discovered they were ill-pre-
pared for such a baptism by fire. Way back in another soccer lifetime,
Bruce Arena remembered sitting in the stands at Florence watching
the U.S. get spanked by Czechoslovakia in the opener, 5–1. "I shook
my head, and I don't mean that as disrespect," Arena said. "It was clear
we had a long way to go." It was an utter shellacking—and an unfortunately accurate predictor of future World Cup results against Central and Eastern European sides. The Americans would suffer chronic

problems against these physically imposing, short-passing teams. They were bumped off balls too easily, thrown off stride and pace. The U.S. fared better against more finely skilled, higher-ranked opponents. The Czechoslovaks fired an unrelenting twenty-three shots at Tony Meola, who was arguably the Americans' player of the match despite that score line. "A rude awakening," said defender Desmond Armstrong. "When there were ten minutes left, I was thinking, 'Come on, just blow the whistle.'" Skuhravý scored twice—the first goal in the twenty-sixth minute from twelve yards after a lovely tic-tac-toe series of passes. A penalty kick by Michal Bilek followed fourteen minutes later after a borderline call against Mike Windischmann. Eric Wynalda put an ugly cap on the match by getting himself ejected. His earlier elbow to the head of a Czech in the first half had gone unnoticed. When he petulantly shoved Jozef Chovanec in the fifty-second minute, a linesman flagged the infraction this time and Wynalda was expelled. "A lot of us went into the game thinking we were going to war, and that was wrong," Wynalda later said. Caligiuri scored the only American goal, not nearly as important as the one he netted in Trinidad.

Considering the scope of this disaster, the match in Rome against the hungry host, Italy, figured to be apocalyptic. Instead, it proved to be a somewhat redemptive and buoyant experience. The Olympic Stadium was filled to the brim with 73,000 Italian flag-waving fans, all heaping great amounts of pressure on the home team. The scene was unforgettable for the Americans, who somehow rediscovered their equilibrium in the midst of this spectacle. Gansler's insertion of Jimmy Banks, Marcelo Balboa, and John Doyle revitalized the defense. There was one early goal in the eleventh minute by Italy, a beauty, when Giuseppe Giannini zipped past both Windischmann and Harkes before beating Meola. A foul in the box by Caligiuri in the thirty-third minute yielded a penalty kick for the Italians. But Gianluca Vialli banged the shot harmlessly off a post. From that failure, the Americans took heart and held their own. Ramos and Harkes, in particular, appeared energized by the occasion. Then in the seventieth minute, the U.S. had a remarkable chance for a draw. The great Italian goal-keeper, Walter Zenga, made a difficult save on a Bruce Murray free kick, and Peter Vermes very nearly beat Zenga on the rebound. As the match wound down to its tight finish, the Italian fans jeered their national team off the field for its narrow victory. The victors were chastened, the losers elated. It had been a long while, forty years, since the Americans were competitive against top-flight opponents in such a meaningful game. "I think we took a giant step tonight," Gansler said. "I've preached all along that you can't be in awe of a team and you can't be in awe of a situation. Both ingredients were there tonight. But I think we showed people we have grown, and we are psychologically tougher than they thought."

The third and final match for the Americans at Italia '90 proved not nearly as catastrophic as the defeat to Czechoslovakia, nor as encouraging as the close loss to Italy. The U.S. entered the game against Austria with a small mathematical chance of advancing out of its group into the Round of 16, requiring a victory by at least three goals. Instead the Americans were clearly outclassed and beaten in a chippy match, 2–1, by an Austrian team forced to play the last fifty-seven minutes of the match one man short. The ejection occurred in the first half, when Peter Artner was red-carded by referee Jamal al-Sharif of Syria for kicking Vermes's leg after a collision. It was at this point that the Americans' inexperience proved fatal. They simply did not know yet how to take advantage of the extra space on the field. The U.S. became impatient and frustrated while the Austrians grew more disciplined and dangerous on counters. Eventually, Andreas Ogris pounced on a loose ball around midfield off a restart, then beat Armstrong, Banks, Windischmann, and finally Meola from twelve yards out early in the forty-ninth minute. Austria scored a second goal in the sixty-third minute by Gerhard Rodax, before a hollow, hopeless goal by Murray from Ramos in the eighty-third minute.

"Obviously we're disappointed," Gansler said. "With the second and third games, though, I feel we showed that the difference between nations who are perpetually here and those like ourselves is not as great as some believe. We can only learn from coming here. I feel we have benefited immensely from the experience."

Gansler, however, wouldn't personally benefit much from the results.

After the harsh results at Italia '90, there was considerable pressure on U.S. Soccer to recruit an established foreign winner as head coach of the national team. Rothenberg heeded his advisers on this count, signing Velibor Milutinovic, a Serbian coach who already had led the Mexican and Costa Rican national teams into the second rounds of previous World Cups. "Bora," as he was known to everyone, was an inscrutable quote and a coach known for his effective but ultra-conservative style of play. Milutinovic could speak many languages, making sense in none of them. He would begin sentences with "My friend . . . ," in the fashion of the politician John McCain. After that start, all meaning and structure were jumbled. Most reporters believed this was a calculated affectation to keep writers at bay. But a couple of the players also confessed at times they could make only limited sense of some commands.

Bora's task was very different than that of other national coaches, because the U.S. was automatically qualified for the 1994 World Cup as host. There was little or no pressure on him, despite largely lackluster results in exhibitions leading up to the big tournament. During one stretch of friendlies from mid-February to late May 1992, the Americans went 1–6–1 and truly appeared lost. In any other nation, fans would have been demanding the head of their national coach after defeats by 4–1 in Ireland, by 3–1 in Morocco, by 2–0 in El Salvador. Nobody seemed to notice in the U.S., and Milutinovic just kept reminding people that the only matches that mattered would be the ones at the World Cup. He demanded and was granted immunity from prosecution until then. As the World Cup approached and the lineup was fortified by the return of America's best players, Bora's side produced some decent results. During one tournament in June 1993, designed to emulate the tight schedule and high level of World Cup competition, the U.S. lost to Brazil, 2–0, in New Haven; routed England, 2–0, in Foxborough; and barely lost to Germany in a wild match, 4–3, in Chicago. Good stuff. And when the

Americans were drubbed, 4–0, by Mexico the following month in Mexico City, high altitude was conveniently cited as the culprit.

All along, this talented group of young players was gaining necessary international experience, learning not to quake at the sight of Brazilian or German uniforms. As the World Cup approached, Milutinovic scheduled easier matches to bolster confidence against the likes of Armenia, Estonia, Moldova, and Iceland (a loss, but you can't win them all). Many of the Americans did not play yet for professional teams, but were kept very busy nonetheless with full-time training and this slate of matches. The lineup was becoming respectable, even formidable. The wide-eyed kids from Italia '90—players like Earnie Stewart, Harkes, Ramos, Wynalda, and Meola, along with relative newcomers Alexi Lalas and Cobi Jones—were peaking at the right time. It was a balanced, talented roster, given an extra boost by FIFA's rule that the host must be granted a number one seeding. That meant there would be no Italy, Brazil, or Germany in the Americans' first-round group. At a kitschy, live television production out in Las Vegas that somehow featured both soul singer James Brown and *I Dream of Jeannie* actress Barbara Eden, the official World Cup draw produced a Group A comprised of the U.S., Switzerland, Colombia, and Romania. Nobody, anywhere, was calling this the Group of Death. Switzerland and Romania were second-tier European sides, while Colombia was ranked well below Brazil or Argentina.

The U.S. lineup was formidable for its 1994 World Cup opener at the Pontiac Silverdome in Michigan against Switzerland, the first-ever indoor match at this tournament. It was a team that was arguably the best ever fielded by the U.S. at any World Cup: In goal, the twenty-five year old Meola, with the very capable backup Brad Friedel; on the backline, Caligiuri, thirty, Alexi Lalas, twenty-four, Marcelo Balboa, twenty-six, and Cle Kooiman, thirty; at midfield, John Harkes, twenty-seven, Thomas Dooley, thirty-three, Tab Ramos, twenty-seven, and Mike Sorber, twenty-three; at forward, Earnie Stewart, twenty-five, and Eric Wynalda, twenty-five. Roy Wegerle, thirty, and Cobi Jones, twenty-four, came off the bench. Dooley and Wegerle were imports of sorts. The others were homegrown, or nearly so. Of that bunch, all but Kooiman would enjoy extended, notable careers on the national team.

"Soccer has changed since then, everything has gotten much better, the players are much better," Ramos said, looking back fifteen years to that roster. "But that team in 1994 was as competitive in its time as any side we've had before or since. I put it right up there. And it was because of a very small number of special players. What I noticed in my twelve or thirteen years on the national team—and what players like Harkes and players who have been in the program for a long time could testify—there were just a group of guys who got it."

Nations prepared painstakingly for the World Cup, but it could be over for them very quickly once they arrived on site. Few teams over the years advanced to the second round after dropping their openers in the three-match first round. A draw, at the least, was generally required. And that was precisely what the Americans managed against Switzerland on June 18, 1994, despite playing well below their potential in Pontiac, MI. Conditions were horrific as temperatures reached 106 degrees on the floor of the Silverdome. Wynalda was suffering from an allergic reaction and several other teammates were near collapse by the end of the match. The Swiss went ahead in the thirty-ninth minute on a goal off a free kick. Just before the half, Harkes was brought down on the full dribble by midfielder Ciri Sforza, creating a free kick for the Americans from twenty-eight yards. Wynalda, whose hands and legs were swollen from the unidentified allergy, curled a gorgeous shot past goalkeeper Marco Pascolo that tipped the underside of the crossbar. Wynalda called it the greatest goal of his career, and it came only hours after he had thrown up his lunch. "This is the World Cup," he said. "No way I wasn't going to play." Wynalda was pulled, at last, in the fifty-ninth minute. Milutinovic's conservative style might have frustrated his own players, but they tamped down play successfully and preserved a draw.

The next match, against Colombia at the Rose Bowl in Pasadena, CA, proved both pivotal and tragic in its own weird way. Milutinovic benched Kooiman for the veteran defender Fernando Clavijo. The reinvented back line was nervous early on, then neutralized Colombia's elegant attackers with pressure in the middle of the field. It was one of the greatest efforts by any American soccer side, a well-earned 2–1 victory on an own goal by defender Andrés Escobar in the thirty-fifth minute and a later one by Stewart—who beat the goalkeeper, Óscar Córdoba, to a lead pass from Ramos twelve yards outside the box in the fifty-second minute. Colombian goalkeepers were known to stray far from the end line. This venture did not end well for Córdoba. Balboa barely missed a spectacular bicycle kick that might have sealed the result and assured him a permanent place in U.S. Soccer lore. But even without that, there was much to celebrate. "A thing that one time seemed like a dream now has come true against a big team," Milutinovic said.

Escobar's famous mistake, however, apparently cost him dearly. Upon his return to Colombia, he was murdered at the age of twenty-seven in Medellin. The killing may have had something to do with the losses suffered by gamblers in that first-round match, or it might just have been part of an ugly bar fight. Colombia was suffering from the worst kind of gangsterism, and it very much impacted the soccer team. Even before the match against the Americans, midfielder Gabriel Gómez was lifted from the Colombia starting lineup after hearing that his family back home had received death threats. Then came the disastrous result. Francisco Maturana, the very same coach who would lead Trinidad and Tobago through the qualifiers in 2009, was furious about the whole defeat. "We basically stunk up the field," he said. "The ideal situation would have been to make eleven substitutions." In any case, the Americans had their first World Cup victory in forty-four years and already were assured of advancing to the second round.

The rest of the tournament was not pretty for the U.S. national team, and Milutinovic was at least in part to blame for impeding his team's significant talents. The Americans were ordered into a defensive shell that destroyed any notion of attacking soccer. Competing in extreme heat at the Rose Bowl, the U.S. required a draw against Romania to avoid facing Brazil in an almost certain dead-end second round knockout match. But when Daniel Petrescu scored for Romania in the seventeenth minute, the Americans did not appear anxious to answer. A crowd of 93,869 was struck numb with boredom as the U.S. sat on a 1–0 defeat, a safe but certain path to a quick end. Romania simply played keep away with its short passing game. As if the loss weren't dreary enough, Harkes committed an extremely stupid mistake by getting his second yellow card of the tournament for dawdling and arguing, instead of taking his place on a simple free-kick defensive wall. The moment that referee Mario van der Ende showed the card to Harkes in the forty-first minute, he became ineligible for the Round of 16 match against Brazil—a disastrous loss at midfield.

The game against Brazil nonetheless was a grand stage for soccer in America, filled with a real sense of kinship and potential. The South American side, always, was everybody's second-favorite team. The Brazilian national squad had claimed the Palo Alto area as its adopted home for the course of the tournament, where Brazilians and wannabe Brazilians gathered and reveled in the gorgeous weather and equally inspirational soccer. The lineup offered pace and quality throughout. It included two very different, but particularly dangerous, attackers: the sly Bebeto and the bulldog Romario. They were far from the best of friends, yet were the perfect offensive combo. "Romario is the Michael Jordan of soccer and Bebeto is the Magic Johnson of soccer," Caligiuri said. To counter, Milutinovic tapped Cobi Jones in place of the disqualified Harkes at midfield. He opted for the aging Hugo Perez at forward instead of Wynalda, who would come on at halftime in place of Ramos.

Tens of millions of Americans watched this Fourth of July match on television, and there were 84,147 fans at Stanford Stadium. Many hoped for a miracle or at the very least, a spirited competitive match. Unfortunately, the game itself proved nearly as dreadful as the previous one against Romania. The Americans packed their own box, hoping desperately to survive ninety minutes plus perhaps thirty more of overtime to reach the fifty-fifty proposition of penalty kicks. In the forty-fourth minute, they received both a crushing loss and an unexpected boost: Leonardo hammered Ramos with a vicious elbow to the head along the left sideline, fracturing the American's skull and causing a concussion. While Ramos was carted off to the hospital, Leonardo was red-carded. Brazil was forced to play short-handed for forty-six minutes. But now the U.S. was without its two best attacking midfielders, Harkes and Ramos, and was unable to build any sort of threat. Milutinovic ordered eight men back in defense of Meola. Inevitably, in the seventy-fourth minute, Romario dribbled past both Dooley and Balboa, then passed to Bebeto on his right. Bebeto sped by Lalas and beat Meola to the far post, beyond the goalkeeper's extended right arm, for the only goal.

The 1994 World Cup in the U.S. had been a great success in many ways. For the first time in memory at this event, true sportsmanship ruled off the field. There was no public animosity whatsoever demonstrated between international fan bases. Some of that was because the cost of traveling throughout the States was just too dire for many of the edgier European fans. Also, England had failed to qualify. Just four years earlier, English hooligans had rampaged over Sardinia, holding the lovely, otherwise serene island hostage during Italia '90. Several of these knuckleheads talked eagerly about trashing the island of Manhattan in 1994, but that never happened. Americans would remember this World Cup as their coming-out ball, yet they also had wasted a unique opportunity. World Cups come to roost in any given host country only once every three decades or so. With a bit more élan and attacking soccer, the U.S. just might have done more than stick close to Brazil with a man advantage.

At the same time, this event sired many other soccer-related ventures. Youth soccer expanded exponentially. Five years later, the U.S. women's team would capture its own World Cup title and everyone's imagination. Organizers had hoped that Major League Soccer would be ready for launching in the fall of 1994, piggy-backing on the enthusiasm and success of the World Cup. The league was conceived and organized in 1993, yet it wasn't until 1996 that the first match was played. When MLS finally kicked off, there was still enough soccer buzz remaining to give the league a substantial average attendance boost, unmatched until David Beckham came to town more than a decade later. "The delay was a function of making sure we got it right and got the right investors in the right places," said Garber, who would become

MLS commissioner in 1999. A portion of the leftover profits from the World Cup, about $5 million, was used as original seed money for MLS—a debt that was later repaid by owners. Without that 1994 World Cup, there would be no MLS, no CONCACAF Champions League. Maybe, too, there would have been no Donovan, no Howard, no Dempsey. And no unexpected run at the Confederations Cup, fifteen years later.

CHAPTER 21

The Dress Rehearsal

THE AMERICANS HEADED TO SOUTH AFRICA IN JUNE 2009, TO test themselves at the Confederations Cup, not knowing what to expect from the experience. They landed in Pretoria, settled into a high-security, three-star hotel where they would have little to do but mingle among themselves. "We get to know each other, become a community," Tim Howard said. "We usually don't get to spend this much time together, because we fly in for games from our teams and then head out right away." They would dine, they would train, and then have the opportunity to preview the atmosphere inside a series of South African soccer stadiums for relatively high-profile matches played on a schedule similar to the World Cup. "The perfect dummy run," Gulati called it. The Americans would learn about the pressure from the Brazilian forwards, about the chilly winter climate, and about the hive-like buzz in the stands of those incessant yard-long plastic horns, the *vuvuzelas*, in the crowds.

The matches themselves figured on paper to be wholly disheartening, regardless of the ambience. The Americans were stuck in a group with Brazil, Italy, and Egypt. Their opener against Italy at Loftus Versfeld Stadium in Pretoria proved to be demoralizing for a number of reasons. In recent meetings, the Americans had played well against this powerful side. Stylistically, they were able to disrupt Italy's short passing game and rarely allowed the *Azzurri* to settle into a comfortable rhythm. There were advantages to playing raw, indecipherable soccer against such a sophisticated team. But this time there would be little hope, because scrappy midfielder Ricardo Clark was red-carded in the thirty-third minute for a sloppy, late tackle on Gennaro Gattuso. The call was questionable, to say the least. Even Gattuso thought that perhaps Clark deserved only a yellow. But after that, playing a man down, the match became a fire drill for the Americans. Little fair analysis could come of it.

The U.S. held its own for the first half, admirably enough. Altidore put together one of his half-gainer cutback moves in the box, pulled down by Giorgio Chiellini for a penalty kick in the fortieth minute. Donovan converted for his fortieth international goal. The second half was a different story. Giuseppe Rossi, the Clifton, NJ, star who had spurned the American team, came on as a substitute in the fifty-seventh minute for Italy, stripped the ball from Benny Feilhaber a minute later, and launched a rocket with his left foot from beyond thirty yards that beat Howard high and to the left. The back line, more confused than ever without the injured Carlos Bocanegra, was in full retreat on the play, to no avail. It was a brilliant strike, changing the whole tenor of the match and reminding Bob Bradley and everyone with U.S. Soccer how unfortunate they were that this kid got away. "Rossi gave us a burst of energy," said Italian coach Marcello Lippi. "He scored a great goal that calmed us psychologically." Danielle De Rossi netted the go-ahead goal in the seventy-second minute. Then Rossi, who was also a teammate of Altidore's at Villarreal, put away the clinching score during the final minute of injury time off a cross from Andrea Pirlo, for a 3–1 victory.

The Americans aimed their wrath primarily at the referee, Pablo Pozo of Chile. They were also understandably frustrated that Rossi, of all people, had shown them up. "The red card made all the difference," Donovan said. "Eleven guys from each team were prepared and ready to play the game, and the guy in the middle with the whistle wasn't." As for Rossi, Donovan didn't wish to speak of the fellow. "If the guy doesn't want to play for us, then I don't really care about him," Donovan said.

Rossi had been raised in Clifton by Italian immigrants, but left home at age thirteen to sign with the development team in Parma. Fernando

Rossi, his father, believed this talented, small-framed child needed to go to Italy, where he would live and breathe soccer, in order to fulfill his potential. Giuseppe Rossi shared the dream, even if at the time it seemed his soccer future was more certain in America. Rossi was a U.S. citizen invited to the pre-World Cup training camp by Arena in 2006. Arena, however, was not about to globetrot around the world on some recruiting mission for a five-foot-eight kid from Jersey yet to prove himself at the international level. "We're not chasing around eighteen-year-old players that can't get games for their club team and tell me they want to play for Italy," Arena said at the time. Arena would continue to embrace that general philosophy, but lived to regret this specific comment. Rossi developed into exactly the sort of attacking star who might have captured the imagination of Americans. By age twenty-two, he was a starter for Villarreal in Spain and the leading scorer for Italy with four goals at the 2008 Beijing Olympics. By 2009, he was coming off the bench for quality time with Italy's senior national team. He was a versatile striker, a threat with both feet and anywhere on the front line. Marcello Lippi, coach of Italy, called him his "little champion," and compared him to Lionel Messi of Argentina. Gulati shrugged, on this matter. There was nothing to be done about the one that got away.

The Americans were simply outclassed against Brazil in the next match at the Confederations Cup, producing their worst result since the loss in Costa Rica. That evolving back line was shakier than ever. Jonathan Spector and Jonathan Bornstein on the back wings offered no solution and Jay DeMerit was only marginally more respectable in the central marking position. At midfield, Beasley appeared hurried on the left side; practically useless with his first touch. Time had now run out on Beasley, as far as Bob Bradley was concerned. This erstwhile core player was simply lost out there, even when he was returned to his customary midfield spot. Enough was enough.

Bradley had warned his team about the efficacy of Brazil's set pieces. Then defender Maicon delivered a perfect free kick from thirty-five yards to midfielder Felipe Melo, who beat Spector for a clear header and a goal. By the twenty-minute mark, the Americans were down by two. Beasley whiffed on a soft, short corner from Donovan, leading to a Brazilian counter-attack from Kaká to Ramires to Robinho for the score. This was quickly becoming a horror show. The Americans didn't shoot once at goal in the entire first half. Then in the fifty-seventh minute, Kljestan made an ugly tackle on Ramires after losing the ball and was red-carded. These expulsions were becoming ritual acts against the U.S. team whenever it played a more polished opponent. There would be one more goal for Brazil in the sixty-second minute by Maicon, making it 3–0. The Americans did not belong on the same field this evening. They might as well have been a youth travel team flighted too ambitiously above their abilities. "I think we were overpowered," Howard said. "Sometimes you just come up against Goliath, and David doesn't win."

Quietly, Bob Bradley took some comfort in knowing his team didn't quit out there, that it kept the score down to a relatively modest thumping when matters might have grown very ugly. This was a reasoned reaction, but these one-sided defeats were demoralizing to a large audience when broadcast live on ESPN back to the States. The U.S. had now dropped three of its last four matches. Its back line was in disarray. And while Americans were not prone to Brazil-style suicidal leaps over such slumps from their soccer sides, there was now a network of websites, bloggers, and fans out there who were placing considerable pressure on team members who cared to pay attention to such things. Gulati himself received two hundred emails, most of them demanding the ouster of Bradley as coach. "I think it's great that Americans have this kind of passion," Gulati said. "I don't think it's great that they have my Columbia University email address." The U.S. Soccer president made a point, almost obsessively, to answer every message. In South Africa, where the wireless connections were extremely slow in hotels, Gulati would power up three laptops at the same time just so that he could utilize the fastest connection.

This torrent of discontent on blogs and message boards became known to both Bradley and to his son, Michael, who took the negative stuff more personally than his father. That's the way it worked with the Bradleys. If you insulted one of them, the other was going to get far angrier. The Bradleys also felt betrayed a bit by ESPN analysts Harkes and Lalas, who were describing these matches and could be brutally frank. Soccer was still a relatively tight little community in America and the Bradleys felt, correctly or not, these commentators had their own agendas or grudges. Harkes was still in search of a coaching position. Lalas had once famously fired Bradley as coach of the MetroStars. In fairness to the two men, Lalas and Harkes were bound by job description to deconstruct some terribly disappointing play early in the summer. "Bob talks to me more often sometimes than other times," Harkes would say, about Bradley's reaction to criticism. "I don't make it personal. He's insecure. He's like a little girl." A similar four-match slump would have meant far greater discomfort to coaches and players in high-pressure places like England, Italy, or Argentina. It was one thing to be criticized by blog posters and Tweeters. It was quite another to be declared an utter incompetent by the *Times of London*, as had happened to many English managers over the decades.

"I don't pay attention," Bob Bradley insisted, though others close to him said that wasn't always the case. "It goes with the territory. I've coached long enough that my ways of doing things are set. You make sure the players understand there will always be stuff that flies around on the outside but none of it can come on the inside and affect what we're doing. The ability on the inside to put a hard shell around things, to establish trust and stick to what we're doing, that's what the job is."

The Americans now moved to a more exotic venue in preparation for what appeared to be a meaningless wrap-up match against Egypt at Royal Bafokeng Stadium in Rustenburg. For three days, they would stay at a hotel on the Pilanesberg game preserve in the North West Province. The players could literally walk outside to contemplate the local fauna, from springboks to brown hyenas, communing with native monkeys by the hotel pool while trying to forget the public relations disaster this tournament had become.

The relocation alone did wonders for their mindset and resolve. This was the real Africa, as they had hoped and imagined it would be. Still, the U.S. placement in the standings was virtually hopeless. In order to finish second and avoid first-round elimination, the Americans needed to defeat Egypt by three goals while Italy lost to Brazil by three. They also hadn't scored a single goal from the run of play. Dempsey, in particular, had been practically invisible. Bradley called him in for a talk, and Dempsey complained outright that he wasn't seeing the ball enough, and that the team required a more aggressive game plan. He wanted to play desperately, despite nagging injuries.

"The next day, you could tell that a certain weight had been lifted," Bradley would tell ESPN.com. "You could sense that [Dempsey] was ready to go. He just needed to get that off his chest. And then he raised his game, right along with his teammates."

Egypt, unlike the U.S., was coming off two splendid matches that had enhanced the African team's international reputation. During an exhilarating 4–3 loss, Egypt gave Brazil all it could handle before falling on a late penalty kick in added time. Then the Egyptians pulled off a shocking 1–0 victory over Italy, leading to a bit of celebratory controversy in the aftermath of the upset. The Egyptian players reported a theft of considerable cash from their hotel rooms, while South African authorities countered with another theory: The players had paid for hookers after the victory over Italy, and were trying to hide the cash expenditures from their own federation. Where there were hookers, there was hope. Bob Bradley took some satisfaction in the notion that the Egyptians had perhaps played themselves out, physically and emotionally, in those first two matches.

"We understood going into the Confederations Cup that our group was very difficult," Bradley said. "But we also knew that meant that the first round was all about three games, not one. And we took different things from each of the first couple of games. One of them was the need to start the game with the right kind of energy, the right kind of intelligence. Try to be the team that takes the initiative in a good way in a game. I think that was incredibly important against Egypt. Egypt had put a lot into their first two games, and we felt strongly that if we could get on top of them, their fatigue might come through."

This was a sound theory in retrospect, but at the time Bradley had little cause for real hope. The U.S. national team's most recent match against an African team in a FIFA tournament did not go well, a loss to Ghana at the 2006 World Cup that knocked them from the competition. Facing much tougher statistical odds on this occasion, Bradley surprisingly chose not to turn the match into a mere test run for lesser, younger players. He employed a classic 4–4–2 formation and kept most of his starting lineup intact, hoping that an early goal for once might reverse his team's fortunes. There were, however, some changes. Charlie Davies, swift and technically sound, was now starting up top next to Jozy Altidore. Beasley was benched, indefinitely. Ricardo Clark was back at central midfield after his suspension, paired with Bradley. Brad Guzan got the start in goal, if only to rest Howard after his two very busy evenings against Italy and Brazil.

What happened over the next two hours, both in Rustenburg and Pretoria, was nothing short of transformational. The U.S. took flight in the sort of way always imagined possible, yet rarely spotted on a grass field. Perhaps this was not elegant soccer, but it was direct and positive. Dempsey's vision had become reality. The Americans set a busy pace early on and capitalized in the twenty-first minute, when Altidore's low cross caused a collision between Egypt's midfielder Ahmed Fathi and goalkeeper Essam el-Hadary. Davies was on the spot and banged the ball off el-Hadary's head for a goal. The Americans went off at the half ahead, 1–0, quite pleased with their own effort.

FIFA requires that the final matches of all its group competitions be played simultaneously, to prevent opponents from arranging some form of advantageous gentlemen's agreement in order to advance to the knockout round. And so at the same time in Pretoria, Brazil was embarrassing Italy, up 3–0 at the half after two scores from Luis Fabiano and Andrea Dossena's own goal in the forty-fifth minute. Bradley told his players about that score, explaining they now had a real chance to make the semifinal round if they tallied two more goals and the Italy score held. "There was a feeling within our team that we had momentum and could keep pushing," he said. Donovan and Michael Bradley combined on a nicely-timed give-and-go to set up a ten-yard score by Bradley in the sixty-third minute. Then in the seventy-first minute, Spector's Beckham-like cross from forty yards was headed by Dempsey past el-Hadary for the 3–0 lead. The Americans had reached their goal quotient. And when Brazil's 3–0 victory over Italy was official, the U.S.

found itself, impossibly, in a semifinal against Spain. The Americans reacted to this news with predictable joy on the field, hugging and tossing jerseys about in all directions. "This is one of the things Americans are capable of," Donovan said. "We have a spirit a lot of people don't. We showed it tonight."

While Donovan's reaction was constructive, Michael Bradley demonstrated a bitter side after the match that caused new concern from U.S. Soccer officials. Even as his stock had risen dramatically as a player, Michael Bradley's reactive nature was becoming a real problem, on and off the field. He was angry with criticism aimed at his father, as much as anything. Michael had about him an us-against-the-world attitude that augmented his amazing work ethic. But it was causing him problems with referees and wasn't exactly the sort of friendly salesmanship still required of this sport's participants in America. He was his father's son—only without the filter.

Any newspaper reporter knows that the best quotes after a match do not come in the interview room, where players sit stone-faced next to their coach and will never say anything even remotely controversial. The mixed zone is a far more productive site. Players there walk past writers' notepads and broadcast microphones in chaotic fashion, not long after the match has expired. It was in this setting, for instance, where Hope Solo so famously blasted her coach, Greg Ryan, and fellow goalkeeper, Briana Scurry, after the U.S. women's team was beaten by Brazil in the 2007 World Cup. And it was in the mixed zone where reporters would find Michael Bradley at his most unguarded and bitter. "When everything is against you, everybody wants to say how bad you are, everybody wants to write you off . . . ," Michael Bradley said. "All the fucking experts in America, everybody who thinks they know about soccer, can all look at that score tonight and let's see what they have to say now."

This was a wonderfully candid quote, yet it hardly seemed the right place or time for such aggressive bravado. After all, the U.S. team had thus far compiled a very modest 1–2 group mark at the Confederations Cup. The Americans had been quite fortunate to advance with such a record, the result of a perfect permutation of events out of anybody's control. They had barely squeaked past Italy in the standings on the goals-scored tiebreaker. A little modesty and self-deprecatory humor appeared in order, at least until the semifinal against Spain at the Free State Stadium in Bloemfontein. That match on June 24 against the European champions figured to be another potential humiliation. Spain, the number one ranked team in the world according to FIFA, was unbeaten in its last thirty-five matches, since November 15, 2006. It featured such international superstars as Fernando Torres of Liverpool, Cesc Fabregas of Arsenal, and Xavi Hernández of Barcelona. If the Americans could simply put up a good show and lose by one or two goals, the tournament would still be considered a relative success.

If nothing else, there had been one momentous shift in personnel. Beasley, still in his playing prime at age twenty-seven and a mainstay during three World Cup cycles, would not see another minute of meaningful action with the national team in 2009. It was a sad development for a significant homegrown talent, nurtured so carefully through America's youth system. Beasley had been part of the whole Bradenton experience, Project 2010. He was one of the golden children, and now he was back on the outside, looking in.

CHAPTER 22

The Boys of Walmart

THERE WASN'T A WHOLE LOT TO DO AT THE IMG SOCCER ACADEMY when DaMarcus Beasley arrived at Bradenton in 1998. He attended the private school off campus, practiced on the complex's many fields (one immaculate pitch was set aside solely for matches), and adhered to the surprisingly strict rules that required significant social adjustment. Beasley had been a star alongside his older brother Jamar at South Side High School in Fort Wayne, Indiana. Soon people were telling his parents, Henry and Joetta, that their younger son could be a great player, that he might make a career out of his talents, and that he needed to go to Bradenton for this new academy program. "The whole idea was for us to get better by living together, training together," Beasley said. "We'd still get the education. I didn't have to convince my parents. It was an easy sell. They let me be a man early." His mother liked innovative notions by nature. She had wanted to name her son Marcus, but decided that wasn't unique enough so she added the "Da." Beasley wasn't supposed to go to Bradenton until the second semester of his junior year, but the local Indiana school district didn't approve of splitting courses, and so he left early, a pioneer.

The facility was actually an assortment of academies sponsored by Nike and IMG, the umbrella consortium of athlete agents and representatives. The tennis academy had been established first, then soccer, later golf. When Beasley and a few others came to scout out the joint, Anna Kournikova was in residence at the tennis academy on the grounds. This caused a considerable stir among the teenage boys. By the time the first class of soccer players arrived, however, Kournikova was gone for good on tour. "The boys were absolutely crushed," said John Ellinger, who supervised practices at Bradenton.

This was a whole new claustrophobic world for the newcomers. In order to travel off campus, a player's parent had to fax his or her approval. Curfew was set at 11 p.m., with bed checks for verification. There were no girls allowed in the dorms; no holding hands on campus. "It was a lot to endure," Beasley said. "But I didn't know many people down there anyway." In mid-term, early 1999, Beasley suddenly had more company. Landon Donovan, Bobby Convey, and Oguchi Onyewu arrived, among others. "I got to show them the ropes," Beasley said. He had his own bedroom in a suite with four others that included Onyewu, and there were now planned trips into town. "You'd have to sign up for the big Wal-mart visit," Beasley said. On Sunday nights, everyone would pile into yellow school buses and drive to the superstore for a ninety-minute shop. That was the big expedition. If life sounded tedious, it really wasn't bad at all. Beasley and the others embraced it. They went to the private school from 8 a.m. to noon. Then while their classmates stewed with envy, they were picked up two and a half hours before the end of classes and transported back to the soccer campus. They would eat lunch, take a nap, practice from 3 o'clock until around 4:30, then shower.

Ten years after the boys from Kearny had transformed American soccer into something international again, the new golden generation of young national players was being nurtured in less organic fashion. These kids had been funneled from all over the country into Bradenton, where they would be carefully programmed into world-class athletes. Donovan, Beasley, Onyewu, and Convey came first; Altidore, Adu, and Michael Bradley would follow in later years. Ellinger chaperoned these crews with his U-17 team around the world to collect all varieties of trophies. They already had begun this process, even before Bradenton.

"At the beginning, we had a camp in December of '97 where we felt we had some definite stars developing in Landon and DaMarcus," Ellinger said. "You could see their quality every session, every game. But it wasn't until the summer of '98 in Austria when we beat Germany, 4–3, in the Little Toto Cup that we knew we had something really special."

In 1999, that national squad would finish fourth at the world championships. Donovan was awarded the Golden Ball, voted the best player in the tournament. Beasley received the Silver Ball as runner-up. "We were all confident, arrogant," Beasley said. "We were the best in the country. All of us had a chip on our shoulders. It made us all fit together."

If Beasley had been less good-natured, his competition with Donovan might have created some bitter feelings. Beasley had been the youth team's center midfielder. Then Donovan joined the club down in Pensacola, Florida. Ellinger prepared the players for the arrival of this new star, told them that Donovan was an amazing forward. He didn't disappoint, scoring twice in his very first match. That was fine with Beasley. "But then the next game Ellinger says to me, 'You're on the left. Landon is in the middle.' He took away my position and I've never gotten it back." Beasley laughed at the whole situation. He and Donovan weren't just teammates, they had been travel buddies since they were seventeen years old, playing up in age at times with the U-23s. They roomed together on the road and both dyed their hair blond before the world championship. "Not a great moment for me, not a good look," Beasley said. And out of this midfield marriage came a certain understanding in motion. "When you play a lot of games together, you have a relationship on the field," Beasley said. "We look for each other. We know where the other one is going to be."

Right through the school year at Bradenton, this original bunch had been well-behaved. But then it was the last day, and a mischievous plan was hatched. Nineteen players—all but one goody-two-shoes, Alex Yi—would sneak off campus for a party thrown in their honor. Five students went out first, climbed a fence and crawled through the grass. It looked a lot like a prison break. The escapees then called back to the others. All but Yi followed. "We were all mad at Alex," Beasley said. Eventually, their prank was discovered and Ellinger came to pick them up and return them safely, without penalty. "Of all the groups, that group felt the most like they were all brothers, more than the others," Ellinger said.

The academy life was done for this class in December 1999, and most of the kids headed back to high school for a final few months to get their diploma. It was a tough adjustment to go from such hard-core soccer playing to regular school and relatively low-level club play. Ellinger would learn from this schedule glitch. The academic program was accelerated, so that the players graduated in December and reported straight to their next athletic challenge. Donovan, always ahead of the game, earned his GED early and headed to Germany. Beasley, for his part, would join MLS, then PSV Eindhoven at the top of the Dutch league, scoring four goals in prestigious Champions League matches, an American record. He was loaned to Manchester City in the Premier League, and he signed with Glasgow Rangers of Scotland in 2007 for about $1.2 million. He wasn't getting enough playing time in Glasgow, however, and it showed. Beasley was unhappy with the state of things. He had gained the reputation as an undisciplined athlete, on and off the field. It was a tough rap to beat, once it grabbed hold of a player. Coaches whispered that Beasley wouldn't fit into anybody's system, wouldn't stick to his assigned area of the field. His practice sessions were uneven. It was tough to figure out which came first: the benchings or the lack of preparation. If Beasley became convinced he would not play in an upcoming match, what was the point of working toward an unreachable goal?

"Scottish football, it's so-so for me," he said. "I'm not the biggest guy and the ball is in the air a lot. There are a lot of sliding tackles, too much rough stuff. But it's an open game with a lot of running and I like that. It's just that I would love to play in Spain one day."

Meanwhile, time was ticking down on his footballing career. Bradley benched him at the Confederations Cup with a frightening finality. It seemed suddenly that Beasley might not make it to the World Cup in South Africa, after all those years invested in his development.

"This is probably the toughest year that I've had in my career," Beasley told his hometown paper, the *News-Sentinel* in Fort Wayne, Indiana. "People forget the fact that I've played eighty-nine times for my country and I've played in two World Cups. They say at twenty-seven my best years are behind me, but twenty-seven is where I'm hitting my prime. I had a bad year last year and that's it. It's just going to be how I rebound from this. I just need to play football again. That's all. I just need to find a team and go play for them."

At Bradenton, there had never been such a problem.

CHAPTER 23

The Breakthrough

THE EVENING OF JUNE 24, 2009, AT FREE STATE STADIUM IN Bloemfontein turned into something very different than anticipated. Strangely enough, the U.S. team was not outclassed and humiliated in the Confederation Cup semifinal. Spain's vaunted freestyle attack was stalled by the near-freezing temperatures and the Americans' custom-made defense. Bob Bradley's team had the advantage of both tactical and psychological preparation. The Americans had played Spain during a 2008 friendly in Santander, losing 1–0. They also viewed plenty of films on their opponents from the European championships. And what became patently clear to everyone was that the Spaniards would dominate possession with their superior skills on the ball, as they had done against virtually every quality opponent, from Italy to the Netherlands.

Bradley's ensuing plan was so simply realized, so ingenious, it suddenly seemed ridiculous that other countries hadn't stymied the Spaniards long before with similar tactics. The U.S. clogged the middle, completely shutting off those fanciful, frontal assaults. The Americans did not allow Spain's talented and prolific playmaker, Xavi, to dissect the center of the field, to find Francisco Torres on the run with through passes. Forced out onto the wings, Spain couldn't mount an effective attack. The relatively small European champs were magnificent on the ball, yet not particularly strong in the air. By comparison, Onyewu looked like Mount Everest in the penalty box.

"They can do anything they want with the football, so you have to pick your poison," Howard said. "Do you want them to go up the middle and make it easy on them? Or do you say, 'We'll give you the wings?' We've got some horses willing to scrap and fight in the box. That's where our power is."

Onyewu and DeMerit excelled in these matchups at central defense. Spector and Bocanegra, healthy again, cut off attacking angles from the sides. Spector, grandson of Art Spector, the first player ever signed by the Boston Celtics, was becoming a reliable two-way player. And by starting Altidore and Charlie Davies to complement Donovan and Dempsey trailing, Bradley had the speed and power up front to fluster Spain's defenders. As planned, Spain dominated possession and set the tempo, yet failed to create dangerous odd-man breakaways. The Americans, adept at counter-attacking, patiently awaited their chances. The first real opportunity arrived in the twenty-seventh minute, when Dempsey looped a pass to Altidore in the center of the field. Altidore did a wonderful job of shielding the ball and spinning defender Joan Capdevila, a teammate on Villarreal. The U.S. forward rocketed a shot from the top of the penalty box that was barely deflected by Spain goalkeeper Iker Casillas off the left goal post and into the net. For Altidore, this was the ultimate moment of personal redemption. He had spent far too long on the Villarreal bench, and now he had scored an enormous goal to the dismay of the very country that had ignored his talents. He pulled off his own shirt in celebration, an automatic yellow card. He didn't care in the least.

After the first half came and went, Spain grew more desperate but no more effective. The Spaniards would outshoot the Americans, 29–9; fire eight shots at Howard, compared to just two by the U.S. at Casillas; earn seventeen corner kicks, compared to three for the Americans; and own possession for 56 percent of the time. Yet all that translated into absolutely nothing on the scoreboard. And then in the seventy-fourth minute, Donovan's cross from the right side on yet another counter was bungled by top Spanish defenders Gerard Pique of Barcelona and Sergio Ramos of Real Madrid. Ramos was looking to clear the ball out of the penalty area and failed to spot Dempsey coming at him from behind. Dempsey sneaked up and one-timed a six-yard shot past Casillas for a 2–0 lead. Two shots on goal for the U.S, both in the net.

That score would hold. The Americans, incredibly, were in the Confederations Cup final and had earned one of their biggest international victories ever. The far better team had lost on the day, but for good reason. Afterward, the Spaniards visibly sulked, trudging off the field with heads down. Many of them refused to trade jerseys with the triumphant Americans. "Whatever, it's not my worry," Donovan said. "They're not used to losing. I can see why they would be frustrated. But I did lose a little respect for them for that." To his credit, Francisco Torres, Spain's greatest talent, showed considerable class. He complimented the Americans and spared them the sneering.

"When you play against Spain, everybody is watching the game," Torres said. "So maybe all the people can see they have fantastic players and a fantastic team."

There was one unfortunate development late in the match, another red card and red flag. Michael Bradley flew in late on a tackle in the eighty-seventh minute and was ejected by referee Jorge Larrionda of Uruguay. It was a shame, coming so late in the match when the result was assured. Bradley would now miss the final against Brazil. It seemed as if officials were getting far too comfortable throwing Americans out of soccer matches. The U.S. had lost a player in three of the four matches at the Confederations Cup, and remembered all too well losing two players in three matches at the World Cup in Germany. The Americans were aggressive on defense, and at times they were late on tackles against technically superior players. But they weren't dirty by nature or design. Unfortunately, Michael Bradley exacerbated the situation by confronting Larrionda in the tunnel after the match. When that incident was reported, his ban was increased to five matches and would include an inconsequential stretch at the upcoming Gold Cup back in the States. More importantly, however, Bradley was gaining an international reputation as a hothead that might eventually cost him with referees at some key, future match, perhaps even at the World Cup.

The Americans were now reaching for the impossible, for their first ever title at a meaningful, international FIFA tournament. Michael

Bradley's ban would force his father again into some ad-libbing at midfield, but basically this was the same lineup that faced Spain— only with Benny Feilhaber starting, instead of coming off the bench. The U.S. would lose something on defense, certainly, with Feilhaber instead of Bradley. The plan for this match was similar to that against Spain: pressure the ball, clog the middle, look for the counter. Brazil was a different nut to crack, however. Not only were the Brazilians technically brilliant, they also were more opportunistic inside the box than Spain with their heads and on set plays. Brazil owned a substantial 13–1 edge over the U.S. in matches, for good reason. Still, the American tactics worked well during the first half, in part because of the overwhelming presences of Onyewu on defense and Howard in goal. Supreme talents Kaká and Robinho were deftly neutralized with careful marking. Then on a counter in the tenth minute, Spector curled a gorgeous cross from the right side into the box that was neatly redirected by Dempsey past goalkeeper Júlio César for a 1-0 lead. This was shocking enough. But seventeenth minutes later, the Americans scored again on a perfect counter, one of the prettiest goals in their inglorious history. Davies and Donovan broke out on a two-man sprint downfield. The swift duo passed the ball back and forth precisely, until Donovan brought it down with one touch on his left side and belted a shot past Cesar for a 2–0 lead. In terms of occasion and execution, this goal arguably challenged Clint Mathis's brilliant score against Korea at the 2002 World Cup. The U.S. now had a clear mission. If it could hang onto a two-goal lead for sixty-three minutes, the world would surely take notice of this upstart side.

The Americans survived the first half, walking into the locker room with that improbable two-goal lead. After that, however, form held and panic carried the day. Less than a minute into the second half, Fabiano received a pass from Maicon with his back to the goal at the top of the box. He pivoted, then blasted a left-footed shot through DeMerit's legs and past Howard. "That pretty much killed us," Altidore said. For some reason, teams seemed to react worst to goals scored against them at the very close of the first half or the very start of the second. Coaches dreaded these momentum changers, planned against them in vain.

Goals came when goals came, whenever attacking inspiration was afoot. Brazil rediscovered its resolve and balance in that forty-sixth minute. The wind knocked out of their sails, the Americans grew weary and sloppy. "They have too many guys that are game-changers," Bocanegra said. "I think we ran out of gas, more than anything." Kaká became his old omnipresent self, eventually creating a goal on a cross to Robinho in the seventy-fourth minute, which turned into a rebound for Fabiano. Finally in the eighty-fourth minute, Brazil capitalized on one of its ten corner kicks, a header by Lucio for the winner. Altogether, Brazil had fired thirty-one shots, compared to nine for the Americans, in the 3–2 victory.

"It's just like, 'Here we go again,'" Howard said. "The hardest part and the most frustrating part is that you can't take everything away from that team. It's so difficult, because you think: 'They have eleven players and we have eleven players, so how come they create numbers? How come you can't stop them? How come it seems like they have twenty-two?' They keep you so off balance. You have no idea what they're going to do until they actually do it."

The end result was the one most expected from the start: another FIFA championship for Brazil. The U.S. team had perhaps gained the most from this tournament, in terms of experience and prestige, because of its victory over Spain and its strong effort against Brazil. This was all about perception, not so much wins and losses. The Americans had finished the Confederations Cup with a modest 2–3 mark and blown a two-goal lead in the final. They had been outplayed in all but the match against Egypt. Still, they had shown again the almost limitless possibilities presented by good coaching, luck, and opportunism against the run of play. It was always more important to win than it was to dominate. And it was doubly important to win at the right time. Their FIFA ranking had risen from number fourteen to number twelve. The world was watching, clearly. During the second day of the G-8 meetings in Italy, President Obama was teased by Brazil President Lula da Silva about the Cup final. Lula said he had watched the match intensely, worriedly, and had invoked Obama's campaign slogan, "Yes we can," while cheering on his national team. Obama answered, "We will not lose a 2–0 lead again," getting a hearty laugh out of the South American. When Bob

Bradley heard about Obama's promise, he was somewhat less certain. "That's easy for him to say," Bradley said. "I guess I'd say the same thing if I were him."

The tournament had scrambled the fortunes of several U.S. players. Onyewu's stock soared immensely from this public demonstration of his stalwart skills in the box. He wasn't the most mobile guy in the world, but his positioning was uncanny and the ball just seemed to find his brow in a crowded box. He would soon transfer from Standard Liege to A.C. Milan, traditionally one of the top ten clubs in the world. Several other players—Davies, Spector, DeMerit, and Clark—established themselves as probable starters on the national team. Davies was soon rewarded with a move from his Swedish club to FC Sochaux-Montbeliard, a more prestigious team in the French Ligue 1. Beasley, meanwhile, had played himself off the first squad.

Glories lay ahead, it seemed. More than ever, there was reason to remain in good standing with this national team.

The Gold Cup, the championship of CONCACAF, was the next tournament on the relentless schedule. It followed right on the heels of the Confederations Cup, and would be staged during the summer of 2009 in venues from California to New Jersey. Bradley tried to do the right thing by his top players, shipping them out to their pro teams at home and abroad to kick-start their new seasons, rather than demanding yet another national obligation. Bradley would use more than fifty players in national team matches during 2009. The coach chose to field younger players for the Gold Cup, hoping to develop some depth for the national team pool. "It's more like a C-team than a B-team," was how one U.S. official described the assemblage, and the selection of these lesser players was a gamble. It could create embarrassing results, right after the feel-good Confederations Cup. As a rule, the Americans did not fare well in international competitions without Donovan and their other core players in the lineup. But there was some undiscovered talent in this bunch, and at least one player about to make a stir.

Stuart Holden was a 24-year-old midfielder born in Aberdeen, Scotland who had moved to Houston at age ten and played for Clemson

University. Then in 2005, he signed with Sunderland in England at the tender age of twenty. Before he could participate in a single match for that club, however, he was attacked by a local man outside a pub in Newcastle. His eye socket was fractured and his career in England was short-circuited. Holden soon returned to his hometown MLS team in 2006. He was a cocky, creative kid. During a Gold Cup draw, 2–2, against Haiti at Foxborough, Massachusetts, he scored late on a gorgeous rocket of a shot, while assisting earlier on the other goal. His play in this tournament would earn him a call-up with the A-team and playing time later in Mexico City. Holden, surely, would get his second shot at a professional career in Europe.

Everything went fine with this young crew, better than expected even, as the U.S. marched through its Gold Cup group and captured a semifinal match against Honduras. But this successful run earned the team a high-profile final against Mexico at Giants Stadium, before a sellout crowd of nearly 80,000 fans and FIFA president Sepp Blatter in the stands. Suddenly, the stakes were raised considerably higher than U.S. Soccer had envisioned and it was too late to change course. There was nothing to be done but to compete against Mexico with this inexperienced group and accept the likely setback. As it turned out, the match became a public-relations fiasco; a signal that not all was healthy in the developmental ranks. The U.S. team on the field at Giants Stadium did not have one black or Hispanic player. It was a small sample, but an indication that perhaps U.S. Soccer hadn't mined all the country's resources after all. The Americans held on gamely for a scoreless first half, then were clobbered, 5–0. All five goals were scored during the final thirty-four minutes of the match, when the U.S. back line utterly lost its shape and its way, following a penalty kick goal in the fifty-sixth minute by Gerardo Torrado. Young Mexican talents Giovanni Dos Santos and Carlos Vela baffled the American defenders. The U.S. managed only one shot all match at goalkeeper Guillermo Ochoa. "The second half for us, that's not what we're all about," Bob Bradley said. "It's important we look hard at ourselves and use it the right way."

This one-sided spectacle greatly appealed to the largely Mexican and Mexican-American audience, which had endured a number of soccer setbacks in recent months, plus key losses to the U.S. over the past decade. It was an afternoon custom-made to make Mexicans feel wonderful, at long last, about their treasured national team, *El Tri*—courtesy of a regional nemesis. At the same time, the debacle imposed a tough lesson on U.S. officials, who had lost their gamble with these raw kids. It was the worst loss anywhere for the U.S. team since a 1985 defeat to England in Los Angeles by the same score. The Americans were bidding to host the World Cup in 2018 and 2022, yet had fielded an inferior team at their own regional championship. This could easily be considered an insult to FIFA and to Blatter, who was sitting next to Gulati during this match.

"While that result was very, very disappointing and painful, even more so when we have the FIFA president sitting with us who had seen us play at the Confederations Cup, in great measure we get a chance for redemption very quickly," Gulati said. "That's something you don't normally get, except in a home and away series, and in this case I'm glad it's not an aggregate score issue. We get an opportunity at redemption on August 12th in Mexico City and we'll have a different-look squad. I think the group that played in the Gold Cup for five and a half games did very well. I think a lot of people were surprised that we had that much depth and that players who didn't have the same level of experience as the players who were at the Confederations Cup were able to do as well as they did. Clearly the first goal rattled them, or unnerved some of our team, and we were really chasing the game after that. There were a bad thirty minutes. They were a *very* bad thirty minutes. But I don't think that reverses or undoes the real progress that we've shown."

Gulati had come to call this span of 2009, "The Summer of Soccer." There had been the success at the Confederations Cup, solid television ratings (more than seven million people in America watched Brazil play the U.S. in that Cup final), and incredible crowds all over the country for exhibitions featuring the likes of A.C. Milan, Chelsea and Barcelona. But there was still the matter of this debacle against Mexico, this 5-0 score line that went out across the world. Whenever these two rivals played, some bitter seeds were planted in the soil. The Mexican federation had brought back their old coach, Javier Aguirre, *El Vasco* ("The

Basque"), to revive the national team and he was still full of vinegar. Aguirre characterized the U.S. national soccer style as a few set-play tricks wrapped up in a defensive shell.

"They stack eight in the back and live off the other team's mistakes," Aguirre had said, before the final. "If we do what they do, it's going to be a zero-zero game and that's not my goal."

He wasn't far off on that day at Giants Stadium, where the U.S. side was practically devoid of technical or racial diversity. The Americans appeared a throwback to the times when the national team was a bunch of slow suburban kids. Gulati insisted the sample size was too small to condemn America's youth movement. The U-17 team was a rainbow coalition, he said, coached by a former Colombia international star, Wilmer Cabrera. The Mexicans? They were heroes again at home, at least until the scheduled World Cup qualifier on August 12 against the Americans.

"Tonight I will sleep well," Aguirre said. "Tomorrow, the pressure begins again."

CHAPTER 24

1998 . . .

FOR EVERY STEP FORWARD FOR THIS NATIONAL TEAM, IT SEEMED, there was a kick in the pants. Long before the U.S. was thumped by Mexico at the Gold Cup, it experienced a more significant humiliation at France '98. Bora Milutinovic left his position with the U.S. team after the 1994 World Cup to move on to his next challenge, a second stint coaching the Mexican national team. Bora was a nomad by nature, and was paid generously to follow his muse. In April 1995, U.S. Soccer appointed Steve Sampson as interim coach while considering other options. It was a situation very much like the one involving Bob Bradley more than a decade later. Sampson owned a decent resumé, and was very familiar to American officials. He'd led Santa Clara University to the NCAA championship in 1989, beating the University of Virginia, coached by Arena. In 1993, he became Milutinovic's assistant and unofficial translator with the national team. He was also deeply involved in the organization of the 1994 World Cup. The players knew him, so Sampson seemed to represent a natural progression. When the Americans performed well under his leadership, beating Argentina 3–0 in a major upset and claiming fourth place at Copa America, the "interim" tag was dropped from his job title in August 1995. Sampson was signed through the 1998 World Cup in France.

This new coach inherited the same core of players that had blossomed under his two predecessors, Gansler and Milutinovic. Many of them still did not have professional contracts, and instead were full-time national players—a situation unique to America. But now the original group from this golden generation was no longer at its playing peak. Harkes and Ramos were thirty-one, while Wynalda was twenty-nine. Lalas would be twenty-eight by the World Cup, and not quite up to his impressive form at Padova in the Italian League. To make matters worse, Sampson demanded fresh-faced enthusiasm from his players while offering pep talks and inspirational words of the day. His coaching methods produced considerable eye rolling from the veterans, who felt fairly or not that Sampson was a bit out of his league.

It is debatable whether Sampson ever had a fair chance. He might have arrived at just the wrong moment, becoming the bad guy forced to make the difficult, unpopular transition from an accomplished older group to an unproven, younger generation. The qualifying rounds went smoothly enough, better than expected. The Americans advanced through the usual CONCACAF trials to France without the crises that faced them in 1989. There was even a draw at *Azteca*, the best result ever. But when it came time to select his final twenty-two-man roster for the World Cup, Sampson drove a wedge through the middle of the U.S. team with a forcible changing of the guard.

The coach dropped both Meola and Harkes, who had been captain of the team until his dismissal. Meola's case was straightforward enough. Sampson felt Juergen Sommer was better suited to be the nominal third keeper and cheerleader, behind Kasey Keller and Brad Friedel. Harkes's situation was far more complex and divisive. It wasn't until nearly twelve years later, in February 2010, that rumors from 1998 were confirmed: According to Wynalda and Sampson, Harkes was having an affair at the time with Wynalda's wife, Amy. Wynalda spoke openly about this for the first time on Fox Soccer Channel, comparing the love triangle to a reported affair rocking England's national side between John Terry and the former partner of teammate Wayne Bridge. Wynalda said Harkes's affair dearly cost the U.S. team and his own marriage, which eventually ended in divorce. Sampson, to his credit, had held his tongue about the relationship, taking heat for dumping Harkes on sheer performance criteria until Wynalda broke the silence. "The last thing I wanted to do was drop John Harkes from the team, because I really did believe he was an outstanding leader on the field," Sampson told the *Associated Press*. Of the original three Jersey guys, only Ramos would remain for a third World Cup. Harkes was replaced at midfield by the more elegant Claudio Reyna. Sampson wasn't certain the two St. Benedict's High School alums could co-exist effectively at midfield, because Reyna tended to defer to his elder, Ramos, and the two players were stylistically different. Reyna was a classic possession midfielder. Ramos was more aggressive. Still, they had played well together during the qualifiers. Elsewhere, the roster was loaded with experience: Stewart, Wynalda and Wegerle up front. Dooley, Balboa, Lalas and Jeff Agoos on defense complemented the young shining light, Eddie Pope. In goal, Keller and Friedel were driven by a competitive, creative friction.

That was the blueprint, anyway. But Reyna was never a vocal team leader by nature, not like Harkes or Ramos. And once the tournament began veering the wrong way, a mutiny of sorts among the veterans was inevitable. "That World Cup was just a case of your regular professional guys being pissed off at everything," Ramos said, looking back years later with perspective. "That's what happens when you get all the veteran guys on the wrong side of the coach and it doesn't work. It has happened that way with every professional team all over the world. We were just new at the experience here. But this happens every day, and it happens in other sports all the time."

There were other problems for Sampson in France, not all of his own making. The tournament was held in Europe, where the Americans generally did not fare well. Their grouping this time included Germany, a certain loss, plus Yugoslavia and an inspired Iran. Germany was a hopeless contest, and was scheduled as the first match in Paris. Iran was the second game in Lyon, and that team's national players would surely rise to the occasion when facing their country's ideological nemesis. Yugoslavia presented yet another example of an Eastern European side that always troubled the Americans with deliberate, physical play. Since the expanded World Cup was comprised of 32 teams divided into eight groups, the U.S. now needed to finish first or second in order to advance to the knockout, second round. Then, more trouble: Sampson fell in love with a single striker formation, a 3–6–1 scheme that had produced an unexpected and meaningless 3–0 rout of Austria in Vienna during an April tuneup. He decided to post Wynalda alone up top against Germany, far too large a burden for a player recovering from arthroscopic knee surgery just two months earlier.

The 1998 World Cup experience quickly became a full-blown disaster, almost from the opening whistle at Parc des Princes in Paris. The Americans had buoyed themselves with the far-flung thought that Germany might be vulnerable early in the tournament, before it played itself into form. And there was the further hope of familiarity. Eight members of the U.S. team boasted some Bundesliga experience, and arguably were well-prepared for a physical contest. Yet in the very first minute, Jens Jeremies, Germany's midfield enforcer, threw a nasty elbow in the general direction of Reyna's right kidney, flooring the team's central player and essentially taking him out of the match and the tournament. Reyna was hammered by the Germans throughout the game. He became timid, invisible, and there was no longer any hope at midfield for lengthy possession or the construction of a real attack. The Germans were stronger, faster, better in every department of the game. They stretched the defense clinically with square and cross-field passes, then attacked the seams. An unmarked Andy Moeller scored on a header just eight minutes into the match for Germany. The Americans didn't take a single shot during the first thirty-one minutes. "I think some of us were a little in awe," Reyna would admit. Ramos was fuming at the desultory play of teammates. "I don't think what we saw out there was a step forward for U.S. Soccer," Ramos said. "We're not here to win the World Cup because we know that's not going to happen. But we're here to show that we've improved, and I don't think we did a good job of that." Sampson tried everything. He yanked Mike Burns, the defensive midfielder, at the half for Frankie Hejduk. He subbed Wegerle for Wynalda. Germany scored again, on a goal by Klinsmann, and the Americans were steamrolled, 2–0. "If you can't match them physically, you're in a lot of trouble," Keller said.

It was on to Lyon for a showdown with Iran, and a real madhouse. The game would be the Americans' last chance to rescue this World Cup, if they harbored any hope for the second round. Security forces cordoned off blocks all around the Stade de Gerland, for fear of potential political altercations even though President Clinton had recently called for improved relations between the two countries. Before the start of the World Cup, French officials reported "real and troubling" threats to the tournament by militant Islamists. As it turned out, the only clashes involved French-Iranian refugees versus police, as several thousand expatriates demonstrated inside and outside the stadium with banners and shirts displaying the photos of two Paris-based leaders of an opposition group, the National Council of Resistance. On the field, the Iranian players shook hands with the Americans and handed them white flowers. Then the underdog Middle-Eastern nation beat the U.S., 2–1. Sampson scrapped the 3–6–1 formation, benched Wynalda and started a patchquilt lineup that included Wegerle, Hejduk and Joe-Max Moore. The coach even brought in Preki Radosavijevic, thirty-four, as a substitute, rather than Wynalda. The Americans were unlucky, to be certain. They outshot Iran, 27–15, hit a post and a crossbar. Still, they were unable to score until Brian McBride's header in the eighty-eighth minute. This was the final, crushing insult. The Iranian players kissed the ground at the final whistle, while the Americans stared blankly ahead or sank to their knees. Back in Tehran, Ayatollah Ali Khamenei issued a statement broadcast by state television: "Tonight again the strong and arrogant opponents felt the bitter taste of defeat."

The Americans were already eliminated from the World Cup, with one match left to play. The mess would only get messier. Harkes attacked Sampson in an interview with George Vecsey of the *New York Times*. Other veterans on the team, such as Wynalda and Lalas, began to question Sampson's tactics and competence. Wynalda thought his own benching was personal. The day before the final match, Alan Rothenberg, president of U.S. Soccer, lectured the players to hold their tongues. "Don't say anything you might regret," he said. Not many listened. Ramos called the experience "a shambles," pointing out that Sampson had used seventeen players in the first two matches. "We'll all get older, and we'll all have scrapbooks," Lalas said. "I'm satisfied with myself, even though I didn't play a minute here. I'll be satisfied with my scrapbook.

Steve has to be satisfied with his scrapbook." Considering the mutinous mood on the team, the last match in Nantes was no disaster, just a dreary 1–0 loss to tough Yugoslavia. The Americans finished dead last, 32nd out of 32 teams at the tournament.

Needless to say, Sampson's contract with the national team was not extended. By the third week of the World Cup in France, U.S. Soccer officials were already interviewing potential replacements. There was little time to lose in such matters, because several countries were considering and bidding on a small pool of top international coaching talent. Again there were similarities to the coaching search that would take place in 2006. There were serious talks back then with Carlos Queiroz, the former Portuguese national coach who had worked with U.S. Soccer to develop the so-called "Q-Report"—the developmental plan for soccer in America, the basis of Project 2010. Like Klinsmann years later, Queiroz was a natural. He was a sophisticated, experienced coach with great command of the English language. For some time, it appeared he would be the one. But there was a bit of confusion during the World Cup when Bobby Robson, the respected former English footballer and manager, told a couple of American journalists that he had just hung up the phone with his good friend, Queiroz, and that the Portuguese coach had signed a $1 million contract with U.S. Soccer. Such a source, it seemed, was unimpeachable. But either Robson misheard, or the journalists misunderstood. Queiroz would be getting that million from the U.A.E. (United Arab Emirates), not the U.S.A. Soon enough, Alan Rothenberg and other recruiters were eyeing a more domestic and less glamorous option, Bruce Arena, whose success with D.C. United in the MLS promised considerable knowledge and command over America's young talent pool. For U.S. Soccer, Arena was yet another in a growing line of attractive consolation prizes.

CHAPTER 25

Other Side of the World

BRUCE ARENA WAS BY NATURE A CURMUDGEON, BUT A KNOWL-
edgeable one. The coach did his homework and rarely fielded a lineup
that could easily be second-guessed. He wasn't patient with the media,
but he played few favorites on the field—with the possible exception of
Reyna—and therefore held the respect of team members. When Arena
took over in 1998, the national team was in disarray. Within four years,
the Americans would be playing competitively in a World Cup quarterfinal against Germany. Clearly, he was doing something very right,
despite some substantial bumps in the road. The Americans came
within thirty minutes of elimination in the semifinal qualifying round,
while Arena watched that decisive match in Barbados leaning against a
lamppost, suspended for a previous post-match tantrum. Still, the U.S.
survived all that and headed to Korea in 2002 fervently hoping to fare
better than the 1998 embarrassment.

By this juncture, soccer officials back in America fully understood
the marketing potential of the World Cup and devised a plan at several
levels. In 2000, Garber sat down with MLS deputy commissioner Ivan
Gazidiz and carefully plotted to sign to long-term contracts the top
American players who figured to be important figures at Japan/Korea
2002. Mark Noonan, marketing director for the league, created a whole
ad campaign, "Club and Country," around the so-called MLS strike
force that included young attacking players Donovan, Beasley, and Clint
Mathis. The league bought time during ESPN broadcasts and U.S.

Soccer enjoyed something of a coup when this group was featured, pre-World Cup, on the cover of *Sports Illustrated*.

In December of 2000, Garber went to MLS owners with an ambitious proposal. It was taking too long for the league to generate healthy revenues. It needed to look elsewhere, to form a global broadcasting unit, which would compete for international matches and be called Soccer United Media. Garber pitched the idea of buying the rights to the 2002 World Cup from a German media company, Kirch, which had not yet finalized the sale of those matches. Close ties with FIFA helped close the deal. "If not for that development, MLS wouldn't be here," Garber said. "Our ability to monetize the non-MLS businesses around the country is funding the needs of the league. So that's a massive, pivotal moment in history of this sport in this country. We produced those games, sold it to ESPN, got us into the soccer marketing business. That's all very much World Cup connected."

The 2002 Korea/Japan World Cup was a disjointed affair in a faraway time zone, in many ways confounding. Teams were generally stuck in one country or another, and had no real feel for what was happening over on the other island. American journalists stationed in Korea could not see England or Italy play their first-round matches in Japan, unless they flew over salt water and dealt with airport hassles.

Such inconveniences were lost on the U.S. team, lodged in a fancy J.W. Marriott hotel in Seoul. The Americans were unseeded again, dumped into a fairly hopeless group along with the home side, Korea, plus Portugal and Poland. Every host nation since the start of the World Cup had advanced to at least the second round, so it seemed Korea would probably finish among the top two in the division. Portugal, with star Luis Figo, was ranked number five in the world by FIFA, even if its golden generation of players was a bit past its peak. Poland was another big, physical Eastern European side that presented such unique problems for the Americans. Most experts picked the U.S. to repeat its last-place group finish of 1998.

There was cause for cautious optimism though. A new generation of young stars, some schooled in the nascent MLS, was coming of age. Beasley and Donovan were both swift wing midfield attackers. Clint

Mathis was quirky, but a creative finisher, while veterans Earnie Stewart and Cobi Jones offered speed up top. Eddie Lewis had a left foot, an invaluable asset. John O'Brien, healthy at last, was a technically brilliant midfielder. Brian McBride was a tough man to budge in the box. The defense was anchored by Eddie Pope, Pablo Mastroeni, and Tony Sanneh, each with his own plusses. Brad Friedel was a world-class goalkeeper. There was depth on the bench, providing personnel options for Arena depending on the opponent. But again, much would hinge on the tone set by the very first match. And that first game would be played against Portugal, the highest-ranked team in the group. This could easily have devolved into another Germany-in-Paris disaster. The match was expected to be one-sided and was a tough local sell, as the Koreans filled some seats with volunteers, assigned to cheer on one team or the other.

What happened next at quarter-empty Suwon World Cup Stadium on June 5, 2002, remains astounding in retrospect. The Portuguese were a seasoned group of professionals who had performed in matches at the highest level. Figo wasn't the only international star on this side. There were players in these maroon jerseys from the Italian, Spanish, and Portuguese top divisions. Rui Costa was a thirty-year-old star for A.C. Milan. The back line appeared sturdy enough on paper: Petit was a strong defensive midfielder for Benfica. Beto was a mainstay central defender for Sporting Lisbon, and Jorge Costa was a solid marker for Charlton Athletic in England. Yet despite this sort of high-level professional opposition, the Americans stormed out to a 3–0 lead within the first thirty-six minutes, after an impossibly dreamlike sequence of events. Portugal's famously elegant game unraveled almost from the start, beginning with O'Brien's rebound goal just four minutes into the match. Stewart's corner was redirected by McBride's head flick, and then O'Brien converted the carom after a clumsy save by Portuguese keeper Vitor Baia. Twenty-five minutes later, Donovan's cross deflected off the head of defender Costa for an own goal when Baia failed to protect the inside post. In the thirty-sixth minute, Sanneh delivered a perfect cross to McBride poised in front of the goal. The target man performed his specialty, a header for the third goal.

Arena had prepared his team for many things, but never, ever drilled these American upstarts on protecting a three-goal lead against Portugal. This was, after all, the same U.S. team that had scored exactly once in its previous five World Cup matches, and hadn't defeated a European team in the tournament since 1950. There were inevitably anxious moments as the Portuguese crept back with a goal by Beto in the thirty-eighth minute. Jeff Agoos was guilty of an own goal in the seventy-first minute, when it suddenly seemed things might slip away. Instead of incriminations, however, Agoos was offered only support by teammates. Slowly, surely, time ran out on this 3–2 upset. The Americans righted themselves, then walked off with the biggest upset of the tournament in their first match. "To be ahead three-nothing on anybody, let alone Portugal . . . ," Donovan said. "But we thought, 'Why can't we beat 'em? We're all soccer players.'" There was some logic to the result, once it played out. Portugal was no doubt the technically superior side, and possessed the ball 57 percent of the time. Yet in their own way the Americans, young and direct, were too fast for the Portuguese defenders. Figo was clearly aching, and easily contained on the left side by Sanneh. "The Americans prepared for this for six months, and we just came together," said Antonio Oliveira, the Portuguese coach whose job was suddenly in grave danger.

The U.S. next faced the host, Korea, in a far more charged atmosphere before a sellout crowd of 60,778 at Daegu. Red-clad Koreans gathered outside the stadium hours before the match, playfully taunting American supporters. A small sit-in outside the gates was not a protest against unpopular U.S. Army bases inside South Korea, but rather about disorganized ticket distribution. Arena demonstrated surprising flexibility by starting Mathis in place of Stewart. Mathis was an enormous, distinctive talent, but had long ago alienated himself from the American coaches with his lighthearted approach to practices—and, arguably, to life. When he moved into his new condo in West Paterson, NJ, Mathis spoke with great enthusiasm about building a state-of-the-art bar and party room in the basement that might be featured on MTV. This was the sort of stuff that drove coaches crazy, and then Mathis did himself no favors by shaving his head into a Mohawk for the World

Cup. He looked absolutely deranged, like Travis Bickel in *Taxi Driver*. Mathis found himself benched for the opener. But Arena went with Mathis against Korea, and was rewarded spectacularly. In the twenty-fourth minute, Mathis took John O'Brien's looping pass and scored on a nifty two-touch volley finish. A goal out of thin air—vintage stuff from the lurking Mathis. It was a gorgeous goal, the prettiest of any American score in modern World Cup history. And then the U.S. held on for dear life. The South Koreans flubbed a penalty kick in the thirty-ninth minute, after a marginal call against Agoos. Friedel, the goalkeeper, noticed that the Koreans were unsure among themselves who should take the kick. "They switched three shooters," Friedel said. "It made me feel better. It meant one or two weren't ready." Lee Eul-yong reluctantly stepped to the spot, for a team that didn't really believe in individual heroics. Friedel faked to his left, read the shot to the right, dived, and made the save. A follow by Kim Nam Il went wide. South Korea attacked hard to earn a 1–1 draw. Friedel made two brilliant reaction saves, one with his right glove and the other with his leg. The Koreans were understandably displeased with this result, after firing fifteen shots on goal to six for the U.S. Their players rushed past the media, without speaking. "We deserved to win, 3–1 or 4–1, because we created so many beautiful chances, though not one hundred percent chances," said Guus Hiddink, the Korean coach from Holland. "We were unlucky."

In the end, 60,000 fans emptied from the stadium disappointed, but knowing the Americans had cheated nobody for this tie. The only real sign of resentment came after Ahn Jung Hwan, a late substitute, scored the tying goal in the seventy-eighth minute. Ahn ran to the sidelines for his elaborately choreographed celebration, mimicking the movements of a short-track speedskater. South Korea apparently was finally gaining revenge for the disputed gold medal won at the Salt Lake City Games four months earlier by the American, Apolo Anton Ohno. The show by Ahn didn't really register with the U.S. team. "There are so many sports in the Winter Olympics, I can't even follow them," Arena said. "What's next? Frisbee on ice?" The Americans now required only another tie against Poland, mathematically eliminated, to advance to the second round. "I'm going to take it and get out of town quick and prepare for a very different opponent in Poland," Arena said, of the tie with South Korea. "We didn't just play against the Korean team. We played against a nation."

The match against Poland in Daejon turned into a clumsy paradox. Everything went wrong, before everything turned out right. The Americans fell into utter disarray while yielding two goals in the first five minutes and were defeated, 3–1. Yet the defeat set them up perfectly, somehow, for a winnable second-round match against regional rival, Mexico. "A great day for U.S. soccer," Freidel said. "A lucky day for U.S. soccer." The man of the match was not Friedel, who saved another penalty kick, or Donovan, who finally scored the sole U.S. goal in the eighty-third minute. It was, instead, an Argentine referee named Ángel Sánchez, who quite correctly sent off two Portuguese players more than one hundred miles away in Incheon. By doing this, Sánchez gave South Korea ample opportunity to score against Portugal, which Park Ji Sung eventually did. And because of that result, the U.S. (1–1–1) was able to nip Portugal (1–2) in the Group D standings for second place. The two matches were played simultaneously, creating great confusion in the stadium and on the field. The Korean fans watching the U.S. game cheered mightily at reports of Park's goal. The Americans, even while playing, were trying to sort out the scores. "I'm thinking, 'What the heck's going on?'" Donovan said. "The Korean fans are jumping around. I assumed the Koreans scored and then I looked over to the bench and saw the [U.S.] guys shaking hands congratulating each other. It sure was different." Cobi Jones began to relay the score from the bench to the players on the field, and the Americans walked off knowing they had been given a second life by their hosts. The Americans lost, but they won. And they knew their next opponent, Mexico, very well.

There was now a palpable sense of possibility unprecedented in the history of U.S. soccer. The brackets were wide open, and the U.S. was just plucky enough to take advantage.

The Americans' 2–0 second-round victory over Mexico in Jeonju might easily have turned out differently with a single whistle, because such is the power of the referee in this sport. The key moment arrived in the fifty-fifth minute, with the U.S. nursing a one-goal lead and the

Mexicans relentlessly attacking, creating three successive corner kick opportunities. Finally, as the ball curled inward again toward the goal, John O'Brien, inside the box, clearly punched it out of harm's way with his fist. The world awaited the penalty call and a possible red card from referee Vitor Melo Pereira of Portugal. Inexplicably, they never materialized. The U.S was safe, sound, and on its way to its first World Cup quarterfinal in seventy-two years. "Forty-thousand people saw the hand ball but one didn't," said Aguirre, the fiery Mexican coach. "That would have changed the game. They were lucky." Maybe. But there were plenty of other big plays and turning points. "You know how many calls there are in the tournament?" Arena said. "We weren't lucky."

There were many calls, but few improbable runs like this one from the Americans. Arena had engineered this upset with a switch in formations, and with an important reassignment in responsibilities for a key midfielder. He moved Reyna away from the creative center midfielder role to the right flank in a 3–5–2 formation, a position Reyna had played comfortably with Glasgow Rangers. And at long last, with some space, Reyna lived up to his billing in a major World Cup match. "I'm not a player who's going to break down the defense in the box," Reyna said. "But when I got the ball, I just ran and kept going." He set up the first U.S. goal, the one that turned the match on its ear and sent the low-scoring Mexicans into a panic. Reyna dribbled down the right flank in the eighth minute, beating Ramón Morales, then crossed the ball deep to Josh Wolff, whose one-touch back pass to McBride was knocked in from fourteen yards. Reyna would humble Morales so often along the wing that Aguirre used up one of his substitutions to remove Morales from the match in the twenty-eighth minute. From then on, the Americans relied more on counters than organized attacks to keep their opponents honest.

One of those U.S. forays created the second goal, when Donovan headed in a perfect cross from Lewis on the left side in the sixty-fourth minute. That was enough of a cushion, because Arena's three-center-back plan disrupted the Mexicans' favorite strategy of sending balls into the box for their target man, Jared Borgetti. Mexico became frustrated, committing some chippy fouls, and ended up playing with ten men after captain Rafael Márquez was red-carded for a head-butt on Cobi Jones. Following the final whistle, only the gracious forward Cuauhtemoc Blanco shook the Americans' hands, trading jerseys with Tony Sanneh. "We don't have the best footballers in the world, but we make up for it in heart," Pablo Mastroeni said. "We just wanted the game more."

The Germans, famous for wanting games more than anybody, were next in Ulsan in the quarterfinals. The Americans barely had time to take a deep breath or appreciate their accomplishments. This might have been a truly momentous occasion for the sport in the U.S., given a better staging time and place. Instead, the quarterfinal against Germany would be telecast back to the United States at 7:30 a.m. Eastern Time, played halfway around the world before just 37,337 and plenty of empty seats at Munsu Football Stadium. The match attracted an average of 3.77 million TV homes and a 4.36 Nielsen rating on ESPN—the network's most-watched soccer telecast ever. It could have been much bigger still, if only this had been a World Cup in Europe or the U.S.

Regardless of the hour, the 1–0 loss to Germany was a very good show. The Americans were never outclassed. Arena threw virtually every attacking player he had onto the pitch by the end: McBride, Donovan, Stewart, Mathis, and Jones all had their minutes. The Americans outshot Germany, 11–6; led in shots on goal, 6–2; were even on corners, 6–6. Most surprisingly, the U.S. earned possession 58 percent of the time. The Americans outplayed mighty Germany for much of the match, beat their opponents to the ball, and scared them plenty in the penalty box. Still, they failed to score.

The U.S. had several chances in the first half off counters, as Reyna repeatedly freed Donovan on through passes and loops past the slower German defenders. Donovan, however, had not faced a goalkeeper like Oliver Kahn before in the tournament, and this proved a huge difference. Kahn made a diving glove save off a Donovan left footer in the seventeenth minute, then cut down the angle and saved another Donovan shot in the thirtieth minute on a clear breakaway. Slowly, the Germans played their way back into a match that lacked rhythm, though never effort. Soon, they threatened on a series of dangerous corners and free kicks. In the thirty-ninth minute, after a foul by Eddie Lewis, Christian Ziege curled one of those free kicks in front of the net, where the six-foot, three-inch Michael Ballack found just enough space between Sanneh and Berhalter to launch his header for a goal. Being down a goal to Germany is not unlike trailing by a run in baseball to a young, rested Mariano Rivera. The Germans owned the institutional memory, the legs, and the brawn to lock down a match. Still, this wouldn't prove easy against the Americans.

Down a goal, the U.S. came out hard after the halftime break. A corner kick resulted in a scramble near the German net and Gregg Berhalter squibbed a shot off the fearsome goalkeeper Kahn. The ball struck the left arm of midfielder Torsten Frings, who was standing on the goal line, before it was gobbled up by Kahn. The handball didn't appear to be intentional, and it was unclear whether Scottish referee Hugh Dallas had spotted the contact.

"I don't want to sound like a sore loser, but I saw the play and it should have been a red card and a penalty kick," Sanneh said, of the pivotal non-call in the forty-ninth minute. "It was clear. And the way we had pressure on them, I don't think they could have held with ten men." What goes around comes around. Even Sanneh admitted that. The Americans had been extremely fortunate in their second-round match with Mexico to get away with a non-call on that handball by O'Brien in the box. There was one last, failed opportunity: Sanneh missed a final opportunity in the eighty-eighth minute, when a perfect cross from Mathis grazed Eddie Lewis's hair and caused Sanneh to slightly mistime his own header. The ball crashed into the side of the net, rather than inside the near post.

"The big countries still get a lot more respect than the little ones," Arena moaned, also complaining about five yellow cards. "I didn't realize we were so strong, but the Germans were falling all over the place." The Germans were not pretty to watch but, as usual, the three-time World Cup champions were efficient enough to gain the required result. Again, they relied on superb goalkeeping by Kahn—"The man of the match," said his counterpart, Friedel—and enough headers off set plays to keep them afloat. "It's amazing what fitness and power the Americans had on two days' less rest," Kahn said, looking back at the match. "I was absolutely exhausted."

The tournament was done for the Americans, who exited proudly. In the end, however, precious little had changed. Arena, being an American coach, received no irresistible offers from international clubs and returned with U.S. Soccer for another four years. MLS continued its slow growth, mostly through franchise expansion. And when it was time to seed teams for the 2006 World Cup, the Americans were left out in the cold again.

One thing was different, though. U.S. players now fanned out across Europe to earn good livings on professional teams abroad. An invitation to participate on America's national team was becoming a reward for accomplishments on foreign clubs, just as it was in most other countries.

CHAPTER 26

The Professional

CRAVEN COTTAGE MAY SOUND LIKE EDGAR ALLAN POE'S CREAKY old domicile, but it is really a quaint London soccer stadium on the banks of the Thames, adjacent to verdant, bustling Bishop's Park. Fulham has played its home matches inside this red-brick treasure since 1896, although the place underwent significant alterations over the decades in order to keep up with rising safety standards. The crowd capacity was cut in half to just over 25,000, when a fresh set of league rules required seats and a smidgeon of civility for all spectators. Soccer riots in England were increasingly frowned upon.

Fulham had a recent history of signing American stars like Brian McBride, Carlos Bocanegra, and Clint Dempsey, who arrived at a cheaper price than those from many other countries. It was a club more concerned with maintaining its Premier League status than winning trophies. By sheer economics, Fulham couldn't compete for players with well-financed giants such as Manchester United, Liverpool, Arsenal, or Chelsea. Instead, club officials sought promising alternatives. If these young bargains turned into great successes, Fulham could potentially turn around and sell them for hefty transfer fees. But in the meantime, it was essential for the club to remain in the Premier League, to avoid the final three places that resulted in relegation. Only in this way would Fulham maintain prestige, attendance, and its share in the bounty of television money.

At the start of the 2009–2010 season, Americans Clint Dempsey and Eddie Johnson were both on the roster, though Dempsey's status was far more assured. It was Dempsey's goal against Liverpool in 2007 that rescued Fulham from relegation—a fate that would have cost celebrity owner Mohamed Al Fayed millions in television rights revenue. Dempsey scored six goals the next season, and was rewarded in May 2008, with a contract extension through 2010. The best was yet to come. In the derby against nearby Chelsea that December, he produced his finest match as a Premier professional. Dempsey chested and then knocked a ball past goalkeeper Petr Cech for a 1–0 lead. After the favored Blues went ahead, 2–1, Dempsey scored the equalizer in the eighty-ninth minute on a brilliant, fade-away header off a Simon Davies corner. He scored seven more goals during the 2008-2009 season. Overall, his assimilation since coming over from the New England Revolution had been remarkably smooth. The fit was perfect.

"Just one long, steady step forward," was the way his amiable manager, Roy Hodgson, put it. "Nothing but progress." Dempsey had landed precisely in the right spot, unlike so many other exiled American players. He was playing quality football against top opponents. Fulham was a solid, improving side that had finished seventh in 2009, yet the club did not boast the sort of high-end payroll that supported an endless search for the next great thing. Too many Americans had been buried on benches, or sent out on fruitless loans, when they aspired too high. There was a sense of stability with Hodgson at Fulham.

After a midsummer's training session in the old stadium, Dempsey leaned against a rail by the clubhouse tunnel to speak with a familiar American sportswriter. Dempsey was a homebody by nature, a long way from home. He would have preferred to be playing his soccer in a high-level domestic league—better yet, in Texas. But even when he was seeing only limited time at Fulham back in 2006, Dempsey never thought about returning to MLS. "This is what I want to do," he said. "I already experienced all I could in the MLS. I wanted to learn something new. I'm not going back. I don't see much point in that. You always have to move forward, go as high as you can. Get the most you can out of your career. You don't come back and take the spot of a young kid trying to make it. Of course I say that now. Who's to say when I'm older? But right now my mentality is I'm not coming back. The difference between here and the

States is the passion that the fans have—not to take anything away from the fans in the States. It's growing and it's getting stronger there. But you feel the passion that these people have for each of their clubs and how they can sing in unison. That goes for all the clubs here in England. You don't see that in the States. You'll see sections here and there. But you don't see a whole stadium singing in unison. I think it has to do with tradition. It's difficult to all of a sudden try to make a song for a team and keep with it over time. You have to have your own identity. That's what the American clubs are still trying to find."

Dempsey's media treatment overseas was, if anything, better than at home, where his efforts on defense were sometimes questioned. English reporters covering the team said Dempsey was a player's player. Nothing fancy, but he produced a high work rate and was willing to do anything at any position to see more time on the pitch. "He doesn't really have any tricks, does he?" said Steve Stammers of the *Mirror*. "But he'll play anywhere. He'll give you the effort and never kick up a fuss." Here in South London, Dempsey finally concluded that his best position was at wide midfield, not at forward. By American standards, his first touch was impeccable, practically elegant. The Brits weren't quite satisfied, however. Stammers simply reported his technique was "getting better."

One thing everyone agreed upon: Dempsey had the world's worst game face. He was not Zinedine Zidane, not by a long shot. Dempsey's visage was flat, mopey. His eyes forever appeared tired, world-weary. The first impression, completely deceptive, might lead one to believe Dempsey was unmotivated and lacking in ardor. And maybe that's why people had underestimated him his whole life, how he had fooled them all from East Texas to Craven Cottage. He had never been the chosen one, even within his own family back in Nacogdoches, Texas. There, five children had grown up in a trailer parked in his grandparents' backyard, while his father, Aubrey, took on an assortment of odd jobs. Clint stood third then in the sibling queue behind his older sister, Jennifer, and brother, Ryan. He was eager to perform, to please, but willing to wait his turn.

Dempsey learned his soccer in a fashion more familiar to South and Central Americans than to North Americans. He kicked around any ball he could find on a dirt field, often playing barefoot with and against the local Hispanic kids. At age ten he went with his father to a tryout in Dallas, three hours away, to audition for a team called the Longhorns. Clint was a temperamental kid, his dad warned the coach. But even back then, he had an impressive first touch. He was quickly enrolled, and the family was recruited alongside him to provide transportation and expenses. It was a costly venture for the Dempseys' modest resources. The father sold his boat, sold his guns, to pay for training and commuting costs. "I always felt I had to show my parents that I gave everything I had," Dempsey told ESPN before the 2006 World Cup. "They're the ones who were making those trips, who were sacrificing so much for me. The whole family was. I'd be out on the field, look over, and know that they're the ones busting their butts. That's always motivated me. Still does."

When it became clear that his sister Jennifer had tremendous tennis talent, Clint was forced to drop out of club soccer so that his sister could be afforded the proper coaching. That was the plan, anyway. Jennifer, a state-ranked tennis player, would become the family's world-class athlete. But then in 1995, Jennifer died of a brain aneurysm at age sixteen. The family scrambled to put its lives back together. The tragedy struck Clint Dempsey particularly hard.

"Before she passed away, we had talks about death," Dempsey said. "And I remember her telling me that if something ever happened to her, she'd help me score goals. She'd help them go in the net." Dempsey later wrote a note to his sister and placed it in a vase on her grave. His mother found it, read it. For the rest of his life, he promised, every goal Clint scored he would look to the sky and think about Jennifer. The death might have sapped a good deal of energy and resolve from Dempsey. Instead it inspired him to become the family's new flagship athlete.

When he looked for role models, he was never that interested in the more famous European soccer players, but found himself drawn to the flair of the South Americans. "It's hotter down there, and the pace is slower," Dempsey said. "I loved watching players like Diego Maradona and Carlos Valderrama. Give them space and they can do amazing things." When he was eleven years old, he hoped and planned to watch his idol, Maradona, play in the 1994 World Cup down in Dallas. The Argentine star was disqualified for drug use before that match against Bulgaria in the Cotton Bowl. Dempsey was heartbroken. He kept playing, though, and his uncommon path resulted in an unconventional style not easily classified. Dempsey could effectively play central midfield, wide midfield, or forward. He was rarely the fastest player on the field, but his first step was more than quick enough and his technical skills were strong. He could turn or spin on a ball with considerable craft. His field vision was outstanding. Like Clint Mathis before him, Dempsey was an effective lurker, reading the play as it developed ahead of him and pouncing on scoring opportunities. He was also fearless with his own head in a crowded goal mouth.

Dempsey never attended Bradenton Academy, an efficient enough training ground but a bit formulaic in its own way. So there were creative kinks to his game that were never groomed out of his arsenal. He starred on his Nacogdoches High School team—an outdated notion— leading the hometown school to a 54–2–3 mark during his final three seasons. Then he went straight on to college, playing three seasons for Furman University, scoring seventeen goals with nineteen assists in sixty-two games while the Paladins captured two Southern Conference titles and one Top ten ranking. He finished among the top four scorers on Furman for all three seasons, which was very nice but hardly predicted the sort of career that was forthcoming. Dempsey was drafted eighth by the New England Revolution of MLS in 2004. At the age of twenty-one, he signed a relatively modest four-year contract worth about $40,000 annually. Not exactly a jackpot, but an opportunity to garner attention and gain access to a larger stage.

Dempsey was an immediate hit in Foxborough as an attacking midfielder, scoring seven goals that first season while elected MLS Rookie of the Year. He suffered a broken jaw during the season, playing with the injury for two matches before he was diagnosed. He also blew the decisive penalty kick during a shootout against D.C. United in a semifinal playoff match. But then during the MLS All-Star Game in 2005, he scored the winning goal against Fulham, making an impression with the club that would greatly benefit him later. By 2006, Dempsey was an acknowledged star and beginning to act the part. He coveted a transfer to a European side, and behaved at times in a condescending, volatile fashion all too familiar to MLS coaches. Dempsey had a temper, and was doing nothing to curb it. During that 2006 season, he was twice suspended by the league for violent acts against opponents. In March, he had a significant run-in with his teammate and New England captain Joe Franchino, who collided with Dempsey during a scrimmage. Dempsey threw an elbow at Franchino. They screamed at each other, and then Dempsey punched Franchino several times before the two wrestled to the ground. When the two teammates ran into each other at the training center shortly thereafter, there was another confrontation. Franchino's face was badly bruised, his left eye swollen. Dempsey was suspended for two weeks by the club. Perhaps more punitive: He was dropped from the U.S. national team that traveled to Dortmund in a World Cup tuneup against Germany.

Eventually, Dempsey was included on the national roster by Arena and started the second and third matches at the 2006 World Cup, scoring the only goal by an American in the tournament during a loss against Ghana. He paid for his family to come over to watch those matches, feeling he owed them so much more than that. The World Cup also provided him with an international stage and fresh promotional opportunities. Dempsey was able to combine his love of rap music with a big-time ad campaign. Calling himself by his hip-hop nickname, "Deuce," Dempsey debuted a commercial rap video, *Don't Tread*, for Nike with Texas rappers XO and Big Hawk. He dedicated the song to Jennifer, and the video ended with Dempsey placing a flower on her grave. After his successful World Cup, reports surfaced about interest from European teams. He trained with Feyenoord in the Dutch league. Charlton Athletic offered MLS a transfer fee of $1.5 million. The league turned it down, which did not please Dempsey at all. By this time, he told reporters he'd quit MLS for good at the end of his contract. He hoped this would convince league officials to sell him immediately, while they could still get a decent return. "Let the kid go," said his teammate, Taylor Twellman, who was hoping to negotiate a raise from his own $120,000 salary. Finally in December 2006, Fulham made an impressive offer: $4 million, the largest transfer fee at the time in the history of MLS. A month later, Dempsey had his freedom and a work permit from the United Kingdom.

Dempsey would go about the business of being a reliable professional, speaking his mind only when necessary. He had thought it essential to discuss tactics with Bob Bradley at the Confederations Cup, and their conversation resulted in a revitalized player. Dempsey won the Bronze Ball as the third-best player in that high-level tournament, scoring three goals. In general, he viewed his role on any soccer team very clinically, in a detached manner. These players, these coaches around him—they weren't his family. They were business associates.

"It's the same with Fulham and the national team," Dempsey said. "You have a job to do. Over time, your relationship strengthens if you're around people more often. But what brings you together is the battles out there playing hard on the field. At the end of the day, you have your own family you're spending your time with. When I'm done with training I'm not going out with the guys. I mean every now and then we get together and do something. Maybe one of the guys will play golf. But it's not every single day I'm hanging out with everybody."

Dempsey lived at nearby Wimbledon in Southwest London and now had the financial wherewithal to fly his closest relatives to Fulham home matches every second or third week. He brought them also to national team matches in the States. "I see them more now than when I was in MLS," he said. Dempsey wouldn't talk about his late sister with teammates, however. "I honor her," he said. "And I talk about her when people ask me questions about her. It's not my thing talking about it with every person I see. Someone asks me about it, I have no problem talking about it. But it's not like 'I'm here, news flash, let me tell you about my life.' This is a business, man. You're not making best friends here. You've got friends you're close with, but you're not sitting there telling them all about your family. You keep that to yourself."

Dempsey had come to terms with being a professional soccer player in England. And while he spoke at Craven Cottage, the other American there was still hoping to benefit from such an example. Eddie Johnson was the last man off the practice pitch this day, still juggling balls while others had already showered and changed. He was trying to make an impression with Hodgson, to earn some important minutes again. At one time, not so long ago, he had been America's great hope at forward.

Eddie Johnson arrived at the 2006 World Cup in Germany with great promise and major bling; with fashion accessories never seen before on a U.S. national soccer player: Two diamond earrings. A swooping silver necklace and matching bracelet. A glittering, oversized watch. He was, at last, a fine example of the inner city talent pool that had eluded American soccer scouts for decades. He could run so fast and play attacking soccer so powerfully that he was projected as a national team star of a completely different stripe. Johnson was black, and he was once very poor.

"I was always asking for money from my mom, from my aunts, begging from older people in the projects," Johnson said, about growing up in Bunnell, Florida. "The projects were built around suburban houses, not like New York, not like Queens. But when I got two dollars, that was a lot. It was tough, but I got to learn about life."

This was a standard, urban fairy tale in other American professional sports, which represented the pot at the end of the rainbow for low-income athletes and their families. Soccer, though, was different. It was rarely viewed as a reliable, lucrative escape hatch by inner-city kids with limited exposure to the sport. Johnson's mother, Lewanna, raised three children through fortitude and the aid of food stamps. Then Johnson found a developmental soccer program, the Ormond Beach Jaguars, at age ten, discovered a coach named Bob Sawyer, and clung to the sport like a lifeline. Johnson learned about Pelé, discovered that he was black and a great soccer hero. From then on, when there was trouble, Johnson darted from it. He had a thick scar on his right ear, just behind the gold ring, to remind him about one earlier encounter. He was in a Daytona Beach club when a few cousins—"thugs," he called them, much later—got into trouble with another group of kids. Johnson, fifteen years old at the time, made the mistake of returning to the place again another night, and was recognized by the rival group. "I was jumped by about ten guys," he said. "Needed to get my ears stitched up."

There were surely others like Johnson out in the projects, playing basketball and football mostly, getting lost along the way too often. They could have been soccer stars, too, Johnson believed. They could have ended up with an $875,000 salary, as he did in MLS. He remembered one friend in particular.

"He's incarcerated now, but he was an unbelievable basketball player, an unbelievable athlete," Johnson said. "He started playing soccer with me, and in one year he picked it up so good, I thought he could be amazing. The talent is there in the inner city. It's just a matter of time when those guys will be getting the chance I got."

After Johnson caught the eye of important coaches, he was invited to train at the Bradenton Academy and became a regular call-up on the U-17 team. By age seventeen, he was drafted by the Dallas Burn of the MLS as a Project 40 developmental player in the second round of the 2001 MLS Super Draft. For three seasons, he hardly got off the bench, scoring a total of seven goals in that time. But then he was a star at the 2003 Youth Championship held in the United Arab Emirates, netting four goals to win the Golden Shoe. At age twenty-one, Johnson scored seven goals in seven matches with the senior national team, an unprecedented debut on the international stage. Then he suffered a stress fracture in his big toe, became a father to a daughter, Zoe, and lost considerable momentum. U.S. coaches badly needed Johnson to complement the team's more conventional, slower scoring targets like Brian McBride or Brian Ching. Later, Bob Bradley would use Charlie Davies to fill this speed role. Johnson was 6-feet, 180 pounds, tough to knock off any ball. He didn't have the greatest field vision, yet when he was at his best, in 2005, he could alter defenses. He could score a hat trick against Panama, coming off the bench, as he did at RFK Stadium.

Coaches didn't necessarily trust Johnson's experience at the highest levels of international play. Johnson liked to talk about being "in the zone," but Arena and Bradley were always more concerned about whether a player was "on form," a status measured by recent performances or benchings in MLS or abroad. In Johnson's case, his professional career was extremely uneven. He was successful enough in MLS, scoring a total of 41 goals there over eight seasons. But he could never quite establish himself as a regular player overseas, despite several flirtations and false starts. In August, 2006, he was nearly sent to Real Sociedad of La Liga in Spain on a year-long loan, but then the Kansas City Wizards pulled out of the deal, fearing they would alienate their fan base. He played only limited minutes for the U.S. at the 2006 World Cup in Germany. He agreed to train during the MLS offseason with Reading of the Premier League, and returned to form in 2007 with Kansas City, scoring successive hat tricks in May. Johnson was still a very marketable commodity, but vetoed a deal to go to Derby of the Premier League after MLS had accepted $6 million in transfer fees from the English club. Finally, he completed a complicated three-year contract with Fulham in January, 2008. But Hodgson was not impressed and Johnson appeared in only nine matches, failing to score a single goal. He was loaned out to Cardiff City for the 2008-2009 season, playing in the second-tier Championship division. Even at this level, he was not a starter.

Johnson was back with Fulham in the summer of 2009, hoping to impress Hodgson. He scored a few goals and assisted on others during a series of five exhibitions. He was training hard. "He's finally learning what it's like to be a professional football player in England," Hodgson said. "And that's not easy. I'm starting to see in him the sort of stuff that we saw when we first signed him."

There was hope for Johnson, though time was running out. At the close of 2009, Johnson was loaned by Fulham to Aris Thessaloniki in Greece. He was twenty-five years old, and would be twenty-six in 2010. South Africa would be his last World Cup opportunity, surely. And when Bob Bradley announced his twenty-man roster for the upcoming qualifier in Mexico City, Dempsey was on it. Johnson was not.

CHAPTER 27

Azteca Blues

NEXT ON THE QUALIFYING DOCKET WAS THE BIG ONE, *EL Tamale Grande*, the match at Mexico City on August 12, 2009; a chance to break with history and gain swift redemption for the 5–0 leveling suffered by the young reserves at Giants Stadium in the Gold Cup. Because of his personal history in this rivalry, Donovan was already assured of grabbing center stage down there. Then in the run-up for this match, Donovan became something of a headline magnet. Some of this was sad, some of it was silly, and much of it unfortunately obscured the fact that Donovan was playing the best soccer of his life both for the national team and for the Los Angeles Galaxy.

His three-year marriage to actress Bianca Kajlich was falling apart. *People* magazine broke the unhappy news that Donovan and Kajlich had agreed to an amicable separation. They both were busy working at their demanding careers. The split would allow him, Donovan said, to pursue guilt-free any offers overseas in the winter. "Well, I do have dogs," he said, thinking again. Most other times, such a split with a celebrity wife might be the lead item for any soccer player. In this instance, however, Donovan was making bigger headlines about a feud with that most famous of footballers, David Beckham.

Because of his bent for frankness, Donovan all too commonly became involved in these kinds of combative back-and-forth swipes. Sometimes he threw the first verbal volley, while at other times he merely answered. When Eric Wynalda commented on the Fox Soccer

Channel that Donovan didn't score his goals in the toughest matches, Donovan shot back in *USA Today*, "I think everybody in the soccer world knows the jealousy issues that Eric carries. I don't think two seconds about what Eric has to say."

From an international viewpoint, nobody really cared much what Wynalda thought of Donovan; or Donovan of Wynalda. Beckham was an entirely different story. He was a household celebrity in every nook and cranny of the soccer universe. Donovan had granted a prideful interview with *Sports Illustrated* soccer reporter Grant Wahl, who wrote a comprehensive best seller entitled *The Beckham Experiment*. During their talk, Donovan contended the English star hadn't been much of a teammate on the Galaxy during the 2008 season. Beckham, who had displaced Donovan as captain on the club, skipped optional practices and didn't bother to join the team when he was suspended.

"All that we care about at a minimum is that he committed himself to us," Donovan told Wahl. "As time has gone on, that has not proven to be the case in many ways—on the field, off the field. Does the fact that he earns that much money come into it? Yeah. If someone's paying you more than anybody in the league, more than *double* anybody in the league, the least we expect is that you show up to every game, whether you're suspended or not. Show up and train hard. Show up and play hard. Maybe he's not a leader, maybe he's not a captain. Fair enough. But at a minimum you should bust your ass every day. That hasn't happened. And I don't think that's too much for us to expect. Especially when he's brought all this on us."

A good part of this friction was surely due to the Galaxy's disappointing performance in 2008. And then there was the Brit's decision to abandon the Galaxy for the Italian club AC Milan. Beckham had forced a loan deal from the Galaxy to Milan from January through mid-July, financing his own transfer fee to make it happen. Beckham's motives were admirable enough. He was unashamedly dedicated to England's national team. At the time he first signed with the Galaxy, Beckham had been banished from England's side by the coach, Steve McLaren. Beckham figured he was finished with the national team, and set out on a fresh frontier, America. Then McLaren was fired, Fabio Capello of Italy was hired, and suddenly Beckham was back in favor. He was also playing his pro soccer 7,000 miles away in Los Angeles against competition that wasn't going to impress Capello. He needed to restore his credentials, and the best way was through this loan deal with Milan.

"I'm an honest person," Beckham said, during a press conference at a Hoboken hotel before the Galaxy faced the Red Bulls at Giants Stadium. "If I didn't want to be here, I wouldn't. I'm a very committed person. My whole career, my whole life, is soccer. I want to be involved in the World Cup. I haven't hidden that fact."

Beckham remained a fascinating athlete, a niche midfielder with the unique ability to create goals from a mid-range set piece or a run along the flank. Place a dime on the pitch, Beckman could cross the ball off Franklin Roosevelt's brow. His speed, work rate, and track-back prowess were more questionable, and had commonly soured his relationship with coaches. Beckham sold tickets, he turned Donovan into a scoring machine, but he couldn't always win matches when backed by $30,000-a-year MLS semi-pros on defense. Beckham's early injuries and all the Galaxy's losses severely hampered his relationship with Donovan. Now Beckham and Donovan had become inexorably linked—not only on the field, but as defendant and accuser. Eventually, things were worked out. Beckham met with Donovan after a match against Chivas, at the suggestion and arrangement of Bruce Arena, the Galaxy's coach. Arena was calling himself "Dr. Phil," mediating between these two international stars. The two players forged a peace treaty, although Beckham remained bewildered that a teammate would blindside him like this in the media. Such things rarely happened in Europe, where press access was severely limited and where the most important interviews were generally performed only for a substantial fee.

"Landon apologized," Beckham said. "I told him our view of things. We're both men. We don't take it on the field. Now we go play our soccer. At the end of the day, you get on with it. I've been criticized by Pelé before, by George Best before." The implication, perhaps, was that Donovan was neither Pelé nor Best and had yet to earn the right to snipe.

Beckham and Donovan appeared together and made nice at a post-match podium together, following the Galaxy's 3–1 trouncing of the pathetic Red Bulls. The Galaxy was a harmonious machine, in comparison to its disorganized opponents. Beckham played seventy minutes and his corner kick eventually led to Donovan's seventh goal of the season in the thirty-first minute, a pretty twenty-eight-yard volley, for a two-goal lead. An embrace followed between Becks and Donovan, as if nothing had ever gone wrong between the two fellows. "It was fantastic," Donovan said afterward. "With players like that you don't worry about chemistry because he sees the game the same way." The Galaxy would continue winning plenty of games, nearly capturing the MLS title, mostly because of a revamped defense, led by veteran Gregg Berhalter and rookie Omar Gonzalez on the back line and Donovan Ricketts in goal. Arena did a remarkable job rebuilding this team, earning MLS Coach of the Year honors while Harkes dubbed him, "the manager of managers" on national television. The Galaxy of 2009 allowed half as many goals as it did in 2008. Winning was the greatest ego balm of all. It allowed Beckham and Donovan to believe that each had fully transformed into somebody completely different. Donovan came to think Beckham was now fully committed to the Galaxy, while Beckham felt Donovan now understood the sanctity of teammate relationships.

In late summer, the two stars briefly went their separate ways for national team duties. It was on to Mexico for Donovan, who still had several headlines left in him. The Americans decided to train in Florida, then fly to Mexico City at the last possible moment, which was the afternoon before the match on Wednesday, August 12. Ideally, the U.S. team would have assembled a couple of weeks beforehand in a high-altitude setting such as Denver. This would have given the players' bodies the necessary time to acclimate to the thinner oxygen. But this was an impossible time frame for these athletes, who were all playing club matches on the weekend leading up to the Mexico game.

"We have worked for a long time with different experts regarding altitude training, including the U.S. Olympic Committee," Bob Bradley said. "The research that stuck with us is that if you don't have enough time to acclimatize—which usually takes about ten days—going in late is the best bet." If the U.S. team had practiced in Mexico City for two days, instead of training in Florida, the players would have had a harder time rebounding from the workouts in preparation for the match. Either way, the assignment was difficult. "Until you play in a game there, you don't fully understand what it's all about," Donovan said. "Even the flight of the ball is different. A ball you might think you'll get a head on goes over your head." The assimilation timetable was imperfect at best, but the Americans could take consolation in knowing they were not the only ones taxed by the overcrowded schedule. When it came to World Cup qualifiers, the whole world was inconvenienced. It was always worst, however, for the better national teams in North and South America, because their top players often commuted from Europe. The Americans had joined together for just two days' training in Florida from all over—a dozen from European sides—squeezing yet more soccer into schedules already far too overcrowded. It was no wonder these international matches didn't always live up to the aesthetic standards of club games. But they rattled the very bones of some nations, and Mexico was surely one of them.

"They're always tough. I don't really like making the long trips," said Dempsey, who had hurried over at the last minute after a Europa Cup match at Fulham's home grounds in Craven Cottage. "But you want to qualify for the World Cup, so you go. You give your team the best chance and you help out. Everybody's in the same situation."

Dempsey's club coach at Fulham, like everybody's coach, was not thrilled with the arrangements. Roy Hodgson very much wanted to give Dempsey more rest after the Confederations Cup in South Africa before dragging him into Fulham's preseason, the Europa Cup matches, and then these confounded qualifiers. But injuries on the roster changed those plans and Dempsey already had been worn to a nubbin at Fulham, even before this qualifying match. "Ideally, I'd love to give a player five or six weeks' rest," Hodgson said. "But I couldn't even give Clint three weeks. Fatigue becomes a factor."

There was no letting Dempsey off the hook for this Mexico match, even if he wished. He remained one of six acknowledged core players on the U.S. team, along with Donovan, Michael Bradley, Bocanegra, Onyewu, and Howard. Dempsey had played in ten of the thirteen qualifiers in the 2010 cycle. And this was, after all, the circled date on the calendar; a chance for the U.S. to defeat Mexico in Mexico City—a feat accomplished only once, by Costa Rica. The home team was desperate. Mexico stood at 2–3 in the standings after dropping its first three road matches in the Hex. If Mexico lost or tied at *Azteca*, the regional power would fall into dire qualifying trouble. This was a last stand of sorts; a final opportunity to reestablish Mexico as a dominant player in CON-CACAF. On the front sports page of *Reforma*, a conservative Mexican newspaper, there was a photo of coach Aguirre—the very same coach who had lost to the U.S. at the 2002 World Cup—lecturing his players, accompanied by the headline, "DON'T FAIL!" A cartoon showed a nervous Mexican in sombrero, tightrope-walking and dueling with a re-laxed Uncle Sam.

"I have no margin for error," the cartoon Mexican said.

"I have a parachute," Uncle Sam answered, gleefully.

That parachute was the Americans' 3–1–1 mark, which placed them a full four points atop Mexico. But Mexico had that altitude, had the history. The day before the match, while the U.S. players jetted in from Florida, Gulati held a press conference at *Hacienda de los Morales*, one of the fancier restaurants in Mexico City. Since Gulati had arrived before the team, it fell upon the federation president to represent the squad. He was in a particularly ebullient mood, even for Gulati. He had recently been invited along with FIFA president Sepp Blatter to the Oval Office at the White House for a meeting with President Obama, a supporter of the U.S. Soccer bid to stage the 2018 or 2022 World Cup. Gulati was a big fan of Obama, and was impressed the President had been briefed so well about the bid. "So Sunil, how are we going to make soccer grow in this country?" Obama had asked. It was an occasion Gulati would treas-ure, and he carried this experience and sense of momentum to the Mex-ico City press conference. About sixty journalists, almost all from Mexico, turned out for the session. The news conference was on the surface sup-posed to be a briefing on the World Cup bid. It soon turned into some-thing else: a demand by the local press and television stations for a prediction on the upcoming match. Gulati tried to be as diplomatic as possible, explaining that he firmly believed both sides would ultimately qualify. Eventually, however, Gulati was coaxed into a statement he would later regret: "I think we'll change history tomorrow," he said.

The U.S. team finally landed at the airport, easily surviving the heck-ling of one particular Mexican there who screamed, "*Cinco-zero!*" a ref-erence to the score at the Gold Cup final. The Americans would be housed at the Radisson Paraiso, only about five minutes from *Estadio Azteca*, across from a mall in the southern, urban sprawl of Mexico City. Bob Bradley, Donovan, and Bocanegra held quick interview sessions with American reporters, while avoiding contact with the Mexican media. There were already reports in the local papers that Donovan had predicted a victory, which wasn't quite true. Donovan was asked again what it felt like to be point man in this rivalry. "It used to be a little in-timidating. But what there is now is mutual respect," he said. "They're not bad people. They're always friendly away from the field." Donovan had been on a real tear since the Confederations Cup, aided by the re-turn of Beckham to the Galaxy. During the course of 2009, Donovan would score fifteen goals with seven assists for Los Angeles; five goals with ten assists for the national team. Donovan was named both the U.S. Soccer Player of the Year and Most Valuable Player of MLS—though he would miss a crucial penalty kick that in part cost the Galaxy the title in a tiebreaker loss to Real Salt Lake. Donovan refused to cat-egorize his peak form as a streak. "This is clearly the best I've ever played," he said. "I want to stress this is not something that's going away. This is me now. This is how I play."

On the eve of the match in Mexico City, Uncle Sam's Army gath-ered late into the night at Yuppie's (pronounced You-pee's) Sports Bar in the central *Zona Rosa* of the city. The fans chanted "U-S-A" and sang "Born in the USA." They sparred good-naturedly with the locals, who again countered with the cheer, "*Cinco-zero.*" Police carried semi-auto-matic rifles along the nearby blocks, assuring peace. The next day around 1 p.m. the U.S. team piled into a team bus and navigated the five-minute drive to the stadium that was now a snarled, thirty-minute odyssey through traffic jams and past gesticulating, roadside critics. Some, again, held up five fingers on one hand, zero on the other. Even a private escort of a dozen police was unable to clear the way completely. The area around *Azteca* was a madhouse; the stadium itself a cauldron. The match had been sold out for three weeks. Screeching chants, horns, and whistles bounced around a concrete ocean filled with green and red waves of spectators, more than a hundred thousand of them. Press row accommodations were a bad joke, considering the wealth of the Mexican football federation. There were inadequate power outlets, a dodgy wireless setup. The mixed zone where journalists were to meet the players after the match was dangerously narrow and overcrowded. During the game, writers sat squeezed together among fans, who had the bad habit of hurling full beer cups after every goal.

Bradley might have been expected to field the same lineup as the one that defeated Spain in the Confederations Cup. Instead he made two changes: sturdy Brian Ching would start at forward instead of Altidore, because Bradley felt Altidore was not in game shape to play the full ninety minutes and would be better coming off the bench. And Steve Cherundolo would replace Jonathan Spector on the back line, providing a bit more experience under such high-pressure circumstances. The coach was giving up some attacking dynamics with these otherwise sensible moves. Both Altidore and Spector had proven to be effective weapons in the counterattacks against Spain and Brazil. Altidore was deft at receiving a ball under tight marking, spinning on a defender, and bullying his way into the box. Spector had demonstrated a versatile talent for accurate crosses on the run.

Then, a shocker: just nine minutes into the game, Donovan set up Charlie Davies with an impeccable, in-stride through pass off a counter, catching the Mexicans short on defenders after a failed, aggressive attack. Davies settled the ball neatly with a couple of touches, blasting a twelve-yard right-footer to the far side for a goal. It was beautiful stuff from Davies, a player full of promise and pace, who had come into his own during that same summer. *Estadio Azteca* grew hauntingly quiet. This was the Americans' first lead, ever, in the place. Davies dashed for the corner flag to perform a celebratory dance, but was immediately showered with trash and required rescuing by Michael Bradley. Jubilation was a bad idea here for any opposing player, especially an American.

Such a lead, such a perfect silence, rarely endured in this sort of hostile climate. Still, despite the pressure and the altitude, here was the best opportunity for a historic victory by the visitors. The weather wasn't too hot. The air wasn't too polluted. Under a cloudless sky and on a per-fectly level lawn, the U.S. national team finally owned a lead. But the Americans would soon be pushed back too far on their heels. Control-ling pace demanded controlling the ball—which the U.S. was still un-able to accomplish under this sort of withering pressure. A sunlit moment in U.S. soccer history—the first lead ever in more than four decades playing at this unholy cathedral—lasted only about ten min-utes before Israel Castro rocketed a thirty-yarder down off the crossbar and past Howard. Castro had been given far too much space, and his shot was eerily reminiscent of that by Rossi of Italy in the Confedera-tions Cup. Immediately, Mexico's national team and its fans found their voice again.

To the home team's credit, the Mexicans never panicked despite the score and the occasion. The Mexicans toyed with the U.S. midfield, sprinted down the wings. Efrain Juárez and Giovanni Dos Santos, ar-guably the best young player in all of CONCACAF, were too quick, too technical. They patiently, methodically, employed possession soccer to wear down the weary, oxygen-starved Americans. Even as the clock churned on toward ninety minutes, the Mexicans maintained faith that momentum and field position would deliver a decisive score. And then sure enough, the winner in this 2–1 heartbreaker arrived in the eighty-fourth minute, after a defensive miscommunication between Donovan and Bocanegra just outside the box on the right side. The two Americans eyed each other as Juárez carried the ball past the hesitant Donovan. Jay DeMerit moved in for a tackle on Juárez, but the ball squirted loose to a wide open Miguel Sabah. Sabah, no more than ten yards from Howard, wrecked the U.S. dream right then and there, as beers flew in every di-rection from the stands and a nation released its pent-up frustrations.

"How the ball pops up, I don't know," Howard said. "It just pops up. Then the guy smashes the ball as hard as he can."

It was not so simple to slay this dragon, after all. The Americans showed resolve, demonstrated poise, and still went home with a 0–23–1 record in Mexico City. They had failed again, as they had against Brazil, to protect a lead. The loss wrote a sour ending to Gulati's so-called "Summer of Soccer." It also had a very real impact on the World Cup qualifying standings. The Americans were pushed back into the pack with a 3–2–1 mark and now faced a tricky two months ahead, as they trudged on in CONCACAF qualifying. A few complained about the Panamanian referee, who really had very little to do with the result and might have red-carded a couple of U.S. players if he'd been in a worse mood. Most of the players walked off the field in a snit, avoiding their Mexican opponents. Donovan made a point of hanging around, congratulating the victors. It was always a matter of etiquette and class to Donovan. He figured the U.S. fell to a better team more desperate for points on this day.

"It wasn't a do or die game for us," Donovan said. "It was for them."

Aguirre, for his part, appeared greatly relieved. He had been just ten minutes from a national meltdown. Who knew if he'd have survived the week as coach after a draw? "Today Mexicans can enjoy two tequilas," he said. Maybe three. Thousands of fans partied into the night around the Angel statue in the *Zona Rosa*. The curse of *Azteca* lived on, raising the bar another notch for the next U.S. qualifying squad in 2013. "Like everyone says, it's a magnificent soccer stadium," Bradley said. "The fans are special. That doesn't change anything. It's a tight game and a fair score. A tough loss to have so many guys work so hard and then give up a late goal." Would they ever beat this thing? That was no longer the issue at hand. The Americans headed next toward an inconceivably different place, Salt Lake City, cool and distant, to face El Salvador on September 5.

And yes, there was one more headline from Donovan, who had a great knack for many things, including irony. He had played sick, and it turned out Donovan brought the swine flu with him to Mexico, considered Ground Zero for the disease. Considering how he had flagged in the second half, and his unfortunate role in the decisive Mexican goal, Donovan might have done better to alert Bradley of the illness earlier in the match and summoned a replacement. But it was hard to fault such a competitor for his zeal. Donovan wouldn't be Donovan without that sense of entitlement, and denial.

CHAPTER 28

2006 . . .

IN ADVANCE OF THE 2006 WORLD CUP DRAW IN LEIPZIG, THERE actually was a decent argument to be made for anointing the U.S. national team as one of the eight top seeds. The Americans had reached the quarterfinal in 2002 and had won the hexagonal World Cup qualifying round, ahead of Mexico. They also captured the 2005 Gold Cup, which was the CONCACAF championship. And they were consistently ranked in the top ten by the FIFA computer, before the formula was recalculated to punish CONCACAF teams for weaker opponents. Not all of these factors were considered, however. To the dismay of U.S. Soccer, it was rival Mexico that received a top seeding, along with the host, Germany, plus Italy, Spain, France, England, Argentina and Brazil. The Mexicans would benefit tremendously from this elevated status at the 2006 World Cup. They were placed in a weak Group D, along with Portugal, Angola and Iran. The Americans, meanwhile, were stuck in Group E with Italy, Ghana and the Czech Republic.

Italy was of course considered certain to advance, and would eventually win the championship. The Americans historically had troubles with the Czechs and similar opponents. Only Ghana looked on paper like a winnable match. Arena would later say he knew the Americans had no chance as soon as he saw the draw, but a brave face was maintained as the U.S. headed for its training camp in Hamburg. The lovely city in northern Germany provided a quaint hideaway, although it was a bit geographically inconvenient for the team. Heavy security, much tighter than anything in

Seoul, ringed the team hotel. A back alleyway was sealed off to cars and pedestrians. Practices were closed, for the most part, so the U.S. team conducted interviews at the Hamburg hotel, before relocating south in preparation for its opener against the Czechs in Gelsenkirchen.

What happened next was a great jolt to the confidence of U.S. Soccer, a throwback match to the disastrous 1990 meeting with the Czechoslovaks in Florence, Italy, sixteen years earlier. The Americans had waited four years for this very public moment, to prove there was some real substance to the results at the Korean World Cup. Then five minutes into the first match it was over, kaput, on a goal by the Czechs' new giant, 6-foot, 8-inch Jan Koller—not to be confused with the previous, more graceful Goliath, Skuhravy. The U.S. national team wasn't just beaten, it was drubbed, 3-0. It was as if the Americans had their head on a swivel. They produced no through balls on offense for the purpose of penetration. They missed assignments on defense. The Czechs owned the flanks and, unlike the Spaniards years later at the Confederations Cup, knew exactly what to do with that edge. They produced ten of the best dozen chances to score in this match, throwing in some scrubs at the end to avoid injuries and yellow cards. The defeat was humbling for the Americans, an overwhelming disaster against yet another Central or Eastern European opponent. After the match, Arena lashed out at some of his best players, the sort of public tirade one would never hear from Bob Bradley. "Landon showed no aggressiveness tonight," Arena says. "We got nothing out of Beasley on the night. Kasey (Keller), for whatever reason, puts (the ball) up field when we have nobody." And there you had it: a recipe for the worst defeat in sixteen years, maybe longer.

In 1990, at least, the Czechs had required twenty-five minutes to score their first goal during a 5–1 rout against a completely inexperienced American team. "This wasn't 1990," Arena insisted. "I don't think we looked like the team in 1990." He hadn't yet reviewed the tapes. The Americans, in fact, looked very much like those rookies at Italia `90, only without an alibi. This U.S. team featured eight players and a coach with previous World Cup experience, yet somehow appeared nervous and disorganized from the opening whistle. "It's embarrassing. It never should have happened," Donovan said. "We were a little bit lifeless, a little bit unlucky. For MLS players, this was the date that was circled. It's disappointing. But it's not over. I don't want this memory to carry over. To be fair, we got beat by a pretty good team."

The Czechs had been brilliant though, as it turned out, this was their only solid match of the tournament. Star midfielder Pavel Nedvěd was always in the right place, chasing down loose balls, creating chances. Tomáš Rosický scored twice, once with a swerving right-foot bullet from thirty yards out. After one match, the Americans stood last in Group E, with zero points and a goal differential of minus-three. Now they would have to dig themselves out against Italy, of all countries. The well-funded, well-rested *Azzurri* were coming off a victory against Ghana, and were housed in their own resort villa complete with a journalists' entertainment center. The upholstery on the couches and chairs was adorned with portraits of team stars. A lot of people had invested a lot of money on the Italian national team.

But you never know in soccer. The ball is round. That match against Italy in Kaiserslautern was soon overcome with the same chaos and randomness evident at the small town's train station late that night. The Italians appeared off form from the start, not their sure-footed selves. The Americans took full advantage for once, pressing hard, carrying the run of play. Daniele De Rossi, Italy's midfielder, was ejected in the twenty-eighth minute for a sharp elbow to the cheek of McBride. "Could have broken his face," Arena fumed. McBride returned to the match anyway, with three stitches in his head. Mastroeni was the next one tossed by Uruguayan referee, Jorge Lorrionda, just before the half. "He was looking for an excuse," Mastroeni said. "Anywhere else in the world, it's just a yellow." Then Eddie Pope's tackle from behind on Alberto Gilardino in the forty-seventh minute resulted in yet another expulsion, and in a one-man advantage for Italy—ten-on-nine soccer that only vaguely resembled World Cup play as anyone knew it. This was now a novelty affair.

Two red cards against his team... a shorthanded goal that was nullified on an offside whistle... some exquisite dives by the Italians... the Americans now had every right to wear the dazed look of classic international soccer victims. Arena tried something that looked like a 4–3–1 formation, brought his fleetest players into the match and held his breath. The U.S. coach stomped around the sideline pleading for reason, for sanity, for order, while Keller made some difficult saves down the stretch. "That's natural, the powers in the game get a little more respect from officiating," Arena said. "That's the same in every sport. One day, the U.S. will get some of those calls in their favor." Somehow, under these impossible circumstances, the U.S. held on for the 1–1 draw and remained alive in the tournament. It was not a normal or happy thing, playing shorthanded against a two-time (soon to be three-time) World Cup champion. Arena sometimes had his team practice ten-versus-eleven drills, but never nine versus ten. It was a big field for nineteen men to fill, and it opened like a tulip in direct sunlight, free from all the traps and clutching that so often turn this sport to sludge. Italy and the U.S. traded chances, fast breaks, angled shots. The two sides, stripped to their bare essentials and obvious limitations, went straight to their strengths: The Italians to their pinpoint short passes; the U.S. to its speed and the sure-angled goalkeeping of Keller. The Americans were tested to the extreme. Donovan collapsed on the grass at the end, but the effort had been worth it. The draw was a satisfying one all around, even if the Americans remained fourth and last in their group.

"There were a lot of smiles, a lot of character in the locker room," said Jimmy Conrad, one of the exhausted defenders. "It got to the point where we couldn't cover everybody, we were so tired. But we were the wounded tiger." By the end of the day, the Americans found themselves still alive, somehow, despite earning just one point in two matches, netting zero goals (the score against Italy was an own goal by Cristian Zaccardo in the twenty-seventh minute), and putting just one shot on goal in one hundred eighty minutes. They needed only to beat Ghana to advance while Italy defeated the Czechs.

Italy held up its end of the bargain, but the Americans lost to Ghana, 2–1, convinced they had been robbed by yet another referee. Their persecution complex was now in high gear. The alleged injustice in this match arrived in the form of a penalty call in the box against Onyewu by German referee Markus Merk, just before halftime. Onyewu had bumped against Razak Pimpong, a mere brushing it seemed. In the end, however, that probably wasn't the fatal blow. The U.S. was already losing, 1–0, and should have expected no better than a tie at this pace. When they required one or two goals to stay in the World Cup, it was too steep a challenge. The team finished last in Group E with only one point, two goals (including that own goal by Italy), four shots on goal, two expulsions, five yellow cards and considerable grousing in three matches. Here they went again: "You rarely see something like that called," McBride said about the penalty shot. "They were tussling. They weren't even using their hands." That was true, but so was the futile offense, the nervous touches on the ball. There was no great conspiracy, just an unexceptional World Cup by the Americans. This was neither the disaster of 1998 for U.S. soccer, nor the breakthrough success of 2002. The disappointment merely reflected a general failure of skill and tactics, with an unfortunate barrage of tough opponents and a few careless whistles thrown in the mix.

And so the Arena era ended, after two terms and eight years. His contract expired in December. It should be noted that Arena left the field in character, with a dismissive wave in the general direction of the referee, Merk, and no recognition of the unprecedented, pro-American crowd. To his credit, however, Arena waited inside the stadium to congratulate Ghana coach Ratomir Dujković. He had been let down a bit by his favorite, Claudio Reyna. During that last match against Ghana, Reyna was stripped of the ball by Haminu Draman in the twenty-second minute, a mistake that turned into the first goal. On this one play, the aging Reyna demonstrated all his vulnerabilities and none of his formidable technical skill. He not only lost possession due to a lack of urgency, he also was injured and later replaced. Arena then went to the ungainly Ben Olsen, not the more accomplished John O'Brien. He would also ignore Eddie Johnson, the team's most explosive attacking talent, until the sixty-first minute—despite chants from the crowd to give the swift Floridian a longer run. If the aim of this World Cup was to promote the U.S. team back in the States, Arena had done his players no favors. The coach headquartered the Americans in remote Hamburg, then allowed minimal contact between the press and his players. The result was second-class, packaged coverage, as many U.S. reporters peeled off the American team to focus on other countries. Arena also was too quick to dole out criticism publicly, at players and at referees. He remained fixated on the lousy penalty whistle against Ghana. "That's a big call, by the way, if you haven't figured it out," he said. 'We had to chase the game."

Gulati, president of U.S. Soccer, was given ample opportunity by re- porters after the match to proclaim that Arena had done a good job these past eight years and that he would be returning. Instead, there was obvious unease. Gulati and Arena had endured a practical alliance over time, not based on any notable kinship. By withholding a direct en- dorsement of Arena, Gulati all but confirmed a mutual parting, by de- fault. "We'll sit down and evaluate everything, beginning in about fifteen minutes, informally and with Bruce," Gulati said. "This is not a situation where anyone is panicking. We have a coach, and we'll have a coach at the end of the year."

Arena had suffered plenty in Germany. When he looked back much later on this World Cup, and on his two terms, he would become fatalis- tic about the whole affair. From two very different experiences in 2002 and 2006, Arena came to see the tournament as something of a crapshoot. The Americans had been lucky in Korea, unlucky in Germany. They had joined a slightly easier first-round group in Korea, and even then required a considerable number of happy circumstances to go their way. If Mathis had not scored a remarkable goal against the home team, or if the Kore- ans had let up just a bit against Portugal, or if the Americans had not drawn vulnerable Mexico in the Round of 16, then the 2002 tournament might not have proved so serendipitous. "Our goalkeeper actually made tougher saves in 2002 than in 2006," Arena said. "We knew we were in trouble in 2006 when we saw the draw. We knew we were going to lose to the Czechs. We just hoped we'd get one point against them or Italy, and we did. But the refs don't respect us." Arena thought that expectations for his team—for any U.S. men's soccer team—were unrealistic. "We have a bunch of role players from marginal teams," he said, and they were often facing stars from the greatest clubs in the world.

Arena could be hard on others, and on himself. More generous ob- servers would remember his tenure for the bigger picture, and reflect dreamily on the Korean experience. They wouldn't remember him for Merk's whistle. The World Cup was always much more than a bad call here or there.

CHAPTER 29

Swimming with Minnows

THE QUALIFYING PROCESS COULDN'T RESUME QUICKLY ENOUGH for Bob Bradley, still smarting from that defeat at *Azteca*. In early September 2009, there were back-to-back fixture dates with El Salvador in the U.S. and then at Trinidad and Tobago—against the two teams that had fallen into the cellar of the Hex race, out of contention. Victories were required against both these sides, if the Americans were to fortify their position in the tournament.

The qualifier on September 5 against El Salvador was tucked away like some secret government missile test, in a valley beneath the jutting mountains at *Rio Tinto* Stadium in Sandy, Utah. This marked a return to the accepted practice by U.S. Soccer of hide-and-seek, whenever it came to ethnic fans and key qualifying matches. That game against Honduras at Soldier Field had been a risky exception. For the most part, Gulati remained willing to sacrifice significant gate receipts in order to assure an atmosphere that was not overtly hostile to the so-called home side. Plenty of Salvadorans and Salvadoran-Americans materialized in this suburb of Salt Lake City, anyway. The crowd was split 50–50, even in this remote outpost. But it was all pleasant enough, a low-profile setting for a high-stakes match. Attendance was less than 20,000, with plenty of overpriced tickets unsold. The grass field was picture perfect, despite having provided the base for a monster truck rally less than two weeks earlier. There was no sense of claustrophobic intensity or edginess, yet the place had thrown El Salvador's national team for a bit of a loop.

Twenty-four hours before the opening whistle, the Salvadoran players reportedly were burglarized at the Provo Marriott, of all places. The team had returned from a training session the day before the match to discover cash and valuables stolen from several hotel rooms. Worst hit was midfielder Eliseo Quintanilla, one of the stars, who lost more than ten thousand dollars. He had cashed two paychecks from his professional club, Ermis Aradippou in Cyprus, and planned to bring the money back to his family in El Salvador. Gulati was sympathetic, while insisting the Salvadorans should have been better prepared. These traveling teams made perfect targets for thieves. "When we're on the road, we take on security along with the local groups," Gulati said. "It's happened all over the world."

The U.S. lineup was predictable enough at this late stage of qualifying. Donovan was a wing midfielder again, his usual spot now that Davies had asserted himself at forward next to Altidore—a young combo of speed and power. Benny Feilhaber started in central midfield, offering a bit more offense than Ricardo Clark. Feilhaber, twenty-four, was the ultimate hybrid: Brazilian-born, Scarsdale-raised, of Austrian-Jewish descent, playing professionally in Denmark. He was more comfortable on the attack than tracking back on defense, but the U.S. required goals in this match and reliable Michael Bradley was always on call to pick up any unmarked El Salvadorans. As always, there was some mystery about the left back position, that spot on the field that had haunted American teams for years. Everybody from Hejduk to Eddie Lewis had played there, both out of position, during the last two World Cups. Bradley was using Bornstein for this match again. He'd also tried Pearce, Beasley, and Bocanegra at the position during the seven games of the Hex, never for more than a couple of matches each. The rest of the back line was not all that solid, either. The Americans were playing without their top central defender Onyewu, suspended with two yellow cards, and DeMerit was out nursing a groin injury. Bradley started Chad Marshall, Spector, and Bocanegra alongside Bornstein. Marshall was making his first qualifying appearance; Spector, his second; Bornstein, his third. That was a grand total of six caps for three starters, a dangerous situation that might have worried the Americans more if the U.S. didn't own a 13–1–5 overall mark against El Salvador after shutting them out in the previous five home matches.

The Americans certainly could not afford to draw or lose this home match. The Hex standings had broken the wrong way, with four teams—Costa Rica, Honduras, Mexico, and the U.S.—all battling in close quarters for three-and-a-half spots. The idea in this match was simple enough: Score early. That way, demoralized El Salvador might very well quit. The visiting team was all but eliminated already from World Cup qualifying, standing at just five points with a 1–3–2 mark through six matches. "The longer the score is 0–0, the better it is for them," Donovan said.

Then everything went haywire again. Donovan appeared for much of the match to be the only American player on the field capable of imaginative attack. He could be a wonder to behold in full flight like this, plotting vectors on the run. Meanwhile, his teammates failed to penetrate, or string together meaningful passes. For half an hour, the U.S. mustered no more than half chances. Then, in the thirty-second minute, the Americans found themselves in desperate straits after yielding a sloppy goal by that inexperienced back line. Bornstein began a parade of errors by mis-clearing a ball from the left side back into the box and directly to El Salvador forward Rodolfo Zelaya. Bocanegra backed too far off Zelaya, who centered the ball high to Cristian Castillo directly in front of Tim Howard. Castillo beat defender Spector on the header for a goal, despite a height disadvantage. Bob Bradley was staring into the abyss, possibly throwing away two or three points that were essential down the stretch.

The goal, at least, shocked the Americans into action. They immediately committed more numbers to the attack. Donovan was the difference. He performed the rescue with two gorgeous, head-high crossing passes into the box to Clint Dempsey and Jozy Altidore, for a pair of first half goals. In the forty-first minute, Donovan's free kick from thirty-five yards out on the right side found the brow of Dempsey, charging onto the ball to beat a failed offside trap by the defenders. A couple of peripheral Americans were in an offside position on the play, and the Salvadorans understandably howled about it. Dempsey, however, had begun his run onside. This just underlined the ambiguities of that tricky offside rule, which gives officials leeway to determine whether players posed a decoy threat when they were in an offside position, but not directly involved in the play. The referee, José Pineda, was from Honduras, which might have led some Americans to believe he would lean over backward on behalf of El Salvador. In this instance, he surely did not. CONCACAF had attempted in the past to make certain that officials for the final qualifying phase would not hail from any of the countries involved in the tournament. But the most qualified referees were inevitably from the most developed soccer nations, which were usually participating in the Hex.

In the second minute of added time to close the first half, Donovan's cross set up Altidore for his sixth goal in ten qualifiers, and a 2–1 lead. Both U.S. goals were created by in-stride, head-high passes, the result of Donovan's uncanny trajectory projections. In a way, Donovan was merely making intelligent guesses with these crosses, hoping a teammate would run onto them and do some damage. "It depends," Donovan said afterward. "I'm either looking for somebody who is open, or I'm just trying to put the ball in a dangerous place. Tonight, I was just putting them in a dangerous place."

His instinctive playmaking took the starch, and the stalling, out of the Salvadorans. At halftime in the photographers' work room, a somewhat relieved Gulati met with the press to update reporters on a very relevant topic: the eligibility status of twenty-two-year-old Edgar Castillo, a natural left back who had switched his allegiance to the U.S. from the Mexican national team. As it turned out, the paperwork on Castillo had just been approved by FIFA. Castillo played high school soccer in Las Cruces, New Mexico, then moved as a teenager to Mexico, where he competed for that country in U-23 matches. As a dual citizen, he was called by Sven-Göran Eriksson to be on the 23-man roster for Mexico's senior team, but didn't get into that qualifier match. Castillo played in a couple of friendlies for Mexico, then lost his passport, preventing him from traveling with Mexico to away qualifiers. Gulati never gave up the hunt on Castillo, and eventually the defender decided the path of least resistance was with the U.S. national team. "I have made my decision," Castillo said. "I want to represent the country where I was born, the place where I live." This was also the country, co-incidentally, lacking a decent left back. This change in affiliation was still possible, according to FIFA's latest rules changes, because Castillo had been a dual citizen; because he had only appeared in friendlies (as opposed to FIFA tournament matches) for Mexico at the senior level; and because this was his first footballing change of nationality. In previous years, FIFA only permitted such a switch if the player was under twenty-one years of age.

Considering the problems in the first half created by Bornstein's muff, it seemed the position of left back remained wide open; the sooner Castillo joined the team, the better.

"Can he play in the second half?" asked Grant Wahl, the *Sports Illustrated* writer. Gulati suggested instead Castillo would possibly be ready in October, for the rosters of the final two qualifiers. If not, surely in time for the run-up to the World Cup. In the meantime, Castillo was playing for *Tigres* in Mexico, on loan from Club America. The U.S. national team could wait. He would eventually receive his first call-up from Bradley for a mid-November friendly against Denmark.

The second half began at *Rio Tinto*, and it was a frantic mess. After all this recent international experience against top-flight teams, the Americans remained somehow incapable of killing the clock, at home, against a second-tier foe. Howard called the spectacle "a track meet;" a frightening, back-and-forth relay race with three huge points and possibly a World Cup bid in the balance. An apparent second-half goal by Altidore, on a sliding pass from Clint Dempsey, was disallowed on a foul call that wasn't altogether clear. Altidore asked the ref about it. So did Bradley. Neither got an answer from Pineda. "It's not easy, man," Altidore said. José Francisco Torres came on as a substitute, a welcome sight to Gulati, and very nearly scored for the Americans after a nifty run down the middle of the field. But then in the eighty-seventh minute, the ball somehow found itself in the wrong place, on the foot of El Salvador forward William Reyes, eight yards out. "When he turned to shoot, I was thinking, 'He has the whole goal,'" Howard said. Reyes might have ruined everything. Instead, he spun and struck the ball just a bit to the right of Howard, who made a relatively comfortable save. It had required considerable good fortune, but the U.S. national team grimly held on to further its qualifying run with a scary 2-1 victory over this CONCACAF also-ran. The result was helpful, but not particularly encouraging. If it weren't for Donovan, the Americans surely would have suffered a humiliating upset.

The U.S. (4–2–1) now had three World Cup qualifiers remaining, two of them on the road. The Americans traveled almost immediately to their next match, four days later, to face Trinidad and Tobago, yet another team that had faded from contention.

"If they lay down, great," Howard said. "But you never know."

History was not completely lost on the Americans or Trinidadians at the next qualifier on September 9, 2009. It was inside this same Hasely Crawford Stadium, nearly twenty years earlier, where Paul Caligiuri had scored his famous sun-aided goal that led the U.S. to the 1990 World Cup and dashed T&T's dreams. Former teammate John Harkes was now here as an announcer for ESPN. Russell Latapy, Trinidad's playmaking midfielder back in 1989, was now his national team's coach. So a few familiar faces were on hand for this match, but everything was a bit sad in retrospect. That grand sense of possibility and celebration gloriously present two decades ago was missing from the place, because T&T's World Cup qualifying chances were all but nonexistent. The proud Soca Warriors were 1–4–2 going into this match, tied with El Salvador for last place with just five points. Harkes said that people were telling him the island's soccer mojo had never recovered from the debacle of 1989. That may have been a bit of an exaggeration. Trinidad and Tobago had made a nice run very recently that earned them a cherished spot at the 2006 World Cup in Germany. In any case, the populace was not particularly enthralled with the current situation, and there were empty seats everywhere inside the national stadium. As it turned out, that did not mean the Warriors were prepared to lay down their jerseys. T&T started nine men who played professionally outside their own country, a testimony to the depth of that nation's talent pool. And then the match proved more difficult than expected, another scramble for survival.

Bradley's starting lineup was just a tad more defensive than the one against El Salvador. Clark returned to midfield in place of Feilhaber. "Ricardo has had a lot of games lately for Houston," Bradley said. "We felt that by resting him for the first game and bringing him back for this one, his energy—combined with a little bit of rest—would help us." The back line was fortified considerably by the return of Onyewu from a suspension. As if the Americans didn't have enough to worry about for this road match, there were at least two other concerns: Seven U.S. players entered the game sitting on yellow cards and faced possible suspensions for the next match in Honduras if they received another. Meanwhile, Argentina, of all teams, had fallen into fifth place in the South American qualifying standings. The fourth-place finisher in the Hex faced the dire possibility of facing budding superstar Lionel Messi in a home-and-home playoff situation, leaving even less margin for error. The U.S. clearly needed to remain among the top three in this CONCACAF tournament. By kickoff in Port of Spain, ten national teams already had qualified for the World Cup in South Africa. Paraguay was about to join that group the very same night, to make it eleven. Over in Europe, powerful sides like France, Portugal, Russia, and the Czech Republic were in real qualifying trouble. These races were approaching a climax, everywhere.

After a few minutes of encouraging, positive play by the Americans, T&T took control of the match in such a direct fashion that the U.S. was quite fortunate to hang on for a scoreless halftime. Many things were going wrong again, reminding everyone that soccer was not an easy pastime to figure in advance. Donovan appeared mobile enough on the left side, scooting into the center when presented the opportunity. But Dempsey was isolated and wasted on the right. His usual opportunistic tactics were not paying dividends. Trinidad was giving up a bundle of unnecessary corners, so there was hope that perhaps something might come from one of them. But the run of play was flowing decidedly in the wrong direction. T&T had at least three excellent chances to score in the first half, while the Americans had none. In the twenty-seventh minute, Kenwyne Jones's header from in close was knocked down by Howard. Two minutes later, Cornell Glen—who had played for Bradley with the MetroStars—lost Bocanegra on a long sideline throw-in, then chipped the ball over Howard for what appeared to be a certain goal. Instead, his shot struck the underside of the cross bar and bounced out. "The sound of the crossbar is definitely the best sound in the world," Howard would say. In the thirty-eighth minute, Howard made his most difficult save of the night, diving to block a free kick from Trent Noel.

This was all fresh evidence that Latapy's side was trying very hard, but lacked a finishing touch. T&T had managed only eight goals altogether in eight qualifiers. The Americans were deadlier, more opportunistic. In the sixty-second minute, Dempsey sent the ball to Donovan over on the left, who bought some time, looked for space, and cut back a pass to Clark wide open in the center of the field about thirty yards from the goal. Clark had enough time to set up his right foot with one touch, then came across the ball with a powerful, bending shot that beat Clayton Ince into the right corner of the net. The deciding goal arrived with a touch of irony. At the one-hour mark, as was his custom, Bradley had looked to his bench and told reserve Stuart Holden to warm up. Holden was set to replace Clark at the next opportunity, for the purpose of adding punch to the attack. Thankfully, there was no chance for Bradley to make the move before Clark's powerful shot. After the goal, Bradley opted for a more defensive lineup, sending in Holden for Dempsey and Ching for Altidore. "When the substitution came after the goal, I had a feeling that was supposed to be me," Clark said. "So I thank God I had that opportunity to score a goal." Clark's father was born in Trinidad, and his family was on hand watching this golden moment. "It was something special to have a good showing in front of somebody who has been a part of your life for so long," he said. The Americans were firm believers in sharing the wealth, and the occasion. Clark became the fifteenth U.S. player to score a goal in the 2008-2009 qualifying cycle, the eighth to score a game-winning goal. This was Donovan's eighth assist of the fourteen total goals during the Hexagonal tournament. He said Clark's shot reminded him of Michael Bradley's goal in the first Hex qualifying match against Mexico in Columbus. "Clint did a good job getting in the middle of the field, creating some space and being patient and letting me come into the play," Donovan said. "My first instinct was to put a cross across the goal but I waited and Ricardo made a good late run. Great shot and a great goal."

The match ended in less frantic fashion than the previous one against El Salvador, with fewer nail-gnawing moments. Time ran out, and for the first time in nearly four years the Americans had not earned even a single yellow card during the game from the referee—in this match, Joel Aguilar of El Salvador. The victory represented just the third win for a road team in the 2009 Hex tourney. The other qualifying scores this night were favorable. Mexico beat Honduras. Costa Rica lost at El Salvador. The Americans were now 5–2–1 with sixteen points, alone atop the Hex standings. In the past, that was the magic number considered adequate for qualification. This time, however, the U.S. appeared to need still a few more points from its final two matches to assure itself an automatic World Cup spot among the top three. That feat would become harder now that there were no minnows remaining on the schedule.

CHAPTER 30

The System

ALAN ROTHENBERG WANTED TO MAKE SOMETHING VERY CLEAR: When the United States Soccer Federation began Project 2010 back in 1998, his organization was not promising a World Cup championship by that year. "We were going to develop a team that could be a serious contender," said Rothenberg, the former president of U.S. Soccer. "To say we were predicting we would win, which is what some people think . . . well, even the Brazils and Italys wouldn't have the audacity to predict they're going to win." The thinking back then was that the pool of top players included mostly suburban college kids, an inadequate sample. Federation officials like Gulati and Rothenberg were convinced that a wider array of talent was needed, and that the university system wasn't working because of its limitations on number of games and amateur club participation. "They'd go to college and their skills would decrease, rather than increase," Rothenberg said.

At the time, Carlos Queiroz, a Portuguese coach working with the federation, put together the Q-Report, the inspiration for a fifty million dollar development plan that began just prior to the 1998 World Cup in France. Project 2010 eventually led to Project 40, sponsored by Nike and later by Adidas, a program that guaranteed professional careers in MLS for players who skipped college in order to participate in training. The under-17 residency camp was established in Bradenton, where players such as Donovan and Beasley would develop into mainstays on the national team. That took care of the older kids, but the feeder system still required significant repair work.

When U.S. Soccer officials examined the multi-tentacled monster that had become youth soccer at the start of this millennium, they were not pleased at all. It seemed to them that soccer people weren't in charge anymore. Parents who were attorneys and dentists had somehow installed themselves as instant experts on the sport and programs had been hijacked by well-intentioned, relatively ignorant volunteers. Parents were hiring their own coaches, farming out their kids to the nearest development programs with visions of scholarships dancing in their ambitious heads. And from this surge in demand, a thriving new business erupted. Youth soccer became a boom economy. The pathways through the system fractured and mutated into leagues, academies, camps. Coaches were paid, sometimes directly by parents, to win above all else, in all age groups.

Everywhere, there were confounding options and fresh pressures: the Olympic Development Program, the Super Y League, private academies, Project 40. The great investment of time required for kids and the sheer monetary demands were becoming outrageous. For a sport with minimal equipment, it was no longer unusual for a parent to shell out four figures for her son's soccer education over the course of a year. "It became, who can afford to go to this stuff?" said Jay Berhalter, head of youth development for U.S. Soccer. "We're looking at this thing, and we decided the system is broken. Watching the 2006 World Cup, you could see we hadn't made enough progress. It's been great, but not good enough. Unless we're honest, we're just going to keep painting the pig and not get anywhere."

And so a new, streamlined national academy system was put into play in 2007, modeled after the German system. In Germany, you played and developed through your club, which was a complete social and sporting center. Now it would be that way in America. The environment of the academy was born. A scouting network was developed. Academies across the country were nurtured and staffed with soccer professionals.

Berhalter and other committee members studied the science of expertise, in the broadest sense of that word. They looked at the worlds of music and art in a dozen countries around the world. They interviewed players. In almost every scientific, artistic and athletic field, they discovered training, not one-sided competitions, was the most successful driving force. "It typically takes ten years of training to become an expert in the field and that became an important piece of the puzzle," Berhalter said. The American kids they interviewed were playing too many matches, and training too little. "What we found was they were tired," Berhalter said. "We had kids fourteen, fifteen years old. They said they were playing a hundred games a year and never training. We asked them, 'How many of these games are close, hard, competitive?' They said only five or ten." The youth system had been built around the concept of winning big, often for ego gratification. There had been a huge increase in the amount of soccer activity, but not in the quality of play.

"These kids were being dragged around by the ear to different tournaments, here and there," Berhalter said. "Our motto became, 'Fewer games, more training, more meaningful games.'" Also, lower expenses. Those were the guiding principles of this national academy. U.S. Soccer didn't advertise or promote the new program. Instead, in 2007, the federation placed an open application on its website for a month. A total of 158 clubs applied. As a way to control the soccer sprawl, academy members were not permitted to play in any other programs. There would be thirty matches per season, not a hundred. In accordance with the German system, many of these academy teams would be linked to existing professional clubs in MLS or semi-pro teams. They would be bunched together geographically as closely as possible, to eliminate travel costs. Players would be scouted thoroughly, not in random fashion as they had been under the Olympic Development Program. They might be monitored in twenty matches, instead of one or two. Several academies converged at a combine in Lancaster, CA, and their teams played three matches over four days. The teenaged players were tested for speed, power, agility and quickness before three hundred college coaches. There were professional scouts, too, some from top pro clubs like Mancester United and Chelsea. The scout from Arsenal was a Frenchman, not prone to false flattery. He told Berhalter outright there was nobody at this camp that would make it overseas. "But every year, this looks a little bit better," the scout said. "I can't say that for every country. You can see it happening a little bit."

There were still feuds and fractures. U.S. Youth Soccer was operating separately from the academy system. But the pool of talent was far greater than it had been twenty years ago, even a decade ago. Maybe not as large as those in Europe or South America, but growing. There were more scholarship opportunities, and free programs aimed at inner city athletes.

So why hadn't we produced a Michael Jordan in soccer? For one thing, Michael Jordan chose basketball, as did many of the other great natural athletes in our country. Lacking substantial incentives, fewer talented athletes devoted themselves to soccer. Without celebrity stars playing the sport, soccer struggled to match the popularity and rewards offered by basketball or football. Another problem: children were playing soccer in droves, yet only the most dedicated were watching Donovan and Beckham. Coaches thereby found themselves wasting time explaining things like spacing and in-swing set pieces, without visual reinforcement. Very few nations produced superstars in sports that were not among the three most popular in their country—unless that sport was equally unpopular everywhere else, like swimming. An absence of reinforcement—from high school adulation, to media coverage, to a multi-million-dollar professional contracts—was extremely difficult to overcome.

"American soccer is but a blip on the athletically packed radar of the nation at large," Berhalter said. "Ultimately we need a breakthrough on a real team, in a real league. To start for Bayern, Real Madrid, Barcelona. To start for Arsenal at midfield would be a real accomplishment. We have the population to drive it. It just takes longer. Right now, the NFL is the 800-pound gorilla. But there's not much room to grow there for the NFL. Basketball is becoming a niche sport. You look at hockey, it's a niche sport. You look at soccer, twenty years from now, the demographics . . . it's not a stretch to think this could be far bigger than it is now. Ultimately, we will have a player who is a dominant player. It's going to happen. Not next week. And I'm pretty sure it's not going to be Freddy Adu. But you have to like the dynamics of what's happening."

Jack McInerney, a smallish striker out of Georgia, was a fine example of this evolutionary process. In January 2010 he became the seventh overall pick in the MLS SuperDraft, coming out of Bradenton. But not everybody was so certain there had been great, systemic leaps. The Under-20 national team fared poorly during the world championships in 2009, knocked out in the first round. The U-17 team appeared equally outclassed in the World Cup at Nigeria. Ramos, an assistant coach with the U-20 team, worried that not enough players on the side had come through this expanded youth system. "Half the team I was with in Texas, on the last trip, had never been on a national team before," Ramos said. "What happened to all these other guys we've spent money on? So we're doing something wrong. We've spent tons of money on hundreds of players, and who are they—where are they? Where do our guys go?"

Judging talent in any sport is an imprecise science. If only U.S. Soccer had realized at a nascent stage there were a couple of transformational attacking stars—Vedad Ibešević and Giuseppe Rossi—living within its realm of influence, maybe everything would have been different. Maybe. Even then, probably not. There were many ways to find players, or to lose them. Soccer was a global market; the world spawned and recruited a mother lode of talent. Promising young foreign athletes arrived in America on a regular basis to attend high school or college. It was then up to U.S. coaches and officials, who needed to quickly identify potential stars and convince these players to remain in the American system. Historically speaking, it was easier in the past to rush through citizenship papers on behalf of athletes in this country, or to uncover a FIFA loophole that would allow a foreign-bred player to represent the U.S. at the World Cup. "It used to be we could expedite the process," Gulati said. "It's become much tougher, even tougher after 9/11."

Gulati remained optimistic that Edgar Castillo and the German-American Jermaine Jones would both be a big part of the U.S. team in South Africa. Jones' father was an African-American solder stationed in Germany. Jermaine was raised in Frankfurt, then lived in Chicago and Greenwood, Mississippi, until his parents separated. He returned to Germany with his mother, where he played for Germany's national teams and for the club team, Schalke 04, as a top defensive midfielder. He was arguably the most promising prospect out there for the Americans. His paperwork was approved by FIFA in October 2009, too late for the qualifying run, but in plenty of time to work Jones into the midfield rotation for South Africa.

These eleventh-hour additions to U.S. World Cup teams were not a new concept. The American sides of the 1930s and again in 1950 had their share of immigrants with ambiguous citizenship status. Then in the 1990s, players such as Thomas Dooley, Roy Wegerle and David Regis stretched legal boundaries a bit. There was an ample number of successful imports, but there were also frustrating experiences with a couple of breakthrough players who fell through the cracks. Ibešević, for example, had emerged magically as the leading scorer in the German Bundesliga for equally surprising TSG 1899 Hoffenheim. His parents had moved from Bosnia to Switzerland, then settled in Missouri, where Vedad played for St. Louis University and the St. Louis Strikers of the United Soccer Premier Development League. He was spotted by a scout from Paris Saint-Germain, then moved to the Bundesliga and exploded into a star. Ibešević was one of those rare, gifted attackers who might have lifted the American national team to another level entirely—at least until he tore an ACL during training in January 2009. His sister was an American citizen. He said that U.S. Soccer officials never bothered to recruit him. "I really liked the whole situation with St. Louis, and probably if someone would have approached me I probably would have played for the U.S. national team," Ibešević told the *New York Times* in 2008. "It is difficult now to talk about because it's already past."

Gulati insisted it was considerably more complicated than that. "He's still years away from becoming a U.S. citizen," Gulati said. Ibešević was given a green card, but needed to be a resident of the U.S. at least fifty percent of the time for five years. By playing outside the country, in France and Germany, that progression was halted. FIFA's rules made it even more difficult. Ibešević, born in 1984, played for the U-20 Bosnia and Herzegovina national team. If he had been a dual U.S.-Bosnian citizen at the time, FIFA would have permitted him to switch to the U.S. team before he turned twenty-one. But he became stuck on a national side unlikely to qualify for the tournaments in South Africa or Brazil. In order to have landed Ibešević—short of marrying him off to a U.S. citizen—American coaches needed to identify his brilliance very early on and then convince him to play in MLS for a few years rather than making a fortune overseas—a hard sell, indeed.

Gulati believed he could do little, also, about Rossi. Italy was Italy. Who could resist? Gulati had more regrets when it came to Neven Subotić, a star defender for Borussia Dortmund and a member of the Serbian national team. Subotić was a Bosnian immigrant born to Serbian parents, and played on U.S. youth teams. In 2005, he was considered a marginal prospect at best by evaluators who did not prove prescient. He appeared in four matches with the U.S. national team during the Under-17 World Cup, and was sent off with a pivotal red card during a Round of 16 loss to the Netherlands. He played twice with the U-20 team, but then was not named to that side for the 2007 Under-20 World Cup. By then, Subotić already had made several international connections. He'd signed with Mainz 05 in Germany, where he'd lived until he was ten years old. He wasn't a German citizen, however. His national choices were limited to the U.S. and Serbia. In November, 2006, Subotić was quoted at length on the U.S. Soccer website demonstrating great loyalty to American soccer:

"I've played [for the U.S.], I've been in residency, so I'm an American," Subotić said. "And I've worn the crest, and that's also a thing that you have to respect. If you wear it once you're not going to wear another crest. That would kind of be like back-stabbing, I would say. I'm an American 'til the end." Subotić blamed the disaffection that followed on U.S. coach Thomas Rongen, who left him off his U-20 World Cup side. Subotić came to believe Rongen was bad-mouthing him behind his back. "Well, Rongen certainly said some discouraging and false things about me," Subotić told *ESPNsoccernet* in July, 2008. "Never in my life have I heard that a high-level coach publicly criticizes a player. Professional coaches do that one-on-one with the player... I still don't know what he saw in the other players, and what he didn't see in me."

By 2008, at age 20, Subotić was a top defender for a prestigious European side. By then, it was all too late. Subotić sent a letter to U.S.

Soccer in December 2008, informing officials of his decision. Since he had dual citizenship and he was still under the age of twenty-one, FIFA permitted him to switch national teams without a waiting period.

If you added these three players to the U.S. roster—a healthy Ibisević and Rossi at forward, Subotić on defense—the American team immediately jumped a tier on the contending scale. Yet a full-blown recruiting effort, no matter how deliberate and fawning, might not have worked. And these players might not have turned out as well as they did. You just never knew.

CHAPTER 31

Clinching the Deal

HISTORICAL RESULTS MATTER IN SOCCER. THEY PROBABLY shouldn't, because rosters and conditions change drastically over the course of a few scant years. But institutional memory is stubborn. Italy beats Germany most of the time. The U.S. always loses at Costa Rica. It just happens, and because of that the Americans could take considerable comfort in knowing they had a short, positive track record heading into their next qualifier in San Pedro Sula, Honduras, on October 10, 2009. The U.S. had beaten Honduras there, 2–1, eight years earlier in another key qualifier. In four previous visits to the country dating back to 1965, the Americans were 2–1–1. This wasn't like going to *Azteca* or *Saprissa*. The relatively new Metropolitan Olympic Stadium in San Pedro Sula, the second largest stadium in Central America, housed an audience that was generally less hostile to visitors, and the home team played a clean, commendable style. The *Catrachos* were 8–0 in home qualifying matches during this particular qualifying cycle, yet the U.S. had a shot, simply because history said it did.

The match nonetheless was fraught with intrigue off the field. This was CONCACAF qualifying at its dodgiest. Over the years, unstable governments in Haiti, Nicaragua, and Trinidad and Tobago had produced all sorts of untimely dramas. Now it was Honduras' turn. At a juncture when that country's soccer team was finally performing up to its long-standing potential, Honduras' governing situation had deteriorated at a dangerous clip. On June 28, 2009, President Manuel Zelaya was overthrown in a coup supported by the military, after it became evident he planned to remain in office illegally after his term expired. Zelaya fled, then returned to Tegucigalpa and took haven in the Brazilian embassy there. In mid-September, this stalemate all but shut down the country. The airports were closed and a tight curfew was enforced by interim president Roberto Micheletti. For a short period, it was only possible to enter Honduras through El Salvador, a neighbor that was not always on the friendliest of terms.

Soccer remained an obsession in Honduras, but it was no longer at the top of the tottering government's priority list as the sport unraveled at every professional level. "The coup has hit football," Ramón Maradiago, the former Honduras head coach, told the Chinese news agency *Xinhua*. "Club directors are feeling strain in fulfilling financial obligations to some players. There is a real sense that players are living with constant uncertainty. Football is pain relief. It relaxes and distracts us. It pulls us out of bad feelings. But we have heard lately that the current round of the league has been suspended. All we can do is hope that things are not about to get worse."

The situation imperiled the pivotal World Cup qualifier with the U.S. in October. FIFA briefly debated whether to move the match to another Central American nation, such as Guatemala, but eventually became convinced the crisis was cooling. The U.S. Soccer Federation did not petition for a change. The curfew was lifted and the match would be held in Metropolitan Olympic Stadium after all.

Sadly, very few fans back in the States were able to view this key, exhilarating qualifier. The Honduran federation owned the rights to the broadcast as the host, and sold it to a company, Mediapro, as a pay-per-view package that was aired back in America only in select sports bars. Fans would either have to find a designated tavern in their area or search the internet for a pirated, streaming broadcast by a foreign network. This was the most frustrating arrangement yet. Bradley called it "a shame." U.S. Soccer insisted it could do nothing about these circumstances. England had a similar problem with its qualifier in Ukraine, which was available in Britain only as a paid subscription on the internet. It was simply a matter of dollars. U.S. Soccer had attempted to barter with the Hondurans, when the American federation still owned the rights to the Honduras match in Chicago and retained some leverage. It didn't work. The American federation would have been willing to kick in $100,000 or so to help secure the rights to the match in San Pedro Sula for ESPN. But it would have cost the federation much more than that, Gulati said, perhaps a million dollars. The ratings numbers just weren't guaranteed for ESPN, which didn't even know in advance whether this match would be meaningful.

Bradley had little time to count or consider the number of viewers back home. He faced a terrible coaching dilemma. The Americans likely required a victory in Honduras to clinch immediately a World Cup berth. If they tied or lost, the U.S. would need a draw in the final qualifier four days later at Washington D.C. against Costa Rica. Meanwhile, eight American players on the roster were sitting on yellow cards for the Honduras match. If any one of them received second yellows, he would be suspended for the game against Costa Rica. Bradley could ill afford to lose key contributors for the second match, if he failed to capture the first. "The yellow card situation is a challenging one," Bradley said. "Our discipline is important. We are very pleased that in the last two games we didn't pick up any yellow cards and so we have to do that once again."

In addition to the matter of yellow cards, Bradley was without Dempsey, who had sprained a shoulder while playing for Fulham. Bradley eventually settled on Holden to take that attacking midfield position. A player earning less than $40,000 would thus replace an English Premier League starter. DeMerit was out, facing eye surgery, due to a cornea infection. There was also the now-familiar problem of rust, affecting three pivotal stars. After a brilliant start at his new club, Hull City, Altidore had played few minutes with that struggling team. It was confounding. Coaches all over Europe couldn't seem to look past Altidore's lackluster training sessions. And he didn't help himself a bit. In October, Altidore would show up late for a Hull City match, then Tweet his apologies to the public—a breach of club policy. Meanwhile, Onyewu was getting almost no quality minutes with his Italian super-club, A.C. Milan. Even Michael

Bradley was seeing reduced time with his team in the Bundesliga, Borussia Mönchengladbach.

Bob Bradley's lineup contained one real surprise: Conor Casey, the bald bulldog from MLS, would start at forward in place of Altidore. Casey hadn't scored a single goal in fourteen previous appearances with the national team. But Altidore wasn't merely off form. He was carrying a yellow card and Bradley didn't trust the young man's discipline. If Altidore came off the bench for fewer minutes, he would likely avoid a second yellow and remain available for the match back in Washington. Casey was enough of a physical player to trouble the smaller Hondurans in the box, and his first touch had improved significantly. The shaved head sometimes obscured the notion that Casey did own some subtle technical skills in the box. Casey was also just plain faster than in previous seasons, when his knees were a real problem. "His movement, his ability to hold the ball," Bradley said. "We just felt he's been playing regularly and the qualities he has would be important at the start of the game."

Considering the political backdrop to this match, Metropolitan Olympic Stadium seemed a festive haven from all the nation's troubles. The country was planning a huge celebration, if only it could clinch its first World Cup berth since 1982. The setup was eerily reminiscent of America's spoiler role back in 1989 at Trinidad, only this time San Pedro Sula was swathed in blue, instead of red. The American team awakened at their Hilton Hotel to tooting horns and large headlines in the local papers. "Seven Million Hondurans Are Ready To Celebrate Their New Heroes," wrote *La Prensa*. The match was set to go off at eight o'clock local time that evening. By late afternoon, the stadium was filled with a boisterous crowd of 40,000 ready to party, to forget coups and curfews. In sharp contrast to the scenes in Mexico City and San Jose, this audience stood respectfully and did not jeer "The Star Spangled Banner" when it was played before the match. "We just don't see that very often," Gulati said, admiringly.

The first half provided decent chances for both sides, but no goals—an unsatisfactory score that would have helped neither team clinch a World Cup berth. The final forty-five minutes in that steamy stadium, however, were something else indeed: a wild and crazy spectacle that might have ended in any number of ways. Onyewu started things rolling the wrong way in the forty-seventh minute, sloppily giving away the ball and committing a clear foul that allowed Julio César de León a free kick. De León launched a gorgeous twenty-yard shot that beat Howard, who had no chance. Months earlier, the Americans came storming back successfully from such a deficit against Honduras in Chicago, and now they would do it again. Just nine minutes after falling behind, Davies headed Onyewu's long, lead pass into the box. Casey went high to beat defender Maynor Figueroa while plowing into goalkeeper Noel Valladares. This was Casey playing the role of Frankie Hejduk, hell-bent for leather.

"I kind of speculated that [Davies] would be heading it back in my direction, so I went up and the goalie challenged for it," Casey said. "I don't know if I got my head on it or what, but somehow it went in the direction of the goal and in." Then in the sixty-sixth minute, Donovan produced one of his trademark, in-stride through balls for Casey, who ran onto it and rocketed a low shot past Valladares from twelve yards for the lead. "Landon slipped me a nice ball, and I was alone on goal," Casey said. Donovan was on top of his game again. His free kick from twenty-five yards in the seventy-first minute curled into the upper right corner for a 3–1 lead. The Americans could taste South Africa, could feel eighteen months' of withering work nearing fruition. But once again, the U.S. didn't know how to kill a match, how to take the air out of the ball. As Honduras pressed desperately, the marking by American defenders became almost a random affair. De Leon powered a left-footed goal in the seventy-eighth minute, cutting the deficit to a single goal. All appeared lost when Spector was whistled for a handball inside the box in the eighty-sixth minute. Carlos Pavón, the Honduran forward, bravely stepped up to take the penalty shot that would surely wreck everything.

"You try not to think about all the negative stuff, but it's inevitable," goalkeeper Tim Howard said, recalling that moment. "You just think, 'Where did it all go wrong?'"

The standard game of cat and mouse began between shooter and goalkeeper. Pavon started his run at the ball far to the left, eyeing the left post so that Howard would move to his right. "I thought, 'You're not really going to go there, you know,'" Howard said. "It was too much of a run-up, too much of a look off. I guessed the other way." Howard flew left. As it turned out, it hardly mattered what he did. When Pavón finally took that penalty, he leaned too far back and his shot sailed high over the crossbar. "We're just lucky he missed it," Howard said. Similar mis-kicks on big penalties had been suffered by many greater shot-makers than Pavón over the years, from Roberto Baggio to Beckham. Pavón wrote an exclamation point on his misfortune in this match, lining an open header above the crossbar in the eighty-ninth minute.

The Americans held, 3–2. They now stood 6–2–1 in the Hex standings, in first place, safely ahead of both Honduras and Costa Rica. Mexico, at 6–3–0, also qualified for the World Cup earlier in the day. The two giants advanced, as expected. The Americans popped some champagne bottles in the locker room. They hugged each other and danced about, bursting out with an odd but happy tune, "*Hava Nagila*." Maybe this wasn't the sheer, innocent ecstasy evident back in 1989, in that little Port of Spain locker room. But a World Cup berth was something fresh and new for several of these players and for those who had been there in Germany, it offered a chance at redemption. The victory also avoided the specter of a final, must-draw match against Costa Rica.

"You don't want to go into the last game leaving anything to chance," Donovan said. "As we see around the world, even with qualifiers today, anything can happen in one soccer game and we didn't want to leave that opportunity open. It was nice to get it done. This match was a culmination of a long learning process and we played mature, experienced, a hard-fought ninety minutes, and I was very proud of us."

The Hondurans were heartbroken, but remained hopeful. The *Catrachos* could still capture that third automatic spot with a final victory in El Salvador, combined with a tie or loss by Costa Rica in Washington against the Americans. The respectful crowd in San Pedro Sula applauded both sides as they walked off the field, sensing that this had been a very special match, and the Americans took note of this sporting display. U.S. Soccer officials promised the Honduran coach, Reinaldo Rueda, their team would make a full effort, with an A-team lineup, against Costa Rica in Washington. And so they did.

The match against Costa Rica at RFK Stadium on October 14 was supposed to be something of a celebration, a victory lap. The wearying, sixteen-month qualification process was now ending successfully. Only regional pride was at stake. With a victory, the Americans would clinch first place in the Hex over Mexico, regaining a bit of the bragging rights over their rivals after the Gold Cup fiasco and then the setback at *Azteca*. A loss to Costa Rica at home would be somewhat embarrassing, the first time in thirty-seven years the Americans had been defeated twice by the same team in the same qualifying round. The U.S. also had promised Honduras a good show, and intended to keep its word. This was, after all, Bob Bradley's last look at his team in an official FIFA tournament until the World Cup. Soon, however, all these good intentions took a back seat to a disastrous development.

The Americans flew directly to Washington, D.C. from Honduras, landing early Sunday morning. Then on Monday night, Charlie Davies went out with friends, broke curfew, and was badly injured in a fatal, one-car accident early Tuesday morning in northern Virginia. He required a series of surgeries to repair his right leg, broken in two places, and a ruptured bladder. For days he was listed in serious but stable condition at Washington Hospital Center, after titanium rods were inserted into his tibia and femur bones. Davies had been a passenger in a car driven by an unidentified woman, who was also treated for injuries at the same hospital. A second passenger, Ashley Roberta of Phoenix, Maryland, was killed when the car was split in two after striking a guard rail along George Washington Parkway in northern Virginia after three a.m. The accident itself was under investigation. That stretch of highway was dark, winding, and heavily populated with deer.

Davies, twenty-three years old, had emerged almost from nowhere at the Confederations Cup to become a starting forward with the national team and a successful contributor with Sochaux of the French Ligue 1, which he had joined in the summer of 2009. He combined two elements—blazing speed and steadily improving technical skill—rarely seen in combination on the American roster, with the exception of Donovan. Davies was particularly necessary on a side that played pure, countering soccer against superior opponents. He had been the perfect complement for burlier strikers like Ching, Casey, or Altidore. A former star at Boston College, Davies honed his game by finding competitive matches wherever and whenever possible—commuting from New England to the Westchester Flames in New York back in 2006 to play Under-21 soccer. By the end of that year, he signed with Hammarby of Sweden and went off on another adventure.

"He lived for soccer," said Flames coach Gus Skoufis. "We always knew Charlie would be a star. Losing was not in his dictionary. He would come all the way down from his home in New Hampshire, and he rarely missed a practice. He was a happy kid, a strong kid, and I know he'll come back."

Nobody on the scene in Washington was quite as certain. "Injuries of this nature usually require a recovery period of six to twelve months and extensive rehabilitation," said Dr. Dan Kalback, physician for U.S. Soccer. "Due to Charlie's fitness level, his prognosis for recovery and his ability to resume high-level competition is substantially improved." Davies's family, teammates, and friends were just happy Charlie was alive. Bob Bradley went to visit Davies at the hospital on the day of the match with Costa Rica.

"I heard the doctor say, 'Charles, can you open your eyes?'" Bradley said. "Sure enough, he could." He'd been responsive. That was a good sign. A week later, Davies was out of intensive care and speaking more conversationally with visitors. He would be released from the National Rehabilitation Hospital in mid-November, with no guarantees from doctors about ever resuming his career. "Charlie faces a long recovery from orthopedic injuries," said James DeBritz, director of orthopedic trauma at the Washington Hospital Center, where Davies had been treated. "It will take time and extensive physical therapy for his bones and soft tissue to heal." By Christmas, Davies would be back to Tweeting hopefully. "I'm truly blessed to have survived and have people that care," he wrote. "I'm doing much better and I'm able to walk. Rehab is going very well. So your prayers and mine are being answered," he wrote. "Thank you and Happy Holidays!!!!" By January 2010, Davies was back walking, even training, and more certain than ever he would return in time for the World Cup.

Davies was closest on the team with Altidore, who called him his brother, and with Holden, who was his roommate on the road. The players were informed about the terrible accident on Tuesday afternoon before the match against Costa Rica. Several of them began Tweeting to fans, asking the crowd on Wednesday to give Davies and his family a show of support during the match. When the ninth minute arrived that rainy night in RFK Stadium, thousands of fans sent a choreographed get-well card to Davies. The crowd rose, flashed placards with his number nine jersey number, set off colorful smoke bombs, and sang well wishes to the young player whose World Cup dreams were endangerd. Davies's family was in the stands, appreciative of the salute. It might have been a perfect shout-out, but then Casey blew a wide-open shot from ten yards out, right as the digital scoreboard clock moved to 9:00 minutes into the match.

The U.S. had several opportunities, cashing in on none of them. As often happens, such wastefulness was punished in short order. In the twenty-first minute, Costa Rican forward Bryan Ruiz dribbled easily around Onyewu on the left side and poked the ball past Howard. This was now the sixth time in ten Hex matches that the U.S. had yielded the first goal. The Americans were still recovering from this shock, their defense in disarray, when Costa Rica produced a pretty triangular passing combo that led to a second goal in the twenty-fourth minute by Ruiz from just outside the box. The U.S. was down two goals at the half to a team with much more at stake. The Americans were fit and owned the run of play, yet circumstances appeared nearly hopeless. Bradley had another concern, too: Altidore was cautioned with a yellow in the fourteenth minute. If he received another yellow card and was ejected, Altidore would be forced to sit out the first match of the World Cup in South Africa. Bradley, ever conscious of details, knew that Altidore was wearing a Davies T-shirt beneath his own jersey. If he scored a goal and lifted his jersey for the camera, Altidore would get that second yellow. Bradley warned Altidore about that, just in case.

Altidore never scored, but the U.S. produced another in a series of re-markable comebacks, with a display of admirable attacking soccer under extremely wet, difficult conditions. The Americans outshot Costa Rica, 8–2, in the second half, wearing down the *Ticos* on one foray after an-other. Eventually, Michael Bradley pounced on a rebound off Dono-van's shot to score the first U.S. goal in the seventy-second minute. Then, suddenly, a terrible sight: Onyewu, the team's staunchest central defender, crumpled to the ground in the eighty-third minute after leap-ing for a header. The injury would later be diagnosed as a torn patellar tendon. The Americans had little time to ponder the long-term ramifi-cations of this setback. They would have to play a man short, because Bradley had used his third and final substitution—Kenny Cooper for Casey—in the seventy-ninth minute.

The U.S., still down a goal at the ninety-minute mark, was afforded an unusually lengthy lifeline, five minutes of added time. There had been a great deal of theatrical flopping by the Costa Ricans, contributing to this development. "They got what they deserved," Gulati would say later. The extra time was also in part due to Onyewu's injury, and because of the time-consuming ejection of Costa Rican coach René Simões late in the second half. Simões was sent off by referee Benito Archundia after the coach called for a substitution, only to discover that the fourth referee was signaling on his signboard for the wrong player, Junior Diaz, to come off the field. Simões was understandably infuriated at this sight—Diaz had just entered the match minutes earlier—and pleaded his case at length.

These extra minutes of added time dragged on interminably for the Costa Ricans, who were theoretically just moments from qualifying for the World Cup with a 2–1 victory. In front of that team's bench, play-ers and trainers waved their arms frantically at the referee, pointing to imaginary watches on their wrists, demanding the final whistle be blown. Meanwhile, the U.S. attacked, earning one last corner kick. Rob-bie Rogers, a substitute, booted an in-swinger from the right side. Jonathan Bornstein somehow found a seam and headed in the tying goal, four minutes and fifty-seven seconds into extra time. "I don't usu-ally go for corner kicks," said Bornstein, a defender. "I stay in the back. But I thought, 'I'm going for this one.'"

That single score clinched first place for the U.S. over Mexico, sent Honduras to South Africa, and cost Costa Rica a place at the 2010 World Cup. Four years earlier, the fourth-place finisher in CONCACAF had played off against a pushover also-ran from the Asian region. The rules had changed, however. During this World Cup qualifying cycle, the *Ticos* would be assigned a home-and-home playoff with the tougher, fifth-place finisher in South America—Uruguay—for a final spot at the 2010 World Cup. The Costa Ricans sank to the grass in despair after the ball zipped past their goalkeeper, Keilor Navas. They had come within one clearance of a corner kick from South Africa. Instead they would be traipsing in vain to Uruguay, losing 2–1 on aggregate goals. The U.S. players remained on the field. Bocanegra, the captain, took a microphone and spoke on behalf of the team. He thanked the fans and wished Davies the best. For the Americans, the comeback was ridiculously dramatic but in its own way commonplace. They finished with a 6–2–2 mark in the Hex for twenty points. When they had given up the first goal in those matches, they were 3–1–2.

"First place was a huge significance," Bob Bradley said. "The whole goal was to win the group. Whenever you step on the field, you show what you're about. We showed the mentality, the spirit. They care about each other."

Bradley, for obvious reasons, had mixed feelings about this week. The U.S. had qualified for the World Cup, had won the Hex. At the same time, Davies was in a hospital in serious condition and a team cornerstone, Onyewu, was facing surgery and a long period of rehabilitation. "It's been two days of tough news," Bradley said, estimating the recovery period from surgery for Onyewu to be three to four months. "He's young, he's healthy, our doctors are good." After the operation, however, the rehab estimate for the defender was extended to six months. Over in Italy, A.C. Milan vice president Adriano Galliani would lash out in frustration at the situation. "I'm very angry because once again the national teams take our players and we have to pay the consequences of injuries," Galliani said. "We demand compensation from the American federation because we cannot pay the salary of a player who cannot play for six months." Galliani's stance was absurd. Players often went off to national team matches, and there was of course no way to protect them from injury.

Other countries, other coaches, were qualifying for South Africa this day as redemption and anger spilled from post-match podiums everywhere. Argentina qualified down in Uruguay. Its famous coach Diego Maradona grabbed his crotch, telling critics in the media, in the lewdest of terms, they should now feel free to perform sexual acts upon his nether regions. "I don't forget things," Maradona said, at the press conference. "Those who did not believe—may the ladies excuse me—let them. . . ." Back in D.C., a more filtered Bradley was not about to say such things, but he betrayed a similar resentment. Asked to analyze the play of his own son, he bristled. "I'm not going to assess games," Bradley said. "You can do that. And most of you don't do it very well."

He had earned the right to be both combative and condescending. Another American coach had led another American team on a very difficult journey to its sixth straight World Cup. "I didn't learn Bob Bradley was a good coach," Gulati said. "I knew that going in."

CHAPTER 32

A Different World Cup

DANNY JORDAAN WAS AN EXCEEDINGLY WINSOME FELLOW WITH
a quiet but acerbic sense of humor. If you asked the chairman of the
South African World Cup Committee how he planned to handle hooligans at the upcoming tournament, Jordaan said he had in mind a place
for them somewhere inside the country's game preserves, alongside the
lions and tigers. He would also tell you, in the next breath, that the boisterous, beery European fans had always behaved themselves in his country simply because they experienced such utter soccer rapture—and
maybe, just maybe, because Interpol had weeded out the worst of the
hoolies, holding their passports in abeyance during high-risk travel
matches. Jordaan long ago had mastered the diplomatic art form of the
kiss-and-slap, that perfect blend of praise and veiled threat.

Jordaan was born in 1951, raised during the anti-apartheid movement. He became an activist when he joined Steven Biko's South
African Students' Organization in the 1970's. Later on, as a lecturer and
politician, he worked for the United Democratic Front and the ruling
African National Congress. He was a teacher. He was also a formidable
soccer and cricket player. Voted forty-four among the top one hundred
greatest South Africans by a local network, Jordaan was the driving
force behind this World Cup, nurturing the bid from its conception
back in 1994. He had then just taken part in the country's first free elections, a time of great elation and infinite possibility. With the winds of
African reinvention at his back, he immediately launched an ambitious

bid for the 2006 World Cup. Unfortunately, Jordaan was competing not only against the standard prejudices that face developing nations, but also with a well-funded and inevitably successful bid by Germany. Jordaan's greatest selling point was that a World Cup in South Africa would be far more affordable for fans and teams than one in Germany—a notion that was proven patently untrue. He gained the support of CONCACAF—a you-scratch-my-back kind of agreement—but it wasn't enough. He lost that vote, reorganized quickly and tried again for 2010.

A decade or two earlier, Jordaan wouldn't have stood much of a chance. Sepp Blatter was now the president of FIFA, however, and for Blatter the concept of inclusion had become one of his many crusades. Blatter's regime was rife with monetary scandal and with spontaneous, idiotic statements (his suggestion that women players wear "tighter shorts" was just one of his more outrageous pronouncements). Blatter's appetite for expansion in every direction was limitless. Top players from around the world were wilting under the demands of league play, continental club competition, international qualifiers and tournaments. And under Blatter's reign, ticket scandals festered without significant punishment in the untethered fiefdom of CONCACAF, that confederation of North American, Central American and Caribbean soccer nations theoretically regulated by FIFA. But for all of that, his insistence that the World Cup experience be shared in all corners of the globe was remarkably generous and insightful. Blatter pushed through a federation rotation system mandating that Asia and Africa get their turns at last to play host to a World Cup. And although this rotation would soon be ditched at the demand of the powerful Union of European Football Associations (UEFA), it served its purpose. The decision was made that Africa would be granted a berth in 2010 and South America in 2014.

This meant that Jordaan's organizing committee only needed on this occasion to compete, really, with two other African nations, Egypt and Morocco. The South African national team at the time of the bid showed great promise, although such hopes would dissipate later during a string of disappointing international matches. Back in 2004, there was still considerable promise for the team nicknamed *Bafana Bafana*, or

"The Boys." In addition, sports-crazy South Africa had far more resources than Egypt or Morocco and the backing of a government that
desperately wished to make a major splash. Rugby, cricket and soccer
had always been the lifeblood of South Africa's self-image.

The Springboks were traditionally a powerful force in rugby, a sym-
bol of white South African strength. A sports boycott by most nations
and athletes through the 1980s and early 1990s became one of the most
effective tools for change, eroding Apartheid at its very roots. Now that
a black majority government was in charge, it was time to strut the nation's new image in public. South Africa already had successfully staged
fourteen major international sports events, including the World Cups of
rugby and cricket. A World Cup of soccer in South Africa would represent yet another step forward; a global embrace of unprecedented importance for a nation that had been isolated on playing fields for nearly
four decades because of its racist, minority government.

The history of this land was not pretty. Its internal racial wars tum-
bled into sporting arenas dating back to the 1950s. Ping-pong, of all
sports, first brought the problem to the forefront. Apartheid laws pro-
hibited multiracial competition, which meant no national or club team
with players of color was permitted to face whites anywhere in South
Africa. In 1956, the International Table Tennis Federation confronted
these strictures, refusing to recognize the all-white South African Table
Tennis Union and establishing ties instead with the more liberal South
African Table Tennis Board. The government in turn rescinded the
passports of players from the Table Tennis Board, forbidding them from
traveling abroad. Prime Minister Hendrik Verwoerd also ruled that a
Maori tribesman playing for the All Blacks of New Zealand would not
be permitted to compete against South African rugby teams. The All
Blacks cancelled their tour, announcing they were done with playing in
South Africa forever.

In reaction to all this, the bi-racial South African Sports Association was formed to lobby on behalf of free sports exchanges. The group
was ignored by the apartheid government and went instead to the International Olympic Committee, demanding that South Africa be expelled from the Olympics. The IOC warned South Africa to get its

act together by the 1964 Games. The government was well aware this could become a great public relations disaster and a half-hearted effort was made to make matters better in January, 1963, with the establishment of the South African Non-Racial Olympic Committee. This was not enough for opponents of the ruling regime, who believed that little had truly changed in the makeup of Olympic sports teams. Eventually, South Africa was banished from the 1964 Games in Tokyo, a shock to the system that reverberated throughout the country's white society. South Africa made more concessions for the 1968 Games in Mexico City. The new prime minister, B.J. Vorster, agreed to allow visiting teams with players of color to enter the country. At first, the IOC announced the country's return to the Olympic fold. But Vorster didn't do a thing to integrate South Africa's own teams. By now the international boycott was in full flight, a *cause celebre*. If South Africa were invited to the Games, many other nations would likely bolt. The IOC dis-invited South Africa.

On it went like this, and over the years many white sportsmen from South Africa—including top golfer Gary Player—were thrust into the role of apologist and even worldwide ambassador for Apartheid. Finally, all bans on race in sport disappeared in 1993, not long before the first democratic elections threw out the white settlers from office. The Springboks were permitted to play in the rugby World Cup in 1995, and captured the title unexpectedly to the great celebration of both black and white South Africans. This moment was later captured in the popular film, *Invictus*. Nelson Mandela himself presented the trophy to captain François Pienaar, a white Afrikaner, and all seemed wonderful with the world. But in fact, South African rugby remained very white indeed. It required nearly another decade of evolution before eleven black players were selected in 2004 for South Africa's thirty-three-member squad that would tour Europe.

Soccer was always a very different tale in South Africa. As long as organized sports existed in the country, soccer was embraced by and based in the black community. Because of apartheid, however, the government refused to field a national team until July 9, 1992, when South Africa played its first match in Durban against Cameroon. The event proved both historic and joyful, as *Bafana Bafana* defeated Cameroon, 1–0. The team struggled for the next three years, but then emerged again by winning the 1996 African Nations Cup on home turf with a 2–0 victory over Tunisia in the final. Again Mandela was there to lift the trophy, this time with black athletes around him. The South Africans continued to progress and impress, qualifying for both the 1998 World Cup in France and the 2002 World Cup in Korea, where the national team was recognized as one of the most exciting sides in the tournament. *Bafana Bafana's* aggressive style and wide open matches resulted in a 3–2 loss to vaunted Spain, a 1–0 victory over Slovenia and a 2–2 draw with Paraguay. The team finished with four points but was denied the second round by Paraguay on a goals-scored tiebreaker.

The success, persistence and turmoil of South Africa's soccer team throughout this era were personified by its captain and defender, Lucas Valeriu Radebe, a transcendent player and more recently a spokesman for South African tourism. Radebe was part of *Bafana Bafana* when the team faced Cameroon in the first international match. Before that, he had endured apartheid and all of its limitations. "We only knew our own football teams, our own country," he said. Radebe was one of eleven children raised lovingly in a four-room house in Soweto, near Johannesburg. He was sent as a teenager by his parents to the homeland of Bophuthatswana, to avoid the violence of the Soweto region and to gain an education. "My mother, Emily, she was never satisfied, she wanted me to be a doctor," he said, during one visit to New York in advance of the World Cup. "They saw football as an excuse for parties and women." He had been transplanted to a very rural area, bored beyond belief. He took up soccer in Bophuthatswana—at first as a goalkeeper, until he was kicked in the face and wanted no more of that position. As a young midfielder, he was first spotted by Sylvester Kole, a top South African defender, and offered a contract by the Kaizer Chiefs Football Club. "Kaizer was a big team, a massive team," Radebe said. His parents were not thrilled with the whole notion, nonetheless. There were phone calls back and forth, and finally they agreed to allow him to sign. Then in 1991 his career nearly came to an end, after Radebe was shot by an unknown assailant for mysterious reasons. Radebe believed the shooter was a fan of Kaizer, who was trying to prevent him from transferring to another club. "I was driving home delivering drinks with my brother and cousin," Radebe said. "I hear a gunshot and my leg went numb. There was blood all over. I'd been shot in the back and the bullet came out through my thigh. The first thing I thought was my career was over, but I was lucky. It only went through flesh. That event changed my perspective. I live every day like it is my last day."

Radebe doubled his efforts to launch an international soccer career, and was sold in 1994 by Kaizer to Leeds United in the English Premier League for nearly $400,000. There in England, Radebe became a star. Nicknamed "The Chief," he was appointed captain of Leeds in 1998 and led the small-budget, overachieving club to successive fourth- and third-place finishes. Before leg and ankle injuries slowed him down and forced his premature retirement, Radebe became enormously popular in the English city and was feted during a testimonial at Elland Road in 2005 before a crowd of 37,886. Radebe earned seventy caps with his national team, steadying the defense. Although he wasn't a scorer, Radebe managed a tying goal against Spain in the 2002 World Cup that very nearly put *Bafana Bafana* through to the next round.

Unfortunately, this golden generation of pioneer players grew old and South Africa faltered. "The officials, they stole the limelight," Radebe said. "They didn't invest in grassroots. They got more power and became disrespectful to the players. There is still a lot to sort out." In 2003, *Bafana Bafana* was knocked out in the first round of the 2004 African Nations Cup following a humiliating 4–0 loss to Nigeria. In 2006, South Africa again was eliminated in the first round after suffering three shutout defeats. Desperate officials turned to Carlos Alberto Parreira, the coach of Brazil's 1994 World Cup champions, to lead the national team. Still, South Africa failed to advance past the first round of the 2008 African Nations Cup in Ghana. Parreira resigned unexpectedly in April, 2008, in order to return to Brazil to be with his wife, who was diagnosed with cancer. In his place, officials named another Brazilian, Joel Santana, who had come highly recommended by Parreira. At the 2009 Confederations Cup, a dress rehearsal for the World Cup, the South Africans more than held their own, demonstrating considerable promise. But South Africa failed to qualify for the 2010 Africa Cup of Nations and Santana was replaced in October, as Parreira returned to resume head coaching duties.

Meanwhile, the country's professional league founded in 1997 continued to flourish with sixteen Premier League teams led by the Mamelodi Sundowns, the Orlando Pirates and the Kaizer Chiefs. The Chiefs remained the most popular club. The Pirates had been around since the 1930s. The Sundowns, five-time champions, were operated by mining billionaire Patrice Motsepe and could always buy their way into contention à la Chelsea or the New York Yankees. In 2007, the league inked a $150 million broadcast deal with SuperSport International and signed with major sponsors South African Breweries and Absa Bank for about $10 million per year, over five years. In 2008, cellular company MTN and Nedbank each committed $40 million over five years. The corporate influence became most apparent in May 2008—when the club re-named SuperSport United by an electronic media network captured the Premier League title.

If FIFA required further proof of the country's overwhelming commitment and love of the sport, then it merely needed to consider the Royal Bafokeng in Batswana. That tribe owned rights to land where platinum was discovered, along with gold. Surrounded by poverty, the Royal Bafokeng became relatively rich from these resources, and the king decided after considerable input from tribespeople to invest this windfall in, of all things, a brand new soccer stadium with a seating capacity of 42,000. In this way, the region of Rustenburg would be assured several World Cup matches and a future home for international travel games. The World Cup bid had populist roots and political backing. Jacob Zuma, provisional head of government and president of the African National Congress, signed off on a series of seventeen guarantees with FIFA, involving such issues as safety, transport, health, visas, taxes and infrastructure. Ticket prices were also guaranteed affordable to Africans, because the country froze the exchange rate of its national currency, the rand, at seven rands to a dollar. In this way, the inevitable inflation (the dollar was already worth eleven rands by the close of 2008) would not push ticket prices out of reach of locals. With these pledges in place, FIFA awarded its precious World Cup to South Africa, despite honest concerns about the economic readiness of the country.

This victory in 2004 by South Africa would require an enormous civic commitment of about $4 billion in infrastructure and another $400 million in operations. The investment would create more money, theoretically, but in the meantime there were tremendous costs even beyond the construction of facilities. South Africa needed to supply 41,000 extra police and 40,000 stewards for the event, just for starters. Jordaan saw this all as a unique opportunity to accelerate the political and economic evolution of his nation. He promised "a transport revolution."

"A World Cup demands a world class infrastructure," Jordaan said, sitting in a suite at the Helmsley Park Lane Hotel on Central Park South in New York. "We can use this as a nation. It will be an evolving exercise. It will bring black and white together." After winning the World Cup bid, Jordaan spent much of the next three or four years dousing reports that his country would forfeit the tournament because it was behind schedule in stadium construction, or because it was too dangerous. "Wherever I go, people ask, 'Is the World Cup really going to happen?'" Jordaan said. "I thought it was important for me to answer the public with a resounding 'Yes.' It will happen, and it will happen very, very well. You will see it with crowds and with an atmosphere that will rival any competition we've seen." Jordaan and Radebe spoke lovingly about the buzzing *vuvuzela* horns, about the colorful *makarapa* helmets and the athletic *diski* dancers evident at all South African matches. There were skeptics, nonetheless, many of them residing within FIFA. Concerns about security and stadium readiness led Blatter himself in early 2008 to issue a not-so-veiled threat about possibly relocating the tournament elsewhere, if South Africa didn't get its act together. Particularly troublesome were reports of crimes in the region. Murder rates remained distressingly high. The country's own safety and security minister, Nathi Mthethwa, described the nation as "a killing field" in November 2008. And then in January 2009, two thugs gunned down Jimmy Mohlala, speaker of the Mbombela municipality and a man who fought corruption surrounding the construction of a World Cup stadium.

Officials from CONCACAF and U.S. Soccer always walked a thin diplomatic tightrope regarding the matter of South Africa as host. On the one hand, they backed the South African bid very publicly, with an eye toward receiving payback votes from the African region in future FIFA balloting to determine the hosts in 2018 or 2022. Chuck Blazer, executive committee member of CONCACAF, made a habit in Jordaan's presence to point out his support of South Africa over European competition. At the same time, however, the U.S. wanted FIFA to know it was prepared to take on the responsibilities of an eleventh-hour World Cup assignment, if South Africa failed. Large stadiums and proven security in America could be made available on a moment's notice. Gulati made a point to tell Blatter, whenever possible, that the U.S. would require only two weeks' notice to stage a World Cup. "One week, if we don't need photos on the credentials," Gulati joked.

Blatter put all such speculation to rest in December 2008, which was arguably his last opportunity to steer the tournament away from South Africa. Speaking to reporters in Tokyo before the World Club Cup, he pulled all threats and contingencies off the table. "There is no Plan B, C or D," he said. "For those who still have doubts, I tell you the 2010 World Cup will be organized in South Africa. I will be proud because it is a little bit like my baby. I've had a dream for thirty-four years to bring the World Cup to Africa."

Jordaan assured reporters about security. When one journalist asked him if it would be safe to go out at night, Jordaan cited those 41,000 additional policemen, plus helicopters, surveillance cameras and intelligence from Interpol. He said South Africa was not high on the list of targets by terrorists, that there was no need to fear walking the streets. "It would be a very strange World Cup if people stayed in their hotel rooms," Jordaan said. "Give me your number. I will take you out to dinner."

Jordaan understood correctly that his country was far from perfect, but that many of the suspicions from outsiders were born from ignorance. If he could just bring these people to Johannesburg, he was certain they would see for themselves. The World Cup provided South Africa with the opportunity to greatly alter its image around the globe, from a distant Third World nation to something more familiar and warm. Jordaan called this process "branding." There also would be an architectural legacy. Ten stadiums were being built from scratch or upgraded significantly with new roofs or seats. Already, the South African professional league signed a television contract for $1.5 billion rand, representing a one thousand percentage increase in revenue. The World Cup would produce even more excitement at home about the sport, and with it more fans. There were direct economic boosts, as well: the creation of construction and service jobs; the building of railways and roadways; and tourism growth. Tourism already was expanding by about a million visitors per year. In 2007, 276,491 tourists came from the U.S. alone.

Ticketing would no doubt create the usual problems, although the organizing committee seemed prepared to deal with some of the expected snafus. At the 2006 World Cup in Germany, about sixteen million potential customers were hoping to snag three million available tickets. Foreign fans were often shut out of matches involving their own national team. For the South African World Cup, the percentage of seats available to participating federations in any given match had been raised from five percent in Germany to twelve percent in South Africa. Working with the U.S. embassy, Jordaan set a target of 10,000 tickets for American fans. There were four categories, including team and venue specific packages. U.S. Soccer had its own system of selling allocated tickets. When FIFA opened sales to the public via its website on February 19, 2009, it received requests for 216,975 tickets within 24 hours from 128 different countries. That didn't include thousands more requests from South Africans, who already had submitted paper applications. This sort of initial response went a long way in dispelling fears there might be reluctance from tourists and fans about visiting the country. The greatest deterrents for would-be foreign spectators, it turned out, were the high airfares and hotel rates. "There is a stigma of violence we are trying to eradicate," Radebe said. "It is important for us, for the whole continent, that people will want to go back after the World Cup to invest and enjoy the place."

Even as it was preparing for this journey to South Africa, U.S. Soccer was directing its own campaign to bring the World Cup back home in 2018 or, more likely, 2022. FIFA planned to award those two World

Cups during a single election of the 24-member executive committee in December 2010. The continental rotation that assigned the tournament to South Africa in 2010 and to Brazil in 2014 was now abandoned for a less politically-correct bartering method. Regional federations figured to quietly trade promises and votes. Among those nations campaigning for World Cups in the near future were the U.S., Spain, England, Russia, Australia, Qatar, China, Indonesia, Japan, South Korea plus joint bids by Spain/Portugal and the Netherlands/Belgium. England and Russia were viewed as favorites for the European slot; Australia and the U.S. were the primary contenders for the other. The Americans had many things in their favor—most importantly a ready-made infrastructure of World Cup-worthy stadiums in place for NFL and other sports events. By January, 2010, U.S. Soccer had narrowed its bid to eighteen host cities, including New York and Los Angeles. All venues offered stadiums with capacities greater than 66,000. During a global economic recession, U.S. Soccer had a solid selling point. It would not rely on public financing for massive construction projects. The buildings were already there.

This would be a very different bidding war than the one for the 1994 World Cup, Gulati reminded everyone. There were now a dozen nations vying for the tournament, while back in 1994 there were just three—the U.S., Brazil and Morocco. That previous campaign was small in scope and largely financed by former U.S. Soccer president Werner Fricker, who shelled out the first $200,000 from his own pocket to pay for the bid. This time, a committee was housed in a mid-town Manhattan headquarters supervised by David Downs, executive director of the U.S. Soccer bid, with eight or ten staffers in addition to subcontracted lawyers and marketers. "I'm only donating my cab fare," Gulati said. Downs, a former executive with Univision, accepted the job knowing it might well disappear. If the U.S. were to be awarded the 2022 tournament in 2010, the twelve-year lead time was too long to commit to many definitive plans. The organizing committee would go instead into an odd kind of suspended animation, to be resurrected in full force perhaps five years down the road. "That's one of the reasons Sunil hired me," Downs said. "My mortgage is paid. My kids are in college. I can afford to step away from this for awhile."

Garber, the MLS commissioner, recognized the marketing and growth potential of another World Cup at home. He moved people out of the league's office on Fifth Avenue to make room in one corner for the World Cup committee staffers. "Rather than find offices, let's connect it with us," Garber said. "The patina of the World Cup rubbing off on the professional game is a positive. We have all this time to think of ways to empower the soccer community in the U.S., fusing the World Cup to lift the rest of the sport. In every other country of the world, the sport doesn't need lifting. For them, it's just a matter of infrastructure. We have better infrastructure than any other country in the world. It's not about that. It's how do we use this great event to make soccer more important in the lives of Americans?"

U.S. Soccer unleashed all its diplomatic weapons, from both ends of the political spectrum. Henry Kissinger, a formidable soccer fan, worked his narrowing network of connections. President Obama wrote a letter to Blatter on behalf of the bid, then met with the FIFA president inside the Oval Office. Meanwhile, Americans in dollars and in droves continued to support South Africa 2010. Nobody, anywhere, was paying as much for broadcasting rights to the World Cup. And other than the South Africans themselves, nobody was buying more tickets.

CHAPTER 33

The Draw

SEPP BLATTER COULD NOT HAVE ASKED FOR A MORE GLAMOROUS field of nations or stars than the ones filling his groups at the South African World Cup draw on December 4, 2009, in Cape Town. Several of the top teams—Argentina, France, and Portugal, to name a few—had been in dire trouble during the qualifying cycle, yet managed to pull through in the end. France, in particular, required a tainted hand-ball assist from Thierry Henry to knock out Ireland in a disputed play-off. But now Henry, Lionel Messi of Argentina, Cristiano Ronaldo of Portugal, Francisco Torres of Spain, Kaká of Brazil, Didier Drogba of Ivory Coast, Wayne Rooney of England, and many other glitterati were all included among the impressive rosters. A few highly-rated or re-gional powers had failed to make the cut. Russia, Sweden, the Czech Republic, and Egypt were eliminated in one fashion or another. But really, Blatter had before him a grand international buffet. All seven former champions—Brazil, Germany, Italy, Argentina, Uruguay, Eng-land, and France—had qualified. The U.S. was among a group of just seven teams that had survived to play in their sixth straight World Cup, along with Brazil, Germany, Italy, Spain, Argentina, and South Korea. The participants were all well-rewarded, too. FIFA had increased its total prize money by sixty percent, from $261 million in 2006 to $420 million in 2010. Each one of the thirty-two participating federations would receive a minimum of $9 million for qualifying. The champion would receive $31 million.

The Americans arrived in Cape Town with a twelve-man contingent that included Bob Bradley and Gulati. On the morning of the draw, Gulati gave a presentation before the FIFA executive committee, arguing on behalf of U.S. Soccer's bid to host the 2018 or 2022 World Cups. There were still nine other bidders in the process, and they offered their own productions. Those decisions were still a year away. The 2010 World Cup was a different, more pressing matter. At the time of the draw, before eight groups of four teams apiece were finalized, the online bookmakers William Hill made Spain and Brazil the co-favorites to win the 2010 title at 9–2 odds; England next at 6–1; Argentina at 8–1; Germany at 12–1; Italy, France, Portugal, and the Netherlands at 14–1; Ivory Coast was 20–1. The U.S., Mexico, and Greece were all listed exactly midway through the table at 80–1; New Zealand, Honduras, and North Korea were the longest of shots at 500–1.

Conspiratorialists often argued the draw was rigged; that the miniature, hollow soccer balls plucked from transparent bowls somehow had been heated or cooled to the touch, so that selectors would recognize and favor the most attractive sides. That was surely nonsense. A far more suspicious process was FIFA's seeding methods, which kept changing every four years. It often seemed the seeds came first; the justifications second. And so France was somehow punished for its handball qualification, noticeably absent from the first pot of eight seeds, despite its seventh-place ranking by the computer, its championship in 1998, and its place in the 2006 finals. FIFA announced it would seed teams this time around by a recent computer ranking, yet not by the most recent. The eight seeded teams, in order of ranking, became Spain, Brazil, the Netherlands, Italy, Germany, Argentina, England, and the host, South Africa. The Americans, ranked fourteenth by FIFA, were plopped into the same Pot 2 along with the relatively weak teams comprised of CONCACAF, Asian, and Oceania qualifiers. This meant, unfortunately, there was no way the U.S. could ever face North Korea or New Zealand, fellow denizens in their own pot. The worst-case scenario had the U.S. in a Group of Death with Brazil from Pot 1, Ivory Coast from Pot 3, and France from Pot 4. The most hopeful group might have included South Africa, Algeria, and perhaps Slovenia.

The 2010 draw was shown live, with considerable trappings, around the world. As was FIFA's quadrennial custom—who could forget Sophia Loren back in 1989?—a native-born actress was paired with an unglamorous official to perform as co-emcee. In this case, Charlize Theron shared duties with FIFA general secretary Jerome Valcke. David Beckham was one of the celebrity athletes asked to select the mini-balls. Back in New York, Beckham's teammate and erstwhile feuder, Landon Donovan, settled into a seat on the mezzanine level of the ESPN Zone in Times Square, looking down through a long glass window at the establishment's restaurant and high-def television screens. ESPN2 was airing a live, three-hour extravaganza on the draw. Donovan made the rounds, sitting for interviews on behalf of Visa and Nike. His agent at this time was negotiating both with MLS and with Everton about Donovan's professional future, and the U.S. star would soon be starting in January 2010 on the right wing at Goodison Park, playing on loan from the Galaxy alongside teammate Tim Howard. That would become another delicate contractual balancing act, because Donovan naturally wanted to stay in England for as long as things there were going well. But what Donovan really cared about on this day in December was taking place on these television sets at the ESPN Zone, beamed from across an ocean. He admitted to some jitters. Donovan didn't really know what result would be best. It was impossible to predict which set of opponents, which schedule, would be easiest on the U.S. team. In recent years, the Americans had fared better against higher-ranked, technical teams like Portugal, Spain, and Italy than against bigger Eastern and Central European sides that were strong on the ball and in the air. It was a simpler tactical task to pack the box on defense and force smaller teams down the flanks, marking tightly against crosses and waiting patiently for an opportunity to counter. "A lot of times it comes down to style," Donovan said. "Against Spain, we knew they'd have possession most of the time. We had to accept that. But that played right into our hands. When we've had to dictate games, we haven't done as well. These other teams, they're not entirely scared of us, but they don't want to draw us. We're not necessarily as talented, but we have American spirit, which can go a long way."

The suspense was short-lived. Just minutes into the draw, John Smith, captain of the South African Springboks rugby team, pulled out a tiny soccer ball with "USA" written on the paper inside. The Americans were placed in Group C with England. Donovan immediately realized the ramifications. He would be paired once more against Beckham. "It never ends," he said, shrugging his shoulders. But there was no disappointment. Quite the contrary. Donovan and the U.S. team still craved the sort of attention that would surely come from such a match against the likes of Beckham, Rooney, Frank Lampard, John Terry, and Steven Gerrard. Even the most casual of American soccer fans could name half of Fabio Capello's projected starting lineup, and its Achilles heel: England was thin up top, after Rooney. An injury to that attacking star would change everything. As for Donovan, his thoughts were mostly about Beckham. And Donovan figured Beckham's immediate thoughts were mostly about him.

"I wish we could have got a shot of his face," Donovan said. "Bet he was thinking the same thing." In the end, it really wouldn't work out that way, because Beckham would suffer a torn Achilles tendon in March, 2010, while playing on loan from the Galaxy for AC Milan, in the closing minutes of that team's victory over Chievo Verona in an Italian league match. Beckham's hopes of seeing quality World Cup minutes for England, already shaky, were completely shattered by the injury.

The draw went on, and it got better for the U.S. and Donovan. Algeria and then Slovenia were added to the group, very close to the best-case scenario. The Americans had never faced either team, but the soccer world was small enough that everyone knew something about everyone else at this level. The most dangerous player on Slovenia, and the most accomplished on a professional level, was Milivoje Novaković, the leading scorer and a potent striker for FC Koln in Germany, where he had netted forty-eight goals in his first ninety-seven appearances, a remarkable production rate. Slovenia, ranked thirty-third by FIFA, had been a surprise qualifier after knocking out Russia in a UEFA region playoff. This would be that federation's second appearance in the World Cup since it became an independent team after the breakup of Yugoslavia.

Algeria was ranked twenty-eighth in the world. It barely squeaked into the finals after a playoff match against Egypt in Sudan, and had failed to advance past the first round in two previous World Cup appearances in 1982 and 1986. The parents of French superstar Zinedine Zidane hailed from Algeria, before moving to Marseille. Several of the Algerians now played in the French League, where Bocanegra promised to scout them while appearing for his own team there, Rennes. He was set to face the very next day Algeria's captain, Yazid Mansouri, a midfielder with Lorient. "France and Algeria are intertwined so much," Bocanegra said. "I'll try to get more information, check out their roster." Mansouri was quite clear on Algeria's view of the draw. "England are the favorites for the group, but the other position is very open," he told Skysports.com in Britain. "I consider that each team has the same chance. Algeria is not inferior to USA and Slovenia, and that is our challenge during next summer."

By ranking, at least, the Americans were favored to advance into the second round along with England. Wynalda immediately called this, "The best draw we've ever had in any World Cup." Other television analysts like Harkes and Lalas agreed. Even the ever diplomatic Bob Bradley was hard-pressed to label it any more formidable than "a fair group." And in England, the notion of facing these three opponents in Group C was enough to send all of London into a state of utter euphoria. *The Sun* termed this, "The best group since the Beatles." The scariest opponent here was the U.S., and the Americans didn't frighten too many Englishmen. True, England had its own ghosts to battle, a streak of thirty-four years without a major title and that 1-0 loss to the Americans back in 1950. But England had soundly drubbed the U.S., 2-0, in a friendly at Wembley Stadium in May 2008. The Americans would out-work most opponents, but not England, and their preferred tactics against top-tier opponents were largely useless. Nobody could cede England the flanks and then hope to beat them to headers in the goal mouth. The general feeling out there still was that Americans played English-style football, admirable in their own way, only at a slower pace building from the back and with considerably less polish on the first touch. Roy Hodgson, who coached Dempsey and his share of U.S. stars, saw it exactly that way. "The U.S. are well organized and well drilled, athletically very good and with players with a lot of experience playing in England or Germany," he told *The Guardian*. "But that could be a like-versus-like contest. That could actually be quite good for England. It'll be like a Premier League game, with two teams with a similar style. They'll know how England plays, but we won't be surprised with what they're going to come with. And I think that England have just got far too much quality for the U.S."

The Americans, for their part, had many reasons for caution. It wasn't necessarily a good thing to be facing the group's toughest opponent, England, in the first game on June 12 at Rustenburg. Everyone understood how losing an opening match might completely sabotage a World Cup. The U.S. had never recovered from an opening defeat to advance from the first round, and the Americans weren't the only ones with that history. "It's not just the points. It changes the way you play the matches," Donovan said. "The first game matters to everyone. The second matters more to some than others. The third might mean nothing to some."

The rest of the draw after England was no picnic, either. Against Slovenia, the Americans would face a team that stood up to them physically and marked roughly all over the field. One goal was about all anybody could muster against Slovenia, as Russia learned in two tough matches during qualification playoffs. Then there was the other problem: The U.S. traditionally performed best against teams it recently faced—such as Spain and Brazil at the Confederations Cup, after Bob Bradley had made the necessary adjustments. Bradley would be able to tinker against England in this way, but would not have the same direct experience or preparation against first-time opponents Slovenia and Algeria.

"Bob Bradley and the coaching staff do a really good job of getting the tapes and then breaking them down in a way that's useful to us," Donovan said. "Soccer is not like other sports where you can break down the tape and have an exact idea of how you're going to play, but you can get some sense of what the game is going to look like, and they'll do a good job of that. And it's up to individual players, too, to take time to learn the players, watch them in the coming months if you get a chance to and figure out who exactly you're playing against."

Perhaps the best news for the Americans in this draw arrived in the form of geographic convenience. The three stadiums where they would play first-round matches were all within easy driving distance of the team's selected headquarters, and all at comparable high altitudes. Against considerable odds, the U.S. had played in all three stadiums during the Confederations Cup experience. The first match in Rustenburg would be played at the Royal Bafokeng Sports Palace, which was built by the Bafokeng Nation from their platinum profits. That stadium was the site of the Americans' 3–0 victory over Egypt. It seated only 42,000 at an altitude of 4,920 feet, had an airy feeling to it, and would perhaps take a bit of the nervous edge off the opener. The second match against Slovenia on June 18 would be played in Johannesburg's Ellis Park, with a capacity of 65,000 and at an altitude of 5,750. It was here where the U.S. had lost to Brazil, 3-2, in the thrilling final of the Confederations Cup. The third game against Algeria was set for June 23 at Loftus Versfeld Stadium in Tshwane/Pretoria, where the U.S. fell to Italy. It seated 50,000 at an altitude of 3,980.

The Americans had long ago picked out their headquarters at the serene, oak-lined Irene Country Lodge, centrally located between Johannesburg and Pretoria. They wanted to practice at nearby Southdowns College, just a mile from the lodge. But Italy also had stayed at this lodge and trained at this location during the Confederations Cup, and that country's well-financed federation inquired about possibly booking both places for the World Cup. In the end, an odd arrangement was worked out: The Americans would stay at the Irene lodge, but the Italians would train at Southdowns College, virtually down the street. The U.S. team would bus slightly farther away for their practices, to Pilditch Stadium in Pretoria, a 20,000-seat building and home of Supersport United. Regardless, the Americans' three first round matches were all practically in the neighborhood. From Irene, the first game at Rustenburg was about ninety miles away; the second match in Johannesburg was a twenty-five-mile trip; the third game at Pretoria was a journey of merely twelve miles. Bradley intended to bring his team to the area early for adequate high-altitude acclimatization, the sort of opportunity he would have loved to enjoy for a Mexico City qualifier.

While the Americans were finalizing their plans, thirty-one other nations scrambled to analyze their own brackets and make definitive arrangements. The draw had produced some friendly and cruel twists. In Group A, Mexico was on the way to its typically benign draw, hanging in there with South Africa and Uruguay, when suddenly France was added to the mix from Pot 4. As he witnessed this development, Donovan let out an evil-sounding snicker. On paper, Group A would be the most even, hotly-contested division at the World Cup. Group B was arguably the weakest of the bunch, with Argentina, South Korea, Nigeria and Greece. Lionel Messi, voted player of the year on almost everybody's ballot, appeared to have an easy path into the second round. Group D was of particular interest to the Americans, because it was possible they might cross over and play the first- or second-place finisher here in the Round of 16. Germany and Serbia were the solid favorites, in that order, with Ghana and Australia filling out the group. Group E featured the Netherlands and Denmark, two respected northern European sides, plus Cameroon and weakling Japan. Italy figured to rule Group F, with second place up for grabs between Paraguay and Slovakia. New Zealand was one of those just-happy-to-be-there sides.

All eyes were on Group G, immediately labeled the Group of Death for obvious reasons. Brazil had drawn its linguistic and ancestral motherland, Portugal, plus arguably the best team in Africa, Ivory Coast. In this single group, a fan could expect to watch Cristiano Ronaldo face Kaká; or Drogba versus Brazil's latest attacking sensation, Nilmar. North Korea would be the likely whipping boy, as the other three other sides played every match with ferocity and goal differential in mind. Finally, Group H featured the top-ranked team, Spain, with lesser-lights Chile, Switzerland and the CONCACAF upstart, Honduras.

There were several factors to keep in mind when handicapping this 2010 World Cup. Brazil had captured the previous two non-Europe-based tournaments, and was surely the most logical pick. No European team had ever won a World Cup title when the tournament was held outside its own continent. The host nation had never failed to advance to the second round of this tournament, but the geographical advantage traditionally carried far beyond those borders. Nations from the host continent historically performed quite well. So even if *Bafana Bafana* weren't strong enough to mount a real run, this appeared to be a unique opportunity for stronger sides from the Ivory Coast, Ghana, Cameroon and Nigeria to make their mark. The relatively cold winter weather at some venues, too, figured to be a factor and a possible problem for warm-climate nations. This might have been expected to neutralize some of the advantages held by the Africans and South Americans, because nobody was more comfortable in miserable conditions than players from the Netherlands, Germany, Denmark and England.

As for the Americans, they were a horrific 0–9–1 at four European World Cups. At four non-European World Cups such as this one, they were a far more respectable 6–7–2. The U.S. roster was forever evolving, and the lineup that opposed England in South Africa likely would surely be different than any given scheme from the qualifiers. Bob Bradley had many news events and game tapes to digest. During a single week in January 2010, Donovan became a big hit at Everton; Clint Dempsey suffered a knee injury while playing for Fulham, although it did not appear to require surgery; Ricardo Clark signed a contract with Eintracht Frankurt in the Bundesliga; and DaMarcus Beasley finally was finding some playing time with Rangers in Glasgow.

All American eyes were on that first match against England in Rustenberg, which likely would garner considerable attention and ratings back home, where it would be telecast live in mid-day on a Saturday. At the time of the draw, there were four national team members who were both healthy and getting regular playing time in Premier League matches on frigid, wet pitches. Howard was at Everton, Dempsey at Fulham, Altidore at Hull City and Spector at West Ham. The U.S. was 2–7 overall against England, but anybody with a sense of soccer history knew the Americans had captured the biggest match ever between these two teams—that day back in 1950 at Belo Horizonte, Brazil. Sitting at his home in Pennsylvania, Bahr watched the draw from South Africa and immediately recognized the implications. He was part of the miracle team, part of Gaetjens's goal, that would surely haunt England right through the runup to this match. "I think the U.S. team is well-prepared, organized well, and if all their players are healthy they certainly have a chance," Bahr said. "They said at the time we were 500–to–1 odds and we never gave it a thought. It's different now. People are saying that with the brackets the way they are, the Americans have a chance. There'll be a lot of stories coming out. So many of our players are playing in England now. There's such a long history of soccer. These are different circumstances. But I'll use an old cliché: 'One of the best things about sports is the better team doesn't win all the time.'"

You never know. You chase the round ball, sometimes against the very same side that first gave it a boot.

ACKNOWLEDGMENTS

My father was born and raised in Prague, so I grew up watching and playing this sport above all others, despite the information void. I was there each time Dukla of Prague captured another International Soccer League title on Randalls Island in New York, memories not typically etched into the sporting consciousness of American boys. I played forward in high school, in college, and then midfield on my very own last-place team in the Schaefer Soccer League of New Jersey. Teammates like Francis Ferrara and the Colpitts twins made losing much more fun. Several of my coaches were truly inspiring. They actually let the players play. I am thinking particularly of Robert Simpson at East Brunswick High School in New Jersey and Bill Reddan at the University of Wisconsin, with a club team heading toward varsity status. I can still hear Bill whistling tunes as he merrily lined the field before our matches.

As a reporter, the sport really opened up to me on an international level. I covered the star-studded Cosmos, a gratifying assignment, and then the World Cup qualifiers and World Cup finals for the New York Daily News beginning in 1989. I later chronicled other soccer stories in far-flung places such as Marseille (where I was assaulted by angry motorcyclists), Belfast, Kingston, Mexico City and Doha. By my own reckoning, I finagled soccer trips to fifteen foreign nations, many of which I might never have otherwise visited.

Along the way, there were countless athletes, officials and fellow reporters who made this exotic, demanding travel that much easier and more enjoyable. Soccer has changed, just like every other sport. International stars, overwhelmed by media requests, are not as accessible as they once were when I covered the Cosmos. I never knew, for example, what would happen when I was dispatched to interview Roberto Baggio at an Italian training site. But Baggio gave me the requisite twenty minutes and then some back in 1994, once he heard I was from New York. America has always represented unconquered territory to foreign soccer players, a fresh challenge. They also figured correctly I wouldn't rip them in print. Baggio was no more generous in this way than many other gracious immortals I've been fortunate enough to interview along the way, including Pelé, Franz Beckenbauer and Jack Charlton. The Brazilian coach of the Jamaican national team, Professor René Simões, once gave me a ride back along rickety roads to my hotel in Kingston after his team's practice. I was sorry to see his fate with Costa Rica.

It isn't always easy convincing editors to empty the travel budget for soccer. Hats off to my fellow travelers for pulling off such a stunt, and for all the fine dinners over the past twenty years. I thank Mark Starr and the late, great Shelby Strother for their indispensable company in Italy and France; Charlie Pierce for his ebullient presence at the Asian qualifiers in Doha, the most surreal of assignments; George Vecsey for his wise counsel and rescues almost everywhere; Frank Dell'appa and David Waldstein, for that delightful drive around Sardinia in search of Dutch hooligans during the 1990 World Cup; Chris Cowles, who accidentally locked us both in the claustrophobic press room for the first half of a qualifying match at *Estadio Saprissa* in Costa Rica; the Trekker family, father, son and uncle; my own son, Stefan, who foolishly has found himself in the same business, and helped me to research this book. And the whole gang: Bob and Bonnie Ford, Mark Ziegler, Graham Jones, Duncan Irving, Michelle Kaufman, Phil Hersh, Julie Cart, Doug Cress, Julie Vader, Randy Harvey, Linda Robertson, Charlie Vincent, Roberto Abramowitz, Luke Cyphers, Mike Jensen, Scott Ostler, Ives Galarcep, John Lopez, Amy Shipley, Paul Gardner, Ron Blum, Steve Goff, Mike Woitalla, Lawrie Mifflin, John Powers, Ridge Mahoney, Michael Lewis, Elliott Almond, Jane Havsy, Jack Bell, Steve Davis, Scott French, Paul Oberjuerge, Kelly Whiteside, Alex Yannis, Phil Mushnick, Tom Timmerman, the late Mike Penner, Beau Dure and Grant Wahl, for their company and counsel all those years. Many of these reporters aided me directly or indirectly with this book, with special thanks to Jeff Bradley for his generosity.

It wasn't just reporters, either, who helped me to navigate this world over the decades. There was Tony Signore, a public relations man with a real feel for soccer; Noel Lemon, an incomparable promoter and my personal guide in Belfast; Nick DiBenedetto, a student and supporter of the game; plus U.S. Soccer officials, present and past: Sunil Gulati, Bob Bradley, Mike Kammerman, Elizabeth Sanchez, Jim Moorhouse, David Applegate, Neil Buethe, Bob Gansler and John Polis.

I thank my editor at DaCapo Press, Kevin Hanover, who suggested this book and steadily maintained his enthusiasm for the project; my agent, David Black, and his assistant, David Larabell, who sealed the dream deal (a soccer book? for money?); my editors at the New York Daily News, Leon Carter and Teri Thompson, who patiently put up with my odd journeys and constant whining about the need for comprehensive soccer coverage.

The business of newspapering has not been flourishing of late, but I still hold fast to past and present columnist friends back in New York like Harvey Araton, Johnette Howard, Steve Politi, Lisa Olson, Ian O'Connor, Jay Greenberg, Shaun Powell, Vic Ziegel, George Willis and Mike Vaccaro.

I thank my wife, LynNell, my daughter, Halley, and my mom, Charlotte, for putting up with the Chelsea-Arsenal broadcasts on weekend mornings. And ultimately I thank my dad, for kicking the ball around, and around, and around.

BIBLIOGRAPHY

Books

Allaway, Roger. *Rangers, Rovers and Spindle; Soccer Immigration and Textiles in New England and New Jersey.* Haworth, N.J.: Saint Johann Press, 2005.

Wahl, Grant. *The Beckham Experiment; How the World's Most Famous Athlete Tried To Conquer America;* New York: Crown, July 14, 2009.

Wangerin, David. *Soccer in a Football World.* Philadelphia: Temple University Press, 2008.

Major Magazine, Wire Service and Newspaper Articles

Bell, Jack. "U.S. National Team Will Begin Busy Stretch in England." *New York Times,* May 27, 2008.

Bell, Jack. "Q & A: Hoffenheim Striker Vedad Ibisevic." *New York Times,* December 2, 2008.

Blum, Ron. "Coach says alleged affair hurt '98 U.S. soccer team." *Associated Press,* February 3, 2010.

Dampf, Andrew. "Italy rallies to beat US 3-1 at Confederations Cup." *Associated Press,* June 16, 2009.

Davis, Tom. "Soccer Star's Desire To Play Still Strong." *News-Sentinel, Fort Wayne,* July 2, 2009.

Dure, Beau. "On Field, Donovan Sitting Pretty." *USA Today, October 1, 2009.*

Glanville, Brian. "Sport." *Times of London,* June 6, 2002.

Goff, Steven. "Cuba's Soccer Team Coach Says Two Players Are Missing." *Washington Post,* October 11, 2008.

Kaufman, Michelle. ""Man U Finds Itself a Keeper." *Miami Herald,* November 9, 2003.

Kaufman, Michelle. "Cuban Mystique Awaits Visiting U.S. Soccer Team." *Miami Herald,* September 3, 2008.

Llorca, Juan Carlos. "United States Beats Guatemala 1-0 in World Cup Qualifier." *Associated Press,* August 20, 2008.

Longman, Jere. "Alleging Racism, Soccer Star Seeks 'Moral Compensation.'" *New York Times*, June 14, 2009.

Longman, Jere. "Rossi Helps Italy Kick U.S. While It's Down." *New York Times*, June 16, 2009.

Longman, Jere. "Written Off, United States Moves On in Confederations Cup." *New York Times*, June 22, 2009.

Longman, Jere. "Americans Stun Spain and the Soccer World." *New York Times*, June 25, 2009.

Perez, Renato. "Cuban TV Confirms Defection of Two Booters." *Miami Herald*, October 11, 2008.

John Powers. "Keeping Things in Perspective – Howard Realizes Job Isn't Secure." *Boston Globe*, June 20, 2007.

Scott Wolf. "Eight More than Enough for U.S." *Daily News of Los Angeles*, June 16, 2008.

———. "Italy Subdues U.S. in Soccer Tourney." Associated Press (published in *New York Times*), May 28, 1934.

———. "12,000 See Soccer Yanks Win National Cup Game." *New York Times*, April 6, 1931.

———. "The Canadiens Beaten." *Newark Evening News*, November 26, 1886.

Websites

An effort was made to cite and credit within the text substantive interviews or factual material believed to be exclusive. In addition to the books and newspaper articles listed above, the following websites were also utilized as background material or as sources for quotations:

American Soccer History Archives (//homepages.sover.net/~spectrum/)
ESPN.com
FIFA.com
Hexagonalblog.com
SI.com
SoccerAmerica.com
SoccerbyIves.net
USSoccer.com
Yanks-abroad.com

INDEX

ABC, xi
Abdul-Rauf, Mahmoud, 30
A.C. Milan, 109
   Beckham transfer to, 224–225
   Onyewu at, 259–260
Academy system
   German model for, 250–251
   Ramos on, 144
   youth soccer v., 252
Adidas, 249
Adu, Freddy, 38, 40, 41, 55, 61–62
   Berhalter, J., on, 252
   MLS debut, 39
   overseas, 103
African Nations Cup, 274, 275
Age enforcement, 38
Agoos, Jeff, 206
Aguilar, Joel, 247
Aguirre, Javier, 194–195, 228, 232
   on O'Brien's handball, 209
Al Fayed, Mohamed, 214
Albertini, Demetrio, 109–110
Alcantara, Reynier, 63
Algeria, 284–285
Allaway, Roger, 15
Altidore, Jozy, 41, 42, 65, 146, 153, 230, 259
   Arena on, 54, 55
   background of, 53–54
   on disallowance of his goal against El Salvador, 243
   Donovan on, 128
   Garber on, 57

   goal against Spain, 188
   hat-trick of, 127–128
   on Hejduk, 123
   overseas, 103
   on playing in Europe, 127
   records of, 56
   Reyna on, 55
   strength of, 55
   on U.S. v. Brazil, 190
   yellow card of, 265
Altitude, 79, 80, 99, 287
   Arena on, 100
   U.S. trouble with, 27
American federation, 259
American Football Association, 15
Ammann, Mike, 31
Anspaugh, David, 50–51
Apartheid, 271, 272
Arabella's Favorite Game (James), 16
Archundia, Benito, 266
Arena, Bruce, x, 11, 24, 26, 115, 206
   on Altidore, 54, 55
   on altitude, 100
   Bradley, B., as assistant for, 114
   on CONCACAF, 22
   contract expiration of, 237
   on Donovan, 87
   on Gulati, 4–5
   Gulati on, 4, 5, 238
   as MLS coach of the year, 226
   nature of, 203
   on Rossi, 175
   success of, xi